The Irish RMs

The Irish RMs

The Resident Magistrates in the British Administration of Ireland

Penny Bonsall

FOUR COURTS PRESS

Set in 10.5 on 12.5 Ehrhardt by
Gough Typesetting Services for
FOUR COURTS PRESS LTD
Fumbally Court, Fumbally Lane, Dublin 8, Ireland
e-mail: fcp@ indigo.ie
and in North America for
FOUR COURTS PRESS LTD
c/o ISBS, 5804 N.E. Hassalo Street, Portland, OR 97213.

A catalogue record for this title
is available from the British Library.

ISBN 1-85182-331-X

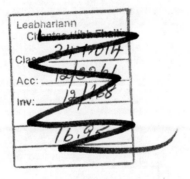
Printed and bound in Great Britain by
MPG Books Ltd, Bodmin, Cornwall

To Ruth Baker and Arthur Ford

The publication of this book has been assisted by a grant from the Scouloudi Foundation in association with the Institute of Historical Research.

Contents

Preface

This history of the resident magistrates explores their role in the British administration of Ireland, and the coincidences and contrasts between the image of the Irish RM and the experiences of the men who held that office. Popular perceptions of the resident magistrates have been shaped by the portrayal of Major Yeates in the Somerville and Ross *Irish RM* stories but little is known of the Major's real-life counterparts. References to their public duties can be found in several scholarly works on the administrative history of Ireland but academic interest has focused chiefly on the resident magistracy at time of crisis or on how their reports on the state of their districts influenced policy in Dublin and London.

This has tended to reinforce the contemporary nationalist view of the resident magistrates as part of the 'foreign garrison', integral to a system of colonial opression whereby alien rule was imposed upon the people. Much of the history of the relationship between the two countries has been written from a similar perspective, within the context of discussion about colonialism and imperialism. No such 'isms' have been utilised in this empirical study of the Irish RMs, which in its scope and content is in line with a recent trend in the historiography away from a dominant interest in political resistance to British rule, towards a growing concern with the extent of Irish participation in governing institutions and a wider consideration of the complex variety of Irish response to the British presence.

Sources for this study include public documents and manuscript collections, contemporary books and newpapers, published memoirs, family memorabilia and some personal reminiscences of growing up in the household of a resident magistrate. The Registered Papers of the Chief Secretary's Office are a major source but all too often the researcher has to rely on the annotation in the annual index rather than on reading and interpreting the original document, because many of the papers themselves have not survived in the National Archives. Documents in the National Archives, Dublin, are reproduced by permission of the Director. I must thank the Council of Trustees of the National Library of Ireland for permission to publish material from the manuscript collection, and the holder of copyright in the Brennan MSS (Mrs Maeve Downey).

Research was undertaken in Ireland, Northern Ireland and England. I was greatly assisted by staffs of the National Archives and the National Library, Dublin; the Public Record Office of Northern Ireland; the Public Record Office, London, and the County Record Office, Trowbridge, Wiltshire. I am also indebted to other institutions and individuals. The Scouloudi Foundation supported my research by grant awards in 1994 and 1995. The management committee of the Institute of Irish Studies at the Queen's University of Belfast enabled me to complete the project as a junior fellow for the academic year 1995-6; my thanks to Professor John Cronin at the Institute, for reading and commenting on an early draft of chapter three, and to others who contributed to shaping my ideas through informal discussion. Mr R. Sinclair, curator of the RUC Museum in Belfast, was unfailingly helpful in supplying information from the constabulary records on those resident magistrates who served in the Royal Irish Constabulary. A special debt of gratitude is owed to Jane Shearer (whose paternal grandfather was John Milling, RM) and her husband, Dr R. Shearer, who have been of great practical assistance to me in a host of ways. Their kindness and generous hospitality to me in Belfast will be long remembered. I am also grateful to my old friend, Ida Hilton, for all she did to make my visits to Co. Louth so enjoyable. Her mother, the late Mrs F. McQuillan (niece of William O'Reilly, RM), was an entertaining informant about her childhood at Knock Abbey and I deeply regret that she did not live to read the finished work.

Origins and Early Years

The resident magistracy had its origins in government response to the perceived failure of county justices to maintain law and order during periods of widespread unrest in the early nineteenth century. The magistrates were key figures in the enforcement and administration of law in rural areas but corruption and inefficiency were commonly believed to be endemic among the Irish magistracy at the time. Justices of the Peace were expected to be men of sufficient social standing to gain the respect of their neighbours, and to exercise some influence over them. In most parts of the United Kingdom they were drawn chiefly from the ranks of country gentlemen and the clergy of the established church but the difficulty in Ireland, from the perspective of English administrators, was twofold. There was a scarcity of individuals regarded as suitable to hold the office, and the religious divide between mainly Protestant gentry and the Catholic mass of the people encouraged popular hostility towards a magistracy often suspected of sectarian bias in carrying out its judicial functions. The high level of absenteeism among Irish landowners was a significant part of the problem but even the resident gentry were unreliable, as they shared a tendency to flee to Dublin or England whenever the country became seriously disturbed. In consequence there were recurring criticisms of the justices as not being truly gentlemen. Men engaged in trade and others deemed unsuitable were allegedly admitted to the commission of the peace because no better candidates could be found. Such men, it was argued, were often lacking in a sense of duty or concern for the public good. It was suspected that they were motivated by self-interest and in hope of benefitting financially from their appointment.

Dublin Castle generally regarded the county justices with a mixture of contempt and mistrust, although differences in attitudes and policies under Tory or Whig administrations have been identified.[1] Tory ministers were often highly critical of the inactivity of some magistrates but they were also constantly aware of the fact that the loyalty of this group accounted for much of their political support in Ireland. This made them sensitive to the magistrates' concerns over any threat to the power and status, and so Tory administrations preferred to rely on the magistracy as the main instrument for keeping the peace. Whig ministers shared the view that many magistrates were idle and inefficient but they believed also that they were likely to be politically disaffected. They suspected that county justices might deliberately neglect their duties and thereby allow the spread of disorder to reflect badly on the government, thus encouraging support for the return to power of the Tories. Whig administrations were therefore more willing to make provision for stipendiary magistrates and military officers to replace ordinary magistrates in exceptional circumstances.

The Lord Lieutenant was given power in 1814 to appoint magistrates 'of police' in any area proclaimed as being in a state of disturbance. These magistrates also had executive functions, as each one had a force of constabulary under his command. They were paid a high salary of £700 per annum and had to be resident in the area to which they were appointed. Further legislation in 1822 enabled the Lord Lieutenant to appoint magistrates to be permanently resident in any specified district, on the application of the justices of a county for such an appointment to be made. These magistrates (paid £500 a year) were not directly connected with the constabulary.[2]

Stipendiary magistrates appointed under the legislation of 1814 and 1822 were forerunners of the resident magistrates proper. The term 'resident magistrate' was not used officially until 1853 but in common parlance it was applied increasingly to magistrates appointed under the Constabulary (Ireland) Act of 1836. The Act repealed those parts of the earlier legislation dealing with magistrates but empowered the Lord Lieutenant to appoint magistrates to reside in such districts as he thought fit. Thereafter the resident magistracy became a permanent part of the administrative system, although critics of the institution claimed that what was contemplated in the provisions of the Act was a temporary response to some emergency relating to the preservation of the peace. This argument was based on an interpretation of Section 32 of the Act, which stipulated that in every warrant issued the Lord Lieutenant should 'state specifically the grounds of the appointment of the magistrate to whom it shall relate'.[3] Returns made to the House of Commons from 1837 to 1844 included reasons for appointments made to meet emergencies during parliamentary election campaigns and in the campaign of opposition to poor rates, or when agrarian outrages increased in the south and west, and when sectarian violence broke out in counties Monaghan and Armagh or in other parts of the province of Ulster. Yet, once appointed, these resident magistrates stayed in office after the emergency had abated. The institution was also continuously expanded by the designation of 'new stations'. A few of these were established at the request of county justices but most appointments in this category were made because the authorities at Dublin Castle considered there to be 'a want of magistrates' in a district.[4] No reasons for appointment were given in any returns issued after the mid-1840s and, in practice, RMs came to be appointed to districts including all Ireland with the exceptions of Dublin city and county.[5]

Governments found it useful to have a core of reliable magistrates in the service of the state, and numbers rose substantially over the decades following the 1836 Act. Prior to the Act there had been twenty-one stipendiary magistrates in office. Fifteen of these were reappointed under the new legislation but the total number of resident magistrates was more than doubled, to 46. Numbers rose to seventy by 1852 and had reached 72 in 1860. This came to be regarded as the full strength of the institution, with numbers being determined by Treasury estimates and the state of the country. Additional RMs were appointed during periods of unrest but numbers were allowed to fall by natural wastage whenever there was comparatively little disorder. Resident magistrates were selected by the Chief Secretary although nominally appointed by the Lord Lieutenant, as head of the executive to which they owed their place and pay. They were always regarded and treated as members of the civil service but this did not ameliorate the suspicions of those who saw them as 'Castlemen' and believed that, far from being impartial law officers, they were influenced in their judicial functions by political instructions from Dublin.

The resident magistrates had the same powers as ordinary magistrates but they could adjudicate over a wider area. County justices were appointed to serve in specified districts but the RMs warrants empowered them to act throughout the counties in which their districts were located and also in adjoining counties. This facilitated the smooth running of the system, by enabling colleagues to cover for others on holiday or sick leave and allowing the Castle to reinforce the magistracy rapidly in any county that became disturbed. Some RMs held additional warrants for Co. Dublin or for Belfast and so could be sent at short notice to those places if the need arose.

The duties of a resident magistrate were not clearly defined. Indeed, the government admitted in a memorandum of about 1846 that 'none but very general instructions for their guidance' could be given. Nonetheless, some twenty circulars issued between 1836 and 1845 directed them on aspects of magisterial functions, such as how to take informations and how to make their reports. They were expected to make themselves generally useful by attending petty sessions courts and accompanying the police to fairs and political meetings or other public gatherings. They were also required to report on their districts and thus formed part of the intelligence network whereby the Castle was kept informed about the state of the provinces; their official diaries had to be kept up to date and submitted to the Chief Secretary's office each month so as to keep the authorities 'acquainted with the whole of the duties performed by the stipendiary magistrates even to their minutest detail'.[6]

Monthly summaries of duty eventually replaced the official diary as a routine means of checking on the RMs and thereafter diaries were only called in during the year if particular proof of a magistrates' movements was required. Leave was granted only on account of ill health or urgent private business, and absence without leave was a sackable offence. Yet despite all this, the resident magistrates' had considerable autonomy and they were not as closely supervised in their day to day activities as the weight of paperwork might suggest. Attendance at petty sessions was not compulsory at this time, and although the RM was theoretically on duty unless on authorised leave it seems highly likely that days recorded in monthly summaries as 'at station' were not wholly taken up by official duties.

The 1836 Act set a salary for the post of £400 per annum but men who had served previously as stipendiary magistrates at a higher salary were given preferential treatment with regard to pay and allowances. Six of those who had been in office prior to 1836 were shown in the 1852 return as receiving up to £461 annually with additional 'lodging allowances' of £100 to £184 a year. Some changes that took place in the 1840s and 1850s can be accounted for by Treasury watchfulness over rising expenditure. Until 1841 all newly-appointed resident magistrates were paid £400 but it then became customary to appoint individuals at £350 per annum, rising to £400 after three years service. Eight of the seventy men in office in 1852 were on the lowest salary scale. In the following year legislation raised the pay of the resident magistrates and brought in a maximum of £500.[7] It was stipulated, however, that no more than twenty individuals at any time should be paid the top rate and that aggregate salaries should not exceed the sum that would have been payable if each one had received £400. Promotion thereafter was not a matter of right but in recognition of merit; some account of seniority was still taken but an increase in pay was seen as essentially an award for good service. Financial considerations may well have delayed promotions after these changes and they certainly pushed down the minimum rate of pay by the early 1870s. The total cost to the Treasury of the annual salaries of the seventy-two RMs in office at April 1872 was (calculated at £400 per head) £29,600 [8] but to keep within the overall limit twenty of them were paid only £300 a year, and this despite the fact that twelve of the lowest-paid had served for more than three years. The salary was supplemented by various fixed allowances which amounted to £159, broken down as follows: for forage and maintenance of two horses, £73; for employing a mounted orderly, £42; for employing a clerk, £36; for stationery, £8. The resident magistrates were also entitled to claim 1s.(5p) per mile travelled outside a twenty-mile radius from their headquarters (unless a railway or other public conveyance was available at less cost), and 15s. (75p) for every night on which they were unavoidably absent from home.

Discontent over rates of pay was growing by the 1870s. In the summer of 1872 the matter was discussed at a general meeting of resident magistrates, after which a deputation met the Under-Secretary and in July a memorial was submitted to the Lord Lieutenant asking for an increase in remuneration. Nothing came of this immediately but the issue was eventually taken up by a Treasury Commission of Inquiry into the civil service in Ireland. Evidence given to the Commission revealed considerable dissatisfaction over pay, allowances, and pensions. It was claimed that rising costs of living had eroded the purchasing power of salaries, leaving many resident magistrates in financially difficult circumstances. George Goold, stationed at Waterford, pointed out that he had been appointed some thirty years ago at £400 a year, the sum then considered 'a proper allowance for the job'. It had not, in his opinion, been over-generous, 'considering that we had to keep a couple of horses, and a certain position', and he claimed that it was now 'totally inadequate'. Goold, like many others, had private means to draw upon and had done so to a limited extent in his early years as a resident magistrate but he explained that latterly all his independent income was absorbed by keeping up his standard of living. 'Without private means', he asserted, 'it would require £800 or £900 a year to keep me at the same level as then.' The importance of maintaining a respectable social position was emphasised by several witnesses including Edward Fitzgerald Ryan, stationed at Wexford, who declared that there were 'no people in the world more sensitive than the Irish people on this point'.

There were further general complaints about expenses and fixed allowances. Some of the RMs claimed that they were out of pocket when obliged to stay away overnight, often having to pay for a servant as well as themselves at a hotel and being charged for stabling their horses. It was acknowledged that resident magistrates often stayed with friends when away from their stations and, by implication, might claim expenses not strictly justified but several never did this as a matter of principle, believing it was important not to socialise with the gentry at the big house when on official duty. The fixed allowances and grievances over pensions were intertwined, as evidence to the Commission revealed. All resident magistrates had to certify each month that they had two horses 'in good and effective condition and available for public service' but in some districts one horse was sufficient, while in Belfast and in Cork city a resident magistrate rarely if ever needed a horse of his own. During the course of the inquiry it also became apparent that for many years no RM had employed a mounted orderly. Nor did any of them employ a clerk, because they either did the paperwork themselves or they made it the responsibility of one of their family. The allowances for orderlies and clerks were therefore really a part of their salaries although neither counted towards superannuation. There was no fixed age for retirement at this time. After thirty years' service a pension of two-thirds of the salary was payable but only after forty years in office could a resident magistrate retire on full pay. George Malony, the RM for Omagh, pointed out that this meant that 'There is now no inducement at all to a man with a family to retire. He must hold on, whether he is able to do the duty or not, the pension is so very small.' The Commissioners agreed that salaries were too low, and that the fixed allowances should be commuted, because they considered it 'unsound in principle' that appointment to the resident magistracy should be 'dependent in any degree on the possession of a private fortune'. Subsequent legislation later in 1874 brought in a retirement age of sixty-five, fixed new rates of pay, and commuted the allowances for forage and postage. It introduced a £100 per annum 'lodging allowance' for the Belfast RMs and it determined the numbers in the higher salary ranges as follows: Class I (not more than twenty), £675; Class II (not more than thirty-three), £550; Class III, £425.[10] These pay scales remained unchanged for more than forty years.

Having traced the development of the institution we now turn to the resident magistrates themselves within the same chronology as above, from 1836 to the late 1870s. Whereas stipendiary magistrates appointed before 1836 had been barristers, no qualifications were required for the office of resident magistrate thereafter. Men were drawn from the upper classes (the aristocracy and landowners) and from the upper-middle classes, particularly the professional middle class. Appointments were made officially on the basis of appropriate legal or administrative experience but there were recurring complaints that the resident magistracy was staffed by the relatives and friends of men of influence, regardless of individual competance or suitability. The majority of those appointed during this period were either former police officers or country gentlemen with no definite career background. It is worth noting that the constabulary in Ireland developed as a quasi-military force with a training system akin to that of the army, and an officer-cadet entry scheme that ensured a gulf was maintained between the elite and the rank and file. The officer class was predominantly Protestant and closely associated with the old ascendancy.[11] Of the forty-eight resident magistrates first appointed under the 1836 Act, twenty-nine had served in the constabulary. By 1860 the proportion of former police officers was considerably less, accounting for twelve of the total of seventy-two. A miscellaneous group of about the same size included men who had administrative experience in the civil service at home or in the overseas empire, some who had been officers in the county militia, a former mayor of Limerick (who had held office during the famine year of 1846), and a sometime supervisor of a school run by the Kildare Street Society.[12] Former army officers accounted for another eight of

the total and a further five had legal qualifications. The overwhelming majority of resident magistrates, however, were men who had previously been
unpaid JPs and of these a small minority had also held other positions in their
home counties, such as grand juror, high sheriff or deputy lieutenant.

Some quarter of a century after the formation of the resident magistracy
government ministers and others were not uncritical of the institution or
entirely satisfied with the efficiency of its staff. Writing to Lord Carlisle in
1862 Chief Secretary Robert Peel [13] observed, 'There are those who incline to
recommend the total abolition of the office of paid magistrate and who think
that its duties might be advantageously transferred to the unpaid Magistracy,
the Country Gentlemen, clergy and others as it is in England.' Peel himself
did not favour radical change in the prevailing circumstances but he went on
to comment upon the ill-feeling among county justices towards the resident
magistrates. JPs resented the close relations that resident magistrates had
with the constabulary and what was seen as their undue influence in a variety
of matters. A particular cause of 'jealousy' was that in cases of outrage when
life was threatened or taken the police were instructed to communicate with
the nearest RM, even if he was many miles from the scene of the crime. Local
magistrates' considered themselves slighted by this, and believed that their
intimate knowledge of a district and its people was not fully exploited in the
effort to apprehend offenders.[14]

The sensitivities of the JPs were of less concern to Peel than the efficiency of the RMs and he was determined on a 'thorough revision' of the list.
He urged that all those 'impartially judged' to be too old or otherwise ineffec-
tive should be encouraged to resign and make way for 'more active and
efficient public servants'. He anticipated that twenty men might be 'weeded
out' in this process.[15] Precisely this number of resident magistrates in office
during 1860 was aged over sixty but by the time Peel undertook his investigation death or retirement had reduced the figure to ten. Far from being
impartially judged, information on the health and fitness of resident magistrates aged sixty or more was provided in the form of self-assessments presented in a parliamentary return of June 1862. All the elderly RMs declared
themselves to be in robust good health and perfectly capable of carrying out
their duties. Only one of them sent a supporting letter from a doctor who had
recently examined him [16] and none, it seems, was persuaded to retire.

The Under-Secretary, Thomas Larcom, was an able civil servant with an
interest in administrative reform, who would have liked the law in Ireland to
have been dispensed on the same principles as in the rest of the United
Kingdom and he strongly disapproved of public offices being awarded by
patronage. With such opinions he was far from being a champion of the
resident magistracy as an institution but he did defend those in office against

some of Peel's criticisms. He suggested that inefficiency was less rife than it had been in the past, and as to the petty jealousies of the JPs he pointed out that they were often reluctant to be called out at night or to accompany the police to riotous disturbances. Moreover, they were inclined to 'throw all the unpleasant duties which the state of Ireland requires' upon the resident magistrates. Larcom himself wished the office could be abolished because he objected to it in principle on the same grounds on which the duke of Wellington, when he was Chief Secretary, had argued against any stipendiary magistracy: 'If you once pay my countrymen for doing their duty they will never do their duty without being paid'. The same might be said of any country, Larcom commented, but he added that he believed the resident magistracy was 'a necessity' in Ireland, where 'the state of the country is such that the gentry mistrust the people and the people mistrust the gentry'.[17]

Accepting the necessity for the institution, Larcom was primarily concerned with the regulations that shaped it and with the calibre of men appointed. He noted that 'the only limitation laid down as a rule is age, which is not to exceed forty'. There was also 'an understood rule not always regularly observed' that men from the constabulary should account for a quarter to no more than a third of the total. He went on to urge that the duties of the resident magistrates were 'of too practical a nature to be made the mere object of political patronage' and he expressed decided opinions about their backgrounds:

> I find constables the best . . . they understand the people, the nature of crime and the machinery for grappling with it. They have graduated in their profession and take a pride in their office. But I am not for excluding other classes of society. We have some valuable men from the Bar – some from the Army – and some from the Country Gentlemen and they all have their merits and disadvantages. They bring knowledge and experience of other former lives and are well suited some to one and some to another district. Country Gentlemen are the most pressed by MPs . . . I certainly think them the least useful generally speaking but I would not be without some of them.[18]

As Larcom noted, former police officers were likely to be exceptionally efficient and they were often notably diligent. It was regarded as promotion for a District Inspector of the Royal Irish Constabulary to be appointed RM, and once in office they were usually posted to the most demanding districts.

It was Larcom's 'least useful' group, the country gentlemen, who dominated the resident magistracy during the Fenian unrest of the 1860s.[19] The emergence of some new organisation was apparent to the authorities as early as the late 1850s but by the mid-1860s Fenianism had developed into a nation-wide movement of threatening proportions, which culminated in the abortive rising of 1867. At the time of crisis, as in earlier and later ones, the resident magistrates came under attack from all sides. They were criticised in some quarters for a lack of determination in dealing with rebels, and elsewhere castigated for brutally suppressing the people. Exceptional measures were taken at the end of 1866 when commissions of the peace were issued to a number of military officers in Cork, 'to enable them to act as Magistrates with the troops on any emergency when it may not be practible to obtain the services of one of the ordinary magistrates'.[20] Who took command when the military was called to the aid of the civil power was a crucial question never definitively answered, it seems, but if a resident magistrate was present the officer commanding troops would usually take directions from the RM. This sometimes proved unsatisfactory, as it did near Templemore, Co. Tipperary, in March 1867. A military report of the action described police and troops encountering sixty or seventy Fenians, armed with an assortment of guns and pikes. At one point in the ensuing clash the RM 'ordered the police party, ten in number, to fire – but would not allow me to fire', wrote the officer. The police fired one volley at 400 to 500 yards whereupon the Fenians ran away through the fields although the whole band might have been captured, according to another officer, if only 'the military had been permitted to take a more determined action'. Lord Strathnairn, Commander-in-Chief for Ireland, also believed that 'weak measures' had lost an opportunity at Templemore and he made it clear that he did not consider the RM a fit person to be in charge of troops at such a time.[21] The RM in question was John Gore Jones, who had been a JP from 1821 to 1831 and then a stipendiary magistrate for five years before being appointed in 1836 as resident magistrate for the Thurles district of Co. Tipperary. He was one of the elderly men Peel had hoped to weed out earlier in the decade but in the special return of 1862 Gore Jones described himself as being in perfect health and claimed that he could daily ride fifty miles and walk twenty, 'without inconvenience'. He was aged seventy at the time of the Templemore incident and he was still in office five years later, in 1872.[22]

It was Lord Naas who was Chief Secretary at the height of the Fenian troubles. He succeeded to the title earl of Mayo while in office, and his surviving papers include numerous applications for the post of RM.[23] Such applications and the references that supported them were not regarded as official papers, and consequently few were saved. This adds to the value of the Mayo papers and although the documents cited below relate only to a brief period in the history of the resident magistrates (1866-8) the scattered evidence from later decades suggests that they are quite representative. They provide some insights into the motives of those who sought the post and what factors influenced the decision to appoint certain individuals.

Men applied for the office for themselves, for their sons, brothers, nephews and cousins, and on behalf of friends and the families of friends. Most were disappointed. There were 120 names on the list of suitable applicants in 1867, and only relatively few of those who wrote up to the Castle actually made it on to the list. Even fewer were translated from the status of prospective candidate to the coveted role of resident magistrate. Many applicants and their supporters were extremely persistent and the place hunters could be a source of annoyance to officials pestered by them. A note of irritation seems to imbue the annotation scribbled in an unknown hand on a letter from a Mr Mackey, which was to be passed on to the Chief Secretary: 'No promise has been made to the gentleman here – who is the son of a neighbour of HE's [His Excellency, the Lord Lieutenant, first duke of Abercorn] in the county of Tyrone . . . the Father is an awful nuisance when in Dublin, always prowling about the Castle.' The influence of family and friends was always important in getting public employment but Mayo's dealings with George Fitzmaurice, RM for Londonderry, indicate that outright nepotism was discouraged. Fitzmaurice informed the Castle that he wanted to retire because of ill health but added that he was 'most anxious' that his son 'should be appointed in my place'. There were sons who followed their fathers into the resident magistracy but rarely into the same district. This was what Fitzmaurice wanted and, moreover, he hoped to arrange the succession before formally resigning. His request was dismissed by Mayo, who wrote that 'it would be impossible to consent to such an arrangement . . . we have made it a rule from which we have never in any instance deviated that we could not consider appointment to any office unless that office was absolutely vacant'.

Personal applicants usually drew attention to talents and experience that might count in their favour but surprisingly few of those who wrote on behalf of others went beyond stating that the candidate was looking for public employment and came from a suitable social background. A correspondent writing in the interest of his nephew explained merely that the young man had been 'invalided from India' and was reluctant to return or even stay in the army, 'as he cannot stand the climate, and thinks soldiering in England does not pay'. He was said to be 'anxious to get the appointment' as resident magistrate because of these circumstances. Similarly, a Mr Reardon wrote on behalf of the son of an old friend to ask if Captain Shiel could be appointed 'as RM or Factory Inspector'. No mention was made of the Captain's suitability but Mr Reardon explained that his young friend was the son of a constabulary officer, and that his mother was 'the sister of a Scotch baronet'. After eleven years in the army the Captain was living at home in Roscommon with his parents, 'whose income is but very limited; so that his dependance upon them is a constant source of sorrow to him'. In conclusion, Mr Reardon offered the information that Captain Shiel was a member of the established church and 'irreproachable in character'.

Able candidates no doubt lost out in the scramble for place. One such was Morty O'Sullivan of West Cove House, Kenmare, Co. Kerry. O'Sullivan, aged thirty-six, had been educated at Carlow College and the University of London. He was a county magistrate and could 'speak and understand the Irish language perfectly', which was a useful attribute in parts of the south and west where it was still often necessary to have an interpreter in court. Also in his favour was his claim that 'both my Father and myself did some service months distant in the Fenian excitement'. In support of his application O'Sullivan sent an impressive set of printed letters of recommendation from referees including two Catholic bishops, two high sheriffs of the county, and the landowners Denis Lawlor JP; Daniel O'Connell JP, deputy lieutenant of the county, of Derrynane Abbey, Cahirciveen; Richard Mahony of Dromore Castle, Kenmare, and the earl of Dunraven. O'Sullivan may have reached the list of likely candidates but he did not become a resident magistrate. It is unlikely that his religion would have been a major handicap, for Catholics were appointed from the outset albeit in a minority throughout the existence of the institution. Social class was more significant than religion in determining who became a resident magistrate, although political patronage also played some part.

The party in power was naturally most sympathetic to candidates who shared its outlook. Yet mere party loyalty was not automatically rewarded with public employment, as the case of a particularly disappointed applicant reveals. Charles Cole of Prospect, Co. Wexford, kept up an unremitting campaign by means of letters to MPs, to Castle officials, and to the Chief Secretary himself during 1866 to 1868. This was, it seems, the culmination of many years of assiduous place hunting. After reading in the *Irish Times* of three vacancies in the resident magistracy, Cole wrote to Mayo in excessively deferential language:

> For upwards of fifteen years, My Lord, I have been anxiously waiting and expecting that some one of the many promised appointments would fall to my lot, but up to the present all my expectations and zeal for the Conservative interest have met with no reward . . . you have now, My Lord, an opportunity of fulfilling your promise, and doing an Act of Justice to a staunch supporter.[24]

Undeterred by rebuffs from the Castle, Mr Cole continued to remind the

Chief Secretary of his existence and his ambitions. News of Mayo's appointment as Governor General of India, in the autumn of 1868, provoked further
appeals from Cole and a final entreaty that before handing over to his succes-
sor Lord Mayo would 'recommend me to that Gentleman for the Appointment of Resident Magistrate'.[25]

On one of Cole's many letters Mayo wrote, 'I cannot think that Mr C has
been in the least badly used'. Recent appointments, he added, had been made
'principally in respect of services performed in connection with the Fenian
movement – Public Service in troublesome times gives in my opinion the first
claim to consideration'. Only three RMs were appointed in almost two years
under Lord Mayo. Two were constabulary officers. George Roche Cronin, a
Catholic born in Co. Kerry, had joined the force at the age of twenty-three in
1857.[26] Thomas Hamilton, from Co. Donegal, had early ambitions to become
a Church of Ireland clergyman but his family could not afford to support him
while he trained for the ministry and so, at the age of eighteen, he joined the
Revenue Police. When that body was disbanded in 1857 Hamilton moved on
to the general constabulary.[27] Both these men were over the official age limit
of forty when they were appointed, in March 1866 and October 1867 respectively, and this despite Mayo rejecting many applicants as 'ineligible' because
of the age bar. What is more, the Chief Secretary stated on occasion that the
limit had been 'strictly adhered to by every government for many years'. This
was blatantly untrue as many exceptions were made over time (usually in the
case of police officers) but the age limit was a useful means of writing off at
least some of the all too numerous applicants. Mayo's third appointee was
Richard Eaton, a barrister from Limerick. He wrote to the Castle on his own
behalf in September 1867 and drew attention to his record of 'some service in
the Fenian unrest'. Eaton was rewarded with remarkable rapidity – within less
than two months he had joined the resident magistracy.

A large part of the attraction of the post was the salary, although it was
not sufficient in itself to maintain a gentlemanly life style. The majority of
resident magistrates at this period and on into the early twentieth century
were men of some means but whose private income or pension was too small
to support their accustomed standard of living. It was undoubtedly the case
that many of the Irish RMs were impoverished aristocrats or impecunious
landed gentry, who were grateful for the salary and pension in a branch of
public employment that was considered appropriate for men of their social
status. The system gave governments a resident magistracy on the cheap, at
salaries well below those paid to the legally-qualified stipendiary magistrates
appointed before 1836, but general recognition of the monetary motives of
place hunters and the patronage involved in making appointments gave rise to
the mocking description of the resident magistracy as 'a system of out-relief

for the Irish gentry'.[28] There was some validity to this, for there were many families like the Catholic Ffrenchs, from Co. Galway, who benefitted from the formation of a permanent resident magistracy. The second Baron Ffrench lost a considerable amount of money, owing to the carelessness of his bank manager[29], shortly before his second son, Martin Ffrench, was appointed RM in 1836. The family fortunes were further strained by the economic consequences of the famine in the 1840s, when no rents were collected on their estates. In 1848 the third Lord Ffrench was forced to sell Castle Ffrench. Another member of the family, Martin Joseph Ffrench, served as a resident magistrate from 1846 until the mid-1850s when he succeeded to the title as fifth Baron Ffrench.[30]

As the Commissioners' who inquired into the Irish civil service noted in their 1874 report, there was always 'an abundant supply of candidates whenever a vacancy occurs' but they also observed that the standard of qualification was 'not as high as could be desired'.[31] This was a recurring criticism and it became more vociferous in the years ahead. Moreover, the close connection between resident magistrates and the landowning class brought into question their impartiality when adjudicating in quasi-criminal or political cases arising out of disputes between landlord and tenant or from the general agitation over land. Hussey de Burgh's compilation of the major landowners of Ireland, published in 1878, included four RMs in office and one retired resident magistrate,[32] while numerous others were the sons, grandsons, more distant blood relatives or in-laws of landowners. This was to become of particular significance from 1879, when the first phase of the land war commenced.

Sporadic violence had disturbed the peace in Ireland since the Fenian troubles subsided in the late 1860s. Troops were deployed during the general election of 1868 and in the Belfast riots of 1872 but on the whole the resident magistrates had enjoyed a period of relative tranquility, going about their routine duties and living comfortable lives akin to those enjoyed by other country gentlemen. Those in Cork and Belfast had heavy work loads, with daily police courts to attend, but in other places the RM was expected to attend the petty sessions only if the clerk had notified him of serious or complex cases scheduled for hearing, or if the local justices could not be relied upon to take their places on the bench. He might be asked to explain his absence on occasion but it was left to his discretion as to which courts he attended. That the job was not a very demanding one was implied by Arthur Mitchell, RM for Ballina, Co. Mayo, in his evidence to the 1874 Commission of Inquiry into the civil service. Mitchell explained that he had taken the post because of his poor health, which precluded him pursuing his career at the Bar. Another witness agreed with commissioner Lord Monck that 'the position of Resident Magistrate on the whole is a pleasant one, taking the round of occupation'. The unionist civil servant, Sir Henry Robinson, aired much the same opinion in his memoirs, where he wrote:

> For anyone who desired to settle down and live a quiet, pleasant country life with a moderate amount of work to occupy him, I doubt whether any more desirable position could have been found than that of an Irish Resident Magistrate up to the end of the seventies. The houses of the leading gentry were open to them, if they were good fellows, and they were nearly always sure of fishing, shooting and social entertainment. They had Petty Sessions to attend on certain days in the month, and on all other days their time was their own. The Government, having appointed them, left them to do their work in their own way, and so long as their diaries showed it was done they washed their hands of them.[33]

Robinson's qualification of the delights of the life of a resident magistrate was of some significance for by the late 1870s Ireland was on the brink of a decade of violent political struggle. During the land war the resident magistrates were 'dragged away from their snipe bogs and the pruning of their rose trees and plunged into a furious agitation which obliged them to go round with the police and read the Riot Act to turbulent assemblies'.[34] The resident magistrates were to acquire exceptional powers during the land war and a reputation for oppression of the people which haunted the institution until its demise, even though a substantial minority never adjudicated in special crimes courts in which the various coercion acts were implemented. The decade of drama that lay ahead was of enormous significance in the history of Ireland and in that of the Irish RMs. The socio-economic and political changes that took place during the 1880s altered the ideology of the nation, and the relationship between Ireland and England. They made some impact on the private lives of those resident magistrates who were landowners, and the polarisation of politics affected every thinking man and woman in Ireland. For the resident magistracy as a whole the significance of the 1880s lay in the bitter legacy of those years.

2

A Decade of Drama

The agitation over land reform was gathering pace during the late 1870s and
it was given added impetus by the dreadful weather of 1879, which was the
wettest year on record and yielded the worst harvest since the famine of the
1840s. An increase in distress and evictions was accompanied by a rise in
agrarian crime and also by the emergence of new forms of organisation and
protest, with the formation of the Land League in 1879 and the formulation
of the Plan of Campaign in 1886. Concessions were made by governments, in
a series of land acts, but coercion was also a part of British policy in Ireland.
In March 1881 the Protection of Persons and Property (Ireland) Act empowered the Irish executive, for a period of eighteen months, to arrest and im-
prison without trial any person reasonably suspected of treasonable practices
or agrarian offences. Later in the same month further legislation brought
another coercion act onto the statute books, in the form of the Peace Preservation (Ireland) Act. In July of 1882 emergency powers were extended by the
Prevention of Crime (Ireland) Act, which was passed in response to the
murder in Phoenix Park of Chief Secretary Lord Frederick Cavendish and
Under-Secretary T.H. Burke. Then, in the second phase of the land war
when the Plan of Campaign was underway, yet another coercion act was
passed. This was no temporary measure but the permanent Criminal Law
and Procedure (Ireland) Act. Commonly known as 'the Crimes Act' or 'the
Jubilee Coercion Act', it became law in the summer of 1887. The decade was
also notable for electoral reform, which enfranchised large sections of the
population, and for the first Home Rule Bill. The Bill was introduced to the
House of Commons in April 1886 but defeated in June. Opposition to Home
Rule provoked serious rioting in Belfast. This major disturbance reflected
and foreshadowed political change in the wider society for during the decade
Nationalism and Unionism emerged as the dominant political ideologies in
Ireland, and the polarisation of politics had a strong religious dimension.[1]

The number of resident magistrates had been allowed to fall to seventy
by the later 1870s but as distress and disorder increased the executive became
concerned to strengthen the institution, particularly after the formation of the
Land League in Co. Mayo during the summer of 1879. From the following

October the League was organised on a nationwide basis and Parnell then
became directly involved, as president of the movement.[2] In December the
Lord Lieutenant's office explained to Treasury officials in London that:

> His Grace regrets to state that in consequence of the present very
> unsatisfactory state of the country, great inconvenience is felt from the
> want of a few more Resident Magistrates, particularly in some dis-
> turbed districts in the West of Ireland where there is a great dearth of
> local magistrates and of duly qualified persons who could be appointed
> as such, and also where owing to the terrorism which exists, local mag-
> istrates have left the country.[3]

It was proposed to again increase the number of permanent RMs to
seventy-two and with the addition of two temporary posts numbers were
brought up to seventy-four in 1880. Six more temporary RMs were appointed
in January 1882. The resident magistracy was maintained above full strength
throughout the decade, although by March 1889 all seventy-five of those in
office were permanent appointments. More than half (forty-two individuals
or 56 per cent of the total) were recognised as legally qualified to adjudicate
in the special crimes courts of summary justice.[4]

The first phase of the land war was notable for the methods of protest
developed by the Land League, such as the communally co-ordinated witholding
of rents, and the effective use of social and economic ostracism as a means of
exerting influence on its opponents. Traditional methods were also employed,
especially in counties Galway and Mayo, which were particularly disturbed
by agrarian crime or 'outrage' as it was termed. Outrage encompassed a wide
range of activities, from the sending of annonymous threatening letters to
violent intimidation or murder. Damage to property included the maiming
and killing of cattle and sheep. Ostracism was not, in itself, a new method of
enforcing the communal will in rural communities but it had not previously
been used against landowners and this non-violent form of protest attracted
much publicity in 1880, when Captain Boycott was subjected to the treatment which thereafter became known as 'boycotting'. Several resident magistrates were involved in this episode of the land war.[5]

Captain Boycott was born in Norfolk in 1832, the son of an Anglican
minister. After a brief career in the army he farmed in Co. Tipperary for a
short period, with his Anglo-Irish wife, before moving to Achill Island (off
the coast of Co. Mayo) where he farmed for eighteen years. In 1873 he
became agent and principle tenant on Lord Erne's Lough Mask estate near
Ballinrobe, Co. Mayo. He first had trouble with his tenants in the autumn of
1879 when he received a written demand, illustrated with a coffin, for a rent

abatement. Nothing came of this but in late September 1880 it became apparent that all but two of the sixty tenants on the estate were planning to withold
their rents. Boycott took proceedings to evict some of them but process
servers were driven off by a stone-throwing crowd of women and children.
Next day, on 23 September, servants and labourers were 'hunted away' from
Lough Mask House and the estate by large numbers of people who were
reported to be 'resolved to starve the agent out of the place'.[6]

The Captain was quickly in touch with the resident magistrate for
Ballinrobe district, John McSheehy, who in turn informed the Castle of developments and arranged police protection on the estate. No violence took
place, but so effective was the boycott that all supplies had to be brought in
from Cong. On 1 November, Boycott appeared at the Ballinrobe petty sessions in a case concerning unpaid wages, and he was 'groaned' and jeered at
by a hostile crowd as he left the court house. The RM judged the situation to
be so serious that he directed Boycott to shelter in the infantry barracks.
McSheehy then called out the constabulary and read the Riot Act, before
escorting Boycott home accompanied by the police.

All of this was widely publicised and funds were raised, by subscriptions
from sympathisers with the Captain's plight, for what became known as the
Boycott Relief Expedition. In order to save the root crops which were beginning to rot in the ground, a workforce of some fifty Orangemen was recruited
from counties Monaghan and Cavan. News of this prompted McSheehy to
request reinforcements for the troops stationed in the barrack town of Ballinrobe.
Infantry and cavalry were sent into Co. Mayo but did no more than patrol the
roads around Lough Mask. Nonetheless, their presence signalled government
support for the relief expedition and this was confirmed when a further 1,000
troops were detailed to escort the Orange labourers to and from Co. Mayo.
The central executive of the Land League held aloof from events at Lough
Mask until after the relief force arrived but they subsequently urged, in
unison with local leaders, that no attempt should be made to interfere with
the harvest. Boycott's crops were saved in the period 12–26 November, without violence but at enormous cost to the taxpayer. It was estimated that
£3,500 was spent to bring in a harvest worth only £350.[7]

Two senior resident magistrates had been sent to assist McSheehy in the
Boycott affair and their involvement continued after the incident officially
closed on 26 November. The Boycotts left Lough Mask next day but, despite
McSheehy's efforts, no suitable transport to the railway station could be
organised because of the continuing boycott and they suffered the indignity
of being carted to the station in an army medical wagon. Thomas Hamilton,
who had been despatched to Co. Mayo from his post at Portarlington, accompanied the Boycotts on the first stage of their journey and travelled with them

up to Dublin, accompanied by a District Inspector. David Harrell, RM for the near-by district of Ballaghaderreen,[8] had also been sent to Ballinrobe during the crisis. He remained on duty at Lough Mask for some time, in charge of 100 troops and police who were left to guard the house and estate. Six months later Harrell was still asking the Treasury for pay owed him for his special duties at Lough Mask.[9]

The conduct of the resident magistrates and the qualifications of men appointed to the post soon came under scrutiny as all aspects of British rule in Ireland were reappraised and challenged. The question of the legal knowledge of the RMs was highlighted by such incidents as that involving Major Traill, who held an impromptu court one Sunday at a police barrack where he imposed sentences from eight days to a month with hard labour. These were overruled on appeal to a higher court, where the resident magistrate's counsel pleaded that Traill had unwittingly exceeded his powers and could not be expected to have much knowledge of the law, as a former army officer. The Major was suspended or perhaps temporarily dismissed but after studying law and being called to the Bar he was reinstated as a resident magistrate.[10] Information about the relevant experience of the seventy-four RMs in office during 1880 was requested by Thomas Sexton soon after he entered Parliament as Home Rule MP for Sligo, the seat he held from 1880 to 1885. It was revealed that almost a third of the total, twenty-five individuals, had legal qualifications but as Sexton was quick to point out very few of them had any practical experience after being called to the Bar. This was to be a recurring criticism in the years ahead. The MP had also asked for information about the petty sessions courts in each district and the resident magistrates' records of attendance. The number of courts varied considerably, from sixty-nine each year in the Moate district to 460 in Limerick district.[11] On average 56 per cent of the resident magistrates had attended over half the petty sessions in their districts during the previous twelve months but some had been to less than one-third of courts held. Throughout the country 6 per cent of scheduled courts had been cancelled for want of magistrates, although the figure was as high as 42 per cent in Ennis district. Most cancellations of courts were caused by the non-attendance of ordinary magistrates but the information in the parliamentary return gave Sexton and other critics evidence that could be interpreted to support allegations of inefficiency in the resident magistracy. It was because of such criticisms that in later years attendance at the petty sessions became the main and most closely supervised duty of a resident magistrate.

Sexton was only one of several Irish Party MPs who were constant critics of the RMs while agitation over the land question continued. In December 1880 counties Mayo and Galway accounted for most of the nationwide total of 153 individuals who were under police protection and those counties, together with Donegal, also accounted for the majority of people who were not constantly guarded but 'specially watched over' by the RIC, to protect them from agrarian outrage.[12] Yet although there were marked regional variations in the level of disturbances, the whole country was to some degree affected by League activities and government response. The situation worsened in 1881, the year in which Fenian dynamiters attacked a military barracks in Lancashire on the mainland, and in which the Ladies Land League was formed in Ireland. Gladstone's second Land Act was passed in that year, as were two coercion acts. In October 1881 Parnell and other leaders were arrested and the League was proclaimed as an unlawful and criminal association.

Some two months later, in December 1881, the Chief Secretary gave greater responsibilities to three of the more efficient RMs. H.A. Blake, Clifford D.C. Lloyd and Captain the Hon. T.O. Plunkett were designated 'Special Resident Magistrates' and put in charge of groups of resident magistrates' districts in the most disturbed counties.[13] All reports from magistrates and police were transmitted to Dublin Castle via the SRMs, who had responsibility for co-ordinating the activities of the resident magistrates, the police, and the military. Three more SRMs were appointed six months later when twenty counties were grouped into special areas with headquarters at Mullingar, Westport, Galway, Limerick, Cork, and Maryborough (Portlaoise).[14]

The SRMs approach to dealing with the crisis was not uniform but Clifford Lloyd became notorious for his ruthless methods in Limerick. Lloyd was born at Portsmouth in January 1844 into a well-known family settled in Ireland. His grandfather had been Provost of Trinity College, Dublin, and his uncle, the scientist Dr Humphrey Lloyd, subsequently held that office from 1867 until his death in 1881. Lloyd was educated at Sandhurst but was diverted from a military career by the offer of an appointment in the Burma police force. He later transferred to the civil administration in the colony, before studying law while on a long leave and being admitted to the English Bar.[15] He was shortly afterwards appointed to the resident magistracy, in 1873. In 1880 he was stationed in Belfast but then posted to Limerick and it was as an ordinary resident magistrate there that he first attracted hostility and praise in equal measure when, in May 1881, he arrested Fr Eugene McSheehy. McSheehy was president of the Kilfinane branch of the Land League and the first priest to be arrested during the land war. Lloyd went on to arrest the entire committee of the Kilfinane branch and it was largely because of these actions that he was selected as a Special RM. His general conduct as SRM was fiercely criticised in the nationalist press, and by both Irish Nationalist and some Liberal MPs in the Commons. He was a popular magistrate with Florence Arnold-Forster (the adopted daughter of the Liberal Chief Secretary), who believed him to be genuinely committed to the good of the country, but like some others who had experience of administration in the overseas empire he was perhaps, as Margaret O'Callaghan suggests, inclined to forget 'that Ireland was a part of the United Kingdom with representatives in parliament, and not a far-flung colony'.[16]

The SRMs existed for only a relatively short time. In September 1882 they were replaced by four 'divisional magistrates', although this was little more than a change of title to reflect more accurately their role in combating the Land League. A fifth divisional magistrate was added in 1885 and the whole country was then reorganised into divisions. Clifford Lloyd did not survive the changes and it has been suggested that his public career was ended because of the sustained criticism of his conduct in the Limerick area.[17] It seems that unsuccessful efforts were made to place him immediately in a colonial governorship, to reduce the political effect of his removal, but as no post could be arranged he was awarded a pension in 1885. The pension was granted on the grounds that Lloyd had retired because of permanent ill health but he was soon appointed Minister of the Interior in Egypt and later served as Colonial Secretary and Lieutenant Governor of Mauritius before ending his career as British Consul in Armenia.[18] He did not draw his pension until 1888, shortly before his death, but many questions were asked in the House as to why he continued to hold public office after being pensioned as unfit.[19]

Lloyd's pension and the administrative posts to which he was appointed in the overseas empire were rewards for his services in Ireland but a suggestion that other SRMs who had reverted to being ordinary resident magistrates should be compensated financially, with an increase in annual pay, was dismissed by the Treasury as: 'preposterous, if only from the point of view that a longer service now as an ordinary magistrate will give a greater reward for the *special* duty . . . A & B get £100 a year each – A dies after 5 years and has received £500. B dies after 10 years and has received £1,000. Yet both did the same work.'[20] The SRMs had been paid the salary of ordinary RMs of their class plus an additional £25 per month for the special work they undertook and an extra monthly allowance of £30 for personal expenses. Treasury officials pointed out that beyond these arrangements nothing had been said about 'rewards' when the scheme for SRMs was first submitted to them in 1881, and no extra payments were granted after the post was abolished.

Another exceptional appointment made during the decade was that of Major Nicholas Gosselin, formerly of the 4th battalion Royal Irish Fusiliers. Gosselin became a resident magistrate in July 1882 but in May of the following year he was given a roving commission to co-ordinate the activities of the

RIC political branch in Britain and to investigate Fenian organisations. There-after he was not listed in returns to the Commons relating to RMs in office but if this was intended to protect his identity it was grossly inadequate, for his name appeared year after year in the list of resident magistrates published in the annual RIC handbooks, where he was shown as 'seconded' on special duty. The Fenian bombing campaign in England petered out after 1885 but Gosselin remained in post as part of the anti-Fenian security measures and he was still warning of dynamite threats shortly before his retirement in 1896.[21]

Meanwhile the resident magistrates found themselves in circumstances familiar to their predecessors in office during the Fenian troubles of the 1860s. Criticised by some Unionists, landowners and Conservatives as ineffi-cient and too lenient, they were castigated in turn by Nationalists, Liberals, and other opponents of coercion in Ireland for being the tools of oppression. They were themselves critical of government policy at times and did not always feel that the dangers they faced were fully understood by Dublin Castle or the general public. As in the 1860s, concern about the efficiency of the RMs led to the compilation of a special return to the Commons. In the spring of 1881 attention focused on those who had been in office for more than twenty years. It was revealed that of the twenty senior RMs there were eight whose length of service exceeded thirty years. Once again there was talk of the need for the resident magistracy 'to be weeded with no sparing hand', as the Lord Lieutenant advised Gladstone in the spring of 1882. Spencer also passed on the opinion of one of the SRMs, who had told him that 'he would not trust a jury of RMs at the moment'. Yet no resident magistrates were forced into retirement and despite his criticisms Spencer made it clear in other correspondence with Gladstone that he regarded the resident magis-trates as 'competent and reliable' on the whole.[22]

As for the RMs, many of them felt that they were unfairly held respon-sible for the state of the country and some were critical of successive govern-ments for allowing the spread of Land League ideas, instead of stamping out the movement in its infancy. Clifford Lloyd recalled one of them saying to him, 'Well, I am a married man, living quietly in the country with my wife and children, and drawing very little pay for the performance of my legiti-mate work, which I do. It is all very well for you . . . walking about here with ten policemen always at your back'.[23] What attracted men to apply for the post was certainly not the prospect of being threatened with violence or pilloried in press and parliament but that was what some of them experienced in the 1880s. Their families might also have to bear the consequences of popular hostility towards a resident magistrate, as the experiences of Captain McTernan illustrate. McTernan was a Catholic who had qualified as a barris-ter and served in the Leitrim Rifles before being appointed in 1876. He was a substantial landowner, with over 4,000 acres in Co. Leitrim and 1,000 acres in parts of counties Kilkenny, Sligo, and Roscommon.[24] McTernan first served as RM at Listowel, Co. Kerry, but in 1878 he was transferred to Ennis, Co. Clare. There he was later instrumental in the arrest and successful prosecution for an agrarian murder of Francis Hynes, which made the RM 'obnoxious to a certain class of persons in Ennis'.[25] McTernan's religion might have proved a useful tie of vertical interest with the lower orders in quieter times but it did not protect him from the anger of priest and people during the land war. He was denounced from the altar of the Catholic chapel, his daughters were threatened on the streets of Ennis, and his life was considered to be at risk if he remained in the district. A transfer to Enniskillen, Co. Fermanagh, was therefore arranged and the RM offered his furniture and effects for sale prior to moving north. The auction was boycotted and not a single item sold.[26]

Different circumstances caused different difficulties for McTernan in his new district. The land agitation was now subsiding but from the old Land League a new National League emerged, as the constituency organisation of the Home Rule party. The League's meetings in the north were countered by Orangemen holding simultaneous demonstrations and in October 1883 Captain McTernan took charge of 300 police and troops at Roslea, where a National League meeting was to be addressed by the Irish Party MP, Tim Healy. Lord Rossmore and Lord Crichton led many thousands of Orangemen to counter what Rossmore spoke of as a rebel assembly. Crichton agreed to the resident magistrates' request to alter his route and thus avoid an encounter between his Orange followers and the nationalists but when McTernan repeated his request to Lord Rossmore, his lordship refused to give way to the RM. He led the Orangemen on to a hillside near the League meeting and there pledged them to resist Home Rule, and condemned the nearby nationalists in violent and extreme language. Rossmore was deprived of his commission of the peace after this incident, although as soon as the Tories were back in power he was quietly reinstated as a county JP.[27]

McTernan's religion would have made him the object of suspicion from bigots like Lord Rossmore and his Orangemen but some of the RMs coreligionists may have welcomed his presence on the bench at petty sessions when they appeared before the court. In 1884 Captain McTernan was the only Catholic among the seventy-four magistrates in Co. Fermanagh.[28] In the wider society, religion and politics became increasingly intertwined during the 1880s, so that by the end of the decade the Catholic-nationalist and Protestant-unionist divide was well established. The Franchise Act of 1884 extended the vote to all adult male householders, thereby increasing the Irish electorate by over 200 per cent between 1884 and 1885 and this spread of democracy coincided with growing support for the nationalist cause. This was countered by the formation of organisations such as the Irish Loyal and Patriotic Union and in the northern counties the Orange Order became closely linked with constituency organisations of the Conservative party. The ILPU was founded in Dublin in 1885 by a group of academics and landowners, as a non-sectarian association of Conservatives and Liberals dedicated to mainte-nance of the union.[29] One of its founder members was the physician and academic, Anthony Traill, who was a brother of Major Traill RM, whose conduct in the early years of the land war had outraged nationalist opinion.[30] Another of the resident magistrates, Cecil Roche, had even closer links with the ILPU. Roche was a barrister who soon attracted notoriety as a 'fanatical firebrand' after his appointment in 1886. The Irish Party MP, John Dillon, raised the question of Roche's association with the ILPU when he asked in the Commons if Roche had been employed as a lecturer for that organisation but was told that prior to his appointment the RM had merely 'delivered some addresses, without remuneration', on behalf of the ILPU.[31] Such was the unpopularity of Roche, however, that there were local protests over his rapid promotion from third- to second-class RM.[32]

Support for the ILPU by a resident magistrate was open to criticism and particularly so because of the religious dimension to the polarisation of poli-tics, when the RMs were overwhelmingly Protestants and unionists. Electoral reform coupled with Gladstone's conversion to support for Home Rule were seen by many people as ominous threats to the Union. As a parliamentary return of 1884-5 showed, there were Catholic majorities in all Irish constitu-encies except for half of the Ulster divisions[33] and it was hardly surprising that strong feelings were aroused by the introduction to the Commons of the first Home Rule Bill in April 1886.

Feeling on both sides was strong in Belfast, where Catholics in general supported the measure and Protestants as a body regarded it with hostility. 'This apparently political question evoked the spirit of sectarian animosity' among the population,[34] and led to the worst riots of the century in the city. Sectarian violence was nothing new in Belfast, where Protestants were con-centrated in and around the Shankill Road and Catholics predominated on the Falls Road, but the 1886 riots were exceptionally lengthy and brutal. Rioting began in the shipyards and docks on 3-4 June and spread quickly to other areas. Before the disturbances ended, in September, thirty people had been killed and nearly 400 injured. The riots were also overtly political for the first time and they were notable for the hostility that the Protestant mobs showed towards the RIC. Moreover, many Protestants of respectable status seemed to sympathise with their rioting co-religionists and to share their attitude to the police force. Wild rumours circulated that RIC reinforcements were all Catholics from distant counties, sent in to slaughter Protestants or at least coerce them into accepting Home Rule, and a fearful antagonism to Catholic nationalism united Protestant unionists of all classes in opposition to any measure of independence that would weaken the union.

Two resident magistrates were stationed at Belfast but as many as twenty were posted temporarily there during the summer of 1886. Three of them were injured in the riots. At an early stage in the disturbances the RMs formed a consultative committee which met from time to time to arrange what measures should be taken to put down the disorder. A larger committee was later formed, to include the mayor and all the borough magistrates. These procedures were criticised by the Commissioners who investigated the riots. They noted in their report that the resident magistrates and the ordinary borough JPs had equal authority and that 'at one of the most trying moments' no fewer than fifty-three magistrates attended a meeting at which, according to one witness, 'there was a good deal of confusion, a great deal of talk, and very little business done'. An executive council was eventually formed but this also 'indulged in long discussions, and was not a body from which prompt and vigorous action was to be expected'. The Commissioners' agreed with a senior RM, Henry Keogh, that the duration of the riots was attributable to 'the divided authority'. They recommended that the Chief of Police in Belfast should be 'free of any magisterial or other control, save that of the Executive Government and the Inspector General of the RIC'. The investigation also led to changes in the responsibilities of the magistrates. The executive and judicial functions of the resident magistrates were intended to be kept separate so, for instance, cases arising out of a riot were not tried by the RM called upon to put down the riot but by resident magistrates brought in from other districts. During the Belfast riots, however, the functions of the resident magistrates had merged unacceptably. Evidence to the commission also revealed a strong body of opinion in favour of relieving borough magistrates of duties in the petty sessions or police courts and the commissioners shared these views: 'We think that the duty of administering justice at the Belfast Petty Sessions Court should be entrusted to two paid magistrates, who should have no duties in the streets, as nothing could be more objectionable than the present system, under which resident magistrates one day take part in the supression of disturbances, and the next preside in the courts.'[35]

It was recommended that the sole jurisdiction at the petty sessions should be conferred on two paid magistrates, who should either be experienced barristers (as were the stipendiary magistrates in Dublin city) or resident magistrates whose duties were judicial only and who 'should not interfere actively against rioters in the street'. Thereafter, the duties of resident magistrates in Belfast were confined to adjudicating in the daily police courts.

When Colonel the Hon. W.F. Forbes was transferred back to the Curragh, in 1889, he was replaced in Belfast by a former practising barrister and it became customary for the two Belfast RMs (usually one Catholic and one Protestant) to be men with legal qualifications and experience.

It was during the year of the Belfast riots that the temporary lull in the struggle between landlords and tenants ended, with renewed agitation prompted by a fall in cattle and dairy prices. Between 1886 and 1891 the Plan of Campaign was underway. The basis of it was that tenants (many of whom were in arrears with their rents and facing eviction) should offer to pay 'fair' or reduced rents. If a landlord refused to accept the offer, no rents at all were to be paid but the monies would be collected by campaigners and used to help evicted tenants. William O'Brien and John Dillon were particularly prominent figures in the movement. Parnell did not himself support the Plan, but it was led by members of the Irish Party or the National League on the 116 or so selected estates where the Campaign was put into effect.[36]

The Irish executive declared the Plan an unlawful and criminal conspiracy in December 1886 and brought O'Brien and Dillon to trial for conspiracy. The trial in Dublin collapsed, in February 1887. The following month the Conservative Prime Minister, Lord Salisbury, appointed his nephew, Arthur Balfour, as Chief Secretary.[37] Balfour was one of the most successful chief secretaries, whose period in office reflected his determination to enforce the rule of law but simultaneously to redress genuine grievances, particularly those relating to landlord-tenant relations. He is remembered mainly for the permanent coercion Bill that he steered through Parliament during his first months in office, and for the repression which followed when the Crimes Act came into force in July 1887. Its severity was criticised by nationalists and by the Catholic church, and it was the cause of some unease among Liberal-unionists. Liberal opinion in England was generally hostile to the Act and opposition to all coercion in Ireland was a concern of numerous radical individuals and organisations throughout Britain. Under the Crimes Act the Lord Lieutenant was enabled to increase the powers of some RMs so that they could prosecute in courts of summary jurisdiction in cases of intimidation and conspiracy. Once again the activities of the resident magistrates' were to come under close scrutiny and several found themselves named in Parliament or in the press, in the context of highly unfavourable criticism of government policy or with reference to alleged misconduct by individual resident magistrates. Arthur Balfour was a resolute defender of the RMs and the knowledge that the Chief Secretary would support the actions of magistrates and the police did much to raise morale among those involved in maintaining law and order.

Some two months after the Crimes Act was in place events at Mitchelstown not only further blackened the name of the Chief Secretary in some circles but also started a chain of events that eventually revealed damning information about one of the resident magistrates. The 'Mitchelstown massacre', as the incident became known, earned Arthur Balfour the soubriquet 'Bloody Balfour' and led to violent anti-government protests in Trafalgar Square, London. It also gave nationalists and Liberals a new rallying cry, 'Remember Mitchelstown'. This encounter between the people and the forces of the state took place on 9 September 1887 at Mitchelstown, Co. Cork, where the National League had organised a meeting to be addressed by John Dillon, to protest over the arrest of William O'Brien and another leading figure in the Plan of Campaign. The demonstrators greatly outnumbered the constabulary and scuffles soon broke out, with the police being driven back to their barrack. From there they opened fire on the crowd, killing two people and wounding several others.[38] In the immediate aftermath conflicting accounts of the event were given and according to one version the RM, Captain O'Neal Seagrave, was 'refreshing himself in the hotel' when the shooting took place. However, Edward Carson (known as 'Coercion Carson' because of his role as a crown prosecutor) was an eye-witness at Mitchelstown and in notes sent to Balfour the day after the incident he stated that when the shooting occurred Seagrave was near the barrack with a group of RIC officers and men.[39] Yet the deaths and injuries were attributable to the authorities' mismanagement[40] and in the circumstances it might have been expected that the RM would resign, as the official who had overall responsibility for the affair. Seagrave acknowledged his lack of experience and his 'want of legal knowledge' to the court of inquiry that investigated the events at Mitchelstown but he stayed at his post and it was an officer of the Royal Irish Constabulary who resigned.

Seagrave then came under scrutiny from people looking for evidence to prove his unfitness for the post of RM. His earlier career in the Cape Mounted Infantry revealed a discreditable past and this was brought to the attention of the House of Commons over a year later in December 1888, by the Irish Party MP for mid-county Cork, the Protestant Dr Tanner. Tanner told the House that he 'did not like to call a man a swindler or thief' but wanted to state a few facts about Captain O'Neal Seagrave and would let MPs judge his character for themselves. He then described how Seagrave had joined the Cape Mounted Infantry as a private and was promoted to lieutenant in 1882. ('Captain' was a spurious title it seems, as no further promotion was mentioned.) In 1883 Seagrave was posted to a remote station in charge of fifty men. Letters complaining about his conduct as commanding officer soon began to appear in leading papers in the colony. Complaints centred on his control and management of a canteen at the 'little African station [where] there was no other place nearer than 100 miles at which anything could be purchased'. Exorbitant prices were said to be charged and no accounts rendered of the profits, which belonged by right to the whole detachment. As a result of investigations steps were taken to get rid of Seagrave but 'friends at the Cape' used their influence on his behalf, and he was merely moved on to another station. There, in November 1884, one of his men going on leave asked the officer to take charge of £5 for him and forward it to his address in England. The money was never received and Seagrave's claim to have purchased a postal order for that amount was disproved by the records of the only post office he could have used. The sordid matter dragged on with more investigations leading to Seagrave's arrest and talk of charges against him of embezzlement. Eventually, in the summer of 1885, he was dismissed from the Cape Mounted Infantry on grounds of gross neglect and breach of trust.[41] Back home in Ireland, he was appointed to the resident magistracy in 1886.

There was no immediate response to complaints about Seagrave, who was later sent on leave while the allegations were investigated, but Balfour gave a robust defence of the Irish RMs in general when they came under attack from one of their most vociferous critics, the Nationalist MP Thomas Sexton. Sexton told the House that the resident magistrates of Ireland ought to be impartial, competent 'by legal training' and independent but he asserted that they were none of these things. They were compromised by their class origins, he believed, for 'out of seventy of them ten could not be named who were not of the landlord class or connected with it by marriage, by social intercourse, or by personal interest'. Consequently, he claimed, the trial of cases arising out of the relations between landlords and tenants might as well be confined to 'any two of the landlords as any two of the resident magistrates'. Although twelve of the RMs had legal qualifications most of these had not practised since joining their profession and Sexton considered this 'a good proof' that they were incompetent. He was scathingly dismissive of the former police officers and 'old soldiers' and he ridiculed the idea of judicial independence from the executive when all the resident magistrates 'could be dismissed tomorrow if they did not give satisfaction'. As evidence of the unfitness of those officially recognised as having sufficient legal knowledge to adjudicate in cases under the coercion acts, he referred to the report of a judgement in the Court of Exchequer in which, he claimed, 'Baron Dowse said they might almost as well ask one of these Resident Magistrates to write a Greek ode as to state a case'. After much more in the same vein Sexton concluded that it was intolerable that the people of Ireland should not only be 'subject to bad law' but that it should be administered 'by persons who were neither impartial, competent, nor independent.'[42]

In response, Balfour suggested that it would be difficult to find magistrates if family connection was to be a disqualification. As to legally qualified

RMs with little or no experience since being called to the Bar, he argued that it was only to be expected that they were not drawn from those 'in good practice' with substantial incomes but he added that 'the fact that those appointed did not possess the lighter arts by which juries were moved, did not show that they were not legally competant to discharge the duties of magistrates.' He went on to assert the independence of the resident magistrates by deriding the notion of their 'abject servitude' and reminding the House that about one-third of cases brought before them recently by the Crown had been dismissed.[43]

The case of the 'hero of Mitchelstown', as Dr Tanner dubbed the Mitchelstown RM, was not allowed to rest although Balfour was adamant that no action would be taken until documentary evidence to support the allegations was received from the Cape. He dismissed the suggestions of some MPs that all the relevant information was readily available in London at the office of the agent-general for the colony. In March 1889 he told the House: 'I am not going so far as to indicate to the public that, because a Resident Magistrate in Ireland happens to be unpopular with honourable Gentlemen opposite, therefore he is not to receive the same meed of justice which would be extended to any other officer . . .',[44] although he added that Seagrave would be dismissed if the evidence sustained the charges. When the papers at last arrived from the Cape the RM was not sacked but allowed to resign, much to the fury of many MPs. Almost six months after the matter was first raised Balfour explained to the Commons in May 1889 that 'Mr O'Neal Seagrave was not dismissed from the office of Resident Magistrate. His resignation was accepted . . . the charges have not been proved in such a sense as to require the Government to dismiss Mr Seagrave.'[45] This carefully worded statement was hardly an endorsement of Seagrave's innocence. It was a political fudge that enabled Balfour to save himself the embarassment of sacking not just any RM, which would have been against his policy of 'backing up' the magistrates, but the very one involved with the incident at Mitchelstown that was forever linked with the name of the Chief Secretary.

During parliamentary exchanges over the Seagrave affair it emerged that prior to going to the Cape colony he had failed in three attempts to pass the examination for a commission in the army, a fact that added to general concern about the calibre of men appointed to the resident magistracy. It was Sir Michael Hicks-Beach (President of the Board of Trade in 1889 but Chief Secretary in 1886) who had appointed Seagrave, 'who was recommended to me as a Roman Catholic gentleman, whose claims to such an appointment had been favourably looked upon by Lord Aberdeen and whose record of service at the Cape was a good one'.[46] By drawing attention to Seagrave's religion, to the approval of his candidature by the Liberal 'Home Rule' viceroy Lord Aberdeen, and to written testimonials that where either deliberately or innocently misleading, Hicks-Beach offered a sub-text that would have been understood by many in the House to mean that under Liberal administrations sympathetic to Home Rule, and eager to bring more Catholics into the judiciary, it was highly likely that unsuitable men would become RMs.

Although Liberal administrations appointed some resident magistrates with Home Rule sympathies most Catholics who were RMs during this period were unionists but what set them apart from many of their Protestant colleagues was that their loyalty to Britain did not include the anti-Catholic prejudice that was a part of the ideology of men such as Clifford Lloyd. The ruling classes in general equated the notion of 'civilisation' with British rule and the spread of the English language but Lloyd's analysis of the socio-economic, cultural and political differences that existed within Ireland was rooted in sectarian bias. In a lengthy letter to *The Times*, written in March 1889, several years after he had left the resident magistracy, Lloyd aired his prejudices in a contribution to debate on the 'Irish Question'. Addressing the issue of Home Rule he confidently asserted that 'The Northerners are essentially an orderly people (Belfast riots notwithstanding); the Southerners are the reverse'. While the former were, he wrote, 'imbued with an intense feeling of civil and religious freedom' and marked by 'an individuality of character', the latter:

> seemed for ever ready to accept the yoke of the strong, provided it is accompanied by appeals to their sentiment and imagination. . . . They have always been the slaves in turn of priests, Governments, or agitators. Some parts of Celtic Ireland are hundreds of years behind the North in Civilization, and in the far West and North-West it is the few who even speak English. It may be a disgrace to us that it is so, but the fact remains. With many qualities that must always appeal to one's heart, the Irish of the south and west are disloyal by tradition, impulsive, reckless, ignorant, emotional, priest-ridden, and willing to be the slaves of the firstcomer who knows how to master them, and, as a consequence, are unstable, poor, and forever in need. The Northerners are hard-headed, thrifty, energetic, free in their religious and social state, loyal to the last degree both by tradition and self interest; they are enlightened and progressive, and therefore a contented and prosperous people.[47]

All this rather overlooked the fact that strong government had demonstrably failed to 'master' the supposedly slavish mass of the people. Substitute 'Protestant' for 'Northerner', and it seems that from Lloyd's perspective, progressive enlightenment and prosperity were equated with Protestantism whereas all that was 'backward' in Ireland was ascribed to Catholicism. Such attitudes were offensive to adherents of the majority faith but it was the equation of Catholicism with nationalism that gave political significance to the religious composition of the resident magistracy.

During the 1880s the mass of the people became more politicised than they had earlier been. The Parliamentary Irish Party developed into a substantial and well-disciplined body in the Commons, supported in the country by its constituency organisation, the National League, and by the nationalist press. In these circumstances in was inevitable that the resident magistracy would become the focus of nationalist criticism. At the end of the decade, in March 1889, another return was called for with the primary purpose of identifying those RMs empowered to adjudicate in the special crimes courts held under the coercion acts. Information was also requested about the 'former vocation' of resident magistrates and the tenure on which they held office. More than half of the RMs had been recognised as competent to hear cases in courts of summary jurisdiction. Many military men and former police officers had been appointed during the decade, because men from those backgrounds were considered particularly suitable to deal with the disturbed state of the country. The structure of the resident magistracy had consequently changed. By 1889 barristers were in a minority and, together with country getlemen and others of miscellaneous experience, accounted for not much over a third of the total. The fact that 64 per cent of the resident magistrates had served in the constabulary or the military added weight to nationalist arguments that the country was virtually under martial law and that the special courts were akin to drumhead courts martial. As to tenure of office, it was well known that resident magistrates' served 'at the pleasure' of the Lord Lieutenant and were potentially subject to instant dismissal. Their independence was, of course, always disputed and the information asked for in the return was intended to add emphasis to that familiar criticism. The tenure of office of all seventy-five RMs, from W.H. Beckett in Athlone to Francis Welch at Kilrush, Co. Clare, was tersely recorded as 'Pleasure',[48] and the RMs were mockingly known among nationalists as the 'Removable Magistrates.'

It had altogether been a difficult decade for the RMs. A fortunate few served in comparatively undisturbed districts and some others were involved in events at a distance, as were A.G. Meldon and George Shannon who acted as legal advisors to successive commissioners for counties Kerry and Clare.[49] Thomas Hamilton, in contrast, had participated directly in several major incidents of the period. After his part in the Boycott affair in Co. Mayo he served in the Chief Secretary's office for some time. This was an exceptional appointment to an extra Class I clerkship at the high salary of £800,[50] and

Hamilton later complained that he had understood that he would be paid at the same rate when he resumed his post as resident magistrate.[51] While serving at the Castle in Dublin he lived under police protection because his physical resemblance to the Under-Secretary, Mr Burke, was believed to put him at risk.[52] He was posted temporarily to Belfast during the 1886 riots and, after somewhat acrimonious negotiations with the Castle, was granted special allowances that brought his income up to the level he had earned as a Class I clerk.[53] Hamilton was subsequently transferred to a district in Co. Donegal where he was a prominent figure in the clashes that took place when the Plan of Campaign was put into operation on the Olphert estate at Falcarragh near Gweedore. The Campaign was led locally by the parish priest, Fr McFadden, with such confidence in his powers that he declared: 'I am the law in Gweedore.' There was considerable violence on the Olphert estate, where battering rams were used to flatten the hovels of evicted tenants, and the RMs, including Hamilton, heard numerous cases involving charges of conspiracy, riot, and assault. Action was eventually taken against Fr McFadden and it seems that it was Hamilton who insensitively suggested that the priest could be taken most easily as he left the Catholic chapel after Mass. The attempted arrest on 3 February 1889 had tragic consequences, for the people in defence of their priest and place of worship resisted McFadden's arrest with such ferocity that RIC District Inspector Martin was murdered by the mob. Shortly afterwards the RIC sergeant at Donegal town wrote to Dublin Castle of 'a very bad feeling existing among nationalists here towards Mr Hamilton, on account of Fr McFadden' (who had subsequently been arrested) and he urged that the Castle should ask the RM to accept police protection although he had previously refused to do so.[54]

Hamilton survived many threats and several physical attacks during his service in the constabulary and the resident magistracy. The 1880s were especially dangerous years for the RMs but only one of them seems to have died as the result of violence and the circumstances of his death are somewhat obscure. Major Neild was RM for the Claremorris district of Co. Mayo for several years prior to his death in late 1887 or early 1888.[55] No contemporary reports of his death have been traced but an annonymous writer to *The Times* claimed, some thirty years later, that Major Neild was 'beaten to death by a mob' as he left a petty sessions court.[56] The land agent, Sam Hussey, gave a different and perhaps more accurate account in his *Reminiscences*, published in 1904. Hussey recalled that Neild was attacked as he left Charlestown on a side car, with his face obscured as he was sheltering under an umbrella. The crowd mistook him for Hussey's son, Maurice Hussey, another unpopular land agent, and attempted to drag the unfortunate RM off the side car. A priest intervened and rescued him but not before the Major had suffered a severe blow on the head, from which he never recovered; he lived on for some six months after the incident.[57]

Nationalists were to recall the 1880s as the period when the RMs 'flourished with greatest obloquy and notoriety' as an adjunct of the RIC, acting as 'political partisans' eager to coerce opponents of the governments of the day.[58] From an alternative perspective, the unionist civil servant Sir Henry Robinson remembered that in the face of fierce hostility most resident magistrates 'administered the law with justice, tact, and firmness', although he conceded that 'some old veterans . . . were rather an anxiety to the Government at times', being inclined to disregard the legal evidence and rely 'on their instincts' in reaching a verdict.[59] Nationalist perceptions of the institution in the years ahead were largely shaped by attitudes formed during the 1880s but the resident magistracy underwent significant change as the end of the century approached. Its strength was steadily reduced and it became less closely associated with the old Protestant ascendancy as more middle class Catholics and Home Rulers were appointed. For a lengthy period in the late nineteenth and early twentieth centuries relations between England and Ireland were considerably more tranquil than they had been in the decade of drama that was the 1880s, and it was during the Indian summer of the Anglo-Irish that the popular success of the Somerville and Ross short stories established an enduring image of the Irish RM, one that was far removed from their portrayal in the nationalist press of the 1880s

3

Major Yeates and the Irish RMs

Major Yeates, RM for the Skebawn district of west Cork, is the central character and narrator of the Somerville and Ross stories, which are comedies of manners and of incident. They are set in the world of the Big House and the hunting field, peopled with mainly Protestant Anglo-Irish sportsmen and mild eccentrics, mostly Catholic or 'mere Irish' comic servants, vulgar middle-class *nouveau riche* and a roguish peasantry. We first meet the Major as he takes up his new post and encounters the 'half-sir' or squireen, Flurry Knox, who is to become his landlord and friend – and chief instigator of many embarrassments for the RM. The Major's duties as a resident magistrate do not feature prominently in the stories but his official position sets up the comic possibilities explored. He arrives in the south-west of Ireland knowing little of the country or its culture, although he tells us he is of Irish 'extraction'. As in many Irish parishes, the RM of Skebawn is one of very few of the Protestant upper class who comes into contact with all of his neighbours from the aristocracy to the peasantry. When he finds himself involved, often with Flurry, in horse stealing, poaching, poteen drinking or other dubious activities the comedy is heightened by the inappropriateness of such conduct by a resident magistrate.

The cousins Edith Somerville (1858-1949) and Violet Martin (1862-1915), who wrote under the name 'Martin Ross', had published various travel journals and several novels before the RM stories. *The Real Charlotte* (1894) is widely regarded as their greatest achievement, and one of the best Irish novels of the period. It is acclaimed for the depiction of its central character, the vindictive and destructive Charlotte Mullen, but its essential subject matter is the values and attitudes of the Protestant Anglo-Irish as they lived through the last stages of their decline.[1] This was the world of the Big House, the world of Somerville and Ross themselves,[2] and of their resident magistrate. The *Irish RM* stories were begun during a holiday in France in the summer of 1898, at the request of the editor of the *Badminton Magazine*. Twelve stories were published at monthly intervals from October 1898 to September 1899 and Longmans then published the collection in November 1899, under the title *Some Experiences of an Irish RM*. The first edition of

3,000 copies sold out within a month, and the immediate success of the collection brought Somerville and Ross an international reputation. Two more volumes followed, *Further Experiences of an Irish RM* (1908) and *In Mr Knox's Country* (1915).

Written for a mainly English middle-class readership, the stories were and are sometimes criticised for Paddywhackery or presenting 'stage Irish' for the amusement of arrogant Anglo-Saxons. This kind of criticism, as Hilary Robinson points out, 'misunderstands both the nature of the comedy of manners and the range of the stories. We meet a wide spectrum of Irish society in the stories, in which class is used to 'place' characters and much of the comedy arises from incongruous encounters between different classes but, as Robinson notes, 'most of the humour deflects on to the narrator himself . . . when we laugh at the other characters we are laughing at the Anglo-Irish far more than at the other Irish . . . [and] the few English present are also objects of mirth.'[3]

One critic has commented that the stories were 'obviously conceived in holiday spirit'[4] but a study of the manuscripts has shown that considerable effort went into the preparatory work for each of them.[5] The cousins gave close consideration to how the language of their Irish characters should be conveyed to readers, which led them to settle for 'the idiomatic phrase' rather than phonetic spelling of dialect or vernacular.[6] The first twelve of the 'accursed *Bad. Mag.* things' kept them 'desperately at work' until August 1899.[7] On the eve of publication of the collected edition Somerville wrote to her brother that she and Martin were 'rather fed up with orders of articles "in the style of your delightful R.M." ones',[8] and she later remarked that 'Even though it cannot be denied that we both found enjoyment in the writing of them, I look back upon the finish of each story as a nightmare effort.'[9]

The Irish writer, Frank O'Connor, regarded *The Irish RM* as 'one of the most lovable books I know' but he considered the tales to be 'yarns, pure and simple', consisting of 'Nothing, certainly, that responds to analysis'.[10] This opinion seems to be widely shared by literary critics, few of whom have given the same serious attention to the RM stories as they have to the novels of Somerville and Ross, especially *The Real Charlotte*. Yet the comedy is rooted in social realism and the darker side of Irish life is not entirely excluded from the sunny world of Major Yeates. There are 'modernizing' references throughout the three volumes, to motor cars, to women riding astride, to the cinema,[11] and social or political change is alluded to in several of the stories. The encroachment of democracy on the power and privilege of the old ascendancy is obliquley touched upon in *Some Experiences of an Irish RM* where, in 'Holy Island', we meet Mr Canty who is a publican and a Poor Law Guardian. In 'Occasional Licences', unionist disapproval of the so-called Morley Magistrates (Catholic JPs appointed in 1892–5 by the Liberal Chief Secretary, in the face of opposition from the lord lieutenants of many counties) is expressed in the Major's description of Moriarty as one of 'the representatives of the people with whom a paternal Government had leavened the effete ranks of the Irish magistracy', and this is followed by various observations from Flurry which hint at the magistrate's corruption.[12] Political content is even more apparent in a close analysis of a story from *In Mr Knox's Country*, 'The Finger of Mrs Knox', where Flurry's grandmother is approached for help by one of her former tenants who is facing foreclosure and eviction after getting into debt to Goggins the Gombeen, a local publican and shopkeeper. Mrs Knox has lost her acres under the provisions of the Wyndham Land Act of 1903, and she at first rejects Stephen Casey's plea by telling him 'I have no tenants . . . the Government is your landlord now, and I wish you joy of each other.' 'When those rascals in Parliament took our land', she adds, 'we thought we should have some peace, now we're both beggared and bothered!' She then relents and her authority proves still sufficient to rescue Casey from his predicament but Goggins is the sort of man who many unionists feared would soon be running a new Ireland, as the Home Rule Bill had been passed by the time this story was written. This gives considerable significance to Casey's lament over land reform, 'it was better for us when the gentry was managing their own business', and to Mrs Knox's condemnation of Goggins for selling timber from a forest planted by her father, thus destroying in a matter of weeks what had taken many years to grow. Goggins might well have answered that it was English invaders and settlers who first deforested Ireland, as Julian Moynahan has commented, but as Moynahan goes on to suggest it seems that in this story the authors are 'trying to locate some essential quality, power, or value associated with the Anglo-Irish tradition at its best, which might survive or outlast what is left of the rapidly liquidating Anglo-Irish economic, social and political base.'[13]

There is only one tragic story in the collection, 'The Waters of Strife', from *Some Experiences of an Irish RM*. In 'The Waters of Strife', the Major attends a regatta where one of the Sons of Liberty crew is struck on the head with a boat hook wielded by a member of another crew competing in the race. The foul is cheered by Bat Callaghan who is immediately set upon by a bystander wearing the green jersey of the Sons of Liberty football team but a fight is prevented by the RIC sergeant. Next morning the Major learns that blood was 'sthrewn' at the crossroads as the crowds made their way home and that the police are looking for a missing man, Jim Foley. A mysterious caller, perhaps Bat Callaghan, taps at the RMs window late one night to whisper that Foley's body might be found in the river. The mid-night visit reminds the District Inspector of Land League days and he follows up the hint passed on to him by Yeates, discovering the corpse in the river with the head smashed in. Callaghan goes missing and is assumed to be the murderer, and his mother calls on the RM to ask him to keep her out of court when the matter is investigated. No information is given to the police, although they believe the murder was witnessed by many people. Nothing more happens but months pass until the Major goes to England, where he is entertained by his old regiment at a mess party to celebrate his forthcoming marriage. Rifle shots bring the party to an end and it is discovered that the sentry, a recent Irish recruit named Harris, has fired at a face that appeared over a wall near his post. The man is clearly distraught and during the night, after taking a fit, he dies. It is evident that no human being could have reached the spot at which the sentry saw a face and it is assumed that it was a ghost he saw. Yeates is asked to look at a letter found in the soldier's pocket, to see if he can decipher the Irish postmark. The letter is from Mrs Callaghan in Skebawn and the dead soldier is her son, Bat Callaghan. This is an oddly unsatisfactory story compared to most of the others. It has been suggested by Stephen Gwynn that the purpose of Somerville and Ross was to show their English readers 'that "the secret half a country keeps" is kept all the same, when the victim is not a baliff, or the tenant of an evicted farm'. Gwynn reads it as showing the 'exclusiveness' of the Irish peasantry and illustrating how little the RM really knows about them.[14] This is a quite convincing interpretation but there is perhaps more to 'The Waters of Strife', which seems to be straining after but never achieving a greater significance than the minor tragedy with which it deals. Yeates is particularly distanced from the people in this story as he approaches the regatta, noting the beauty of the setting but with his mind full of visions of similar events at Oxford, which were orderly affairs watched by crowds in which there were many 'smart parasols' and 'snowy-clad youths.' As he looks down on the reality of the festival of the Sons of Liberty he sees a jumble of overladen boats on the lake and the 'Black swarms of people' who 'seethed' along the shore. The Major is no more than a bystander when Bat Callaghan is dragged down by one of the Sons of Liberty and 'the coming trouble is averted' by a sergeant of the RIC intervening between the combatants. The Sons of Liberty, who justify their title by the 'patriot green' of their jerseys and their 'free interpretation of the rules of the game', perhaps bear some relation to the United Irish League which was founded in the year that 'The Waters of Strife' was written. The UIL title echoed that of the United Irishmen of 1798, whose rising was commemorated in numerous centenary celebrations in May 1898. The year was also notable for a democratic reform which further curtailed the declining power of the old ascendancy when, in August, the Local Government (Ireland) Act replaced the grand juries with a new structure of local government in the form of elected councils. These developments would not have been welcomed by Martin Ross, with her firm unionist convictions and fears for the country if nationalists should take control. She was unwell when the story was written in the second half of November, having been badly injured earlier that month in the riding accident that probably hastened her death, and it is possible that her personal circumstances go some way to account for the dark tone of 'The Waters of Strife'. Nonetheless, there seems to be some political undertone to the tale in which Bat Callaghan is allied with the representative of British rule in Ireland, the resident magistrate, from the opening line. Moreover, the resolution takes place in England where the fate of Ireland will ultimately be settled by the British response to nationalism and unionism. The story closes with the 'appalling peacefulness' of death and the haunting image of a weeping Mother Ireland figure, the Widow Callaghan bereft of her son. It is 'the economical and effectively pathetic depiction of Bat's mother', John Cronin suggests, that gives validity to 'The Waters of Strife' and in the letter from her found in the dead man's pocket Cronin discerns a 'ring of accuracy reminiscent of Synge'.[15] Whatever its deeper meaning, this tragic tale hints at the violence and superstition beyond the seemingly secure world of the Irish RM, which is threatened directly in a later story, 'Oweneen the Sprat'. In this tale, from *Further Experiences of an Irish RM*, the Major and his household are subjected to intimidation after Yeates has apparently injured Owen Twohig in an accident on Christmas Eve. There is a comic resolution in which Twohig and the 'mountainy men' are revealed as fraudsters intent on blackmail but the story reflects the authors' awareness of the real dangers to which resident magistrates were at times exposed.

The Irish RM has evoked much praise from critics for the comic genius of Somerville and Ross but little perceptive analysis, although as John Cronin has pointed out the stories are the 'comic obverse' of the serious novels: 'only the angle of vision is different'.[16] Julian Moynahan has offered a similar reading and he detects an underlying seriousness that gives thematic unity to the major novel written by the cousins, *The Real Charlotte*, and the comic tales on which their popular reputation largely rests. Moynahan considers the RM stories to be 'in an important sense, about the de-anglicizing of . . . Major Sinclair Yeates, and together [they] make a sequel to *The Real Charlotte*, with a new direction indicated for the Anglo-Irish upper classes as they wrestled with the problem of their future in an Ireland that is rediscovering [its] "Celtic" heritage' and moving towards armed conflict with Britain to gain independence.[17] One possible 'new direction' for the old ascendancy was to abandon its privileges with a good grace and accept the incorporation of the emergent Catholic middle classes, which is a recurring theme in the novels. In the RM stories the intrusion of the Catholic middle class into the world of the ascendancy is portrayed through the presence of the prosperous farming family, the Flynns, in 'A Conspiracy of Silence', from *Further Experiences of an Irish RM*, and more particularly through the *nouveau riche* McRorys who represent the urban middle class. Having prospered as a Dublin coal merchant, McRory buys the derelict Temple Braney house where he and his 'enormous family' scandalise the neighbourhood with their vulgarity. The Major, and Dr Hickey, are snobbishly disapproving of the Flynn daughters, with their 'almost unimpeachable English accents' and their pretentious talk of London and Paris, but Yeates is gradually won over by the McRorys. They feature in three of the stories ('The Pug-Nosed Fox' and 'Sharper Than a Ferret's Tooth', in *Further Experiences of an Irish RM*, and 'The Bosom of the McRorys' from *In Mr Knox's Country*') and there is a clearly discernable change in attitude towards the family. The gloomy old father is given little sympathy for his shyness or embarrassment and the boisterous behaviour of his sons earns them disapproval from the Major, but Yeates is quite entranced by Larky, the high-spirited and good-looking daughter. The McRorys manage to cross the 'bounder-y' line, as Yeates puts it, because of their skills and enthusiasm for sports, riding and dancing. They reinvigorate the world of the RM who, from the outset, is somewhat more friendly or at least more tolerant than some of his fellow-Protestant gentry neighbours. He and Philippa cannot bring themselves to regard the McRorys as their social equals but, in 'The Bosom of the McRorys' (*In Mr Knox's Country*, 1915), the Major acknowledges that 'It was clear that our blood brotherhood with the McRorys was fore-ordained and predestined.' No such 'new direction' was taken by Anglo-Irish Protestant unionists in the real world and in the new Ireland that was emerging they were, as a class, to be as ineffectual as the Dysarts of Bruff House in *The Real Charlotte*.

The Major and his social equals could not, however, become sufficiently 'Irish' to fit the cultural definition of Irishness as Catholic, nationalist, and Gaelic. As Julian Moynahan notes, Yeates may be of Irish extraction but he is the very model of a West Briton, a Protestant gentleman 'with his Oxford education and stint at the Sandhurst riding school, his British army service in an English regiment, his monocle and self-deprecating manner',[18] and an English wife. Despite the process of 'de-anglicization' that Moynahan discerns in the RM stories, the Major's experiences merely educate him to a greater understanding and tolerance rather than fundamentally changing his attitudes or values. Indeed, the cultural nationalism associated with the notion of de-anglicization is gently mocked in the stories, through Philippa's interest in learning Gaelic and Leigh Kelway's determination to 'master the brogue'. It was an influential lecture by Douglas Hyde, entitled 'On the Necessity for De-Anglicizing Ireland', that first proposed the notion of reclaiming Ireland from English influences and the idea gained wide currency during the 1890s and the following decade. It was a major concern of the Gaelic League and it was vigorously promoted by the journalist, D.P. Moran, in his weekly paper, the *Leader*. Moran advocated the philosophy of an 'Irish Ireland' and it was he who derisively labelled as 'West Britons' those Irish men and women whose manners and cultural orientation were seen to be derived from English models. The Major's cultural identity is therefore of some importance if a reader turns to the Somerville and Ross stories as a representative portrayal of a typical Irish resident magistrate of the late nineteenth and early twentieth centuries.

What is most interesting about the stories from a historical perspective is not their merit as literary works but their value as documentary evidence in shaping an enduring image of the Irish RM. It would, of course, be foolish to look to these comic tales for a sociological or historically accurate account of the resident magistracy during the period in which Somerville and Ross were writing but our knowledge of the resident magistrates is extremely limited and the term 'Irish RM', if it means anything today, is usually associated with Major Yeates. As the resident magistrate Christopher Lynch-Robinson recalled, *Some Experiences of an Irish RM* rapidly became a classic 'that penetrated to the utmost ends of the Empire until there was hardly a living Briton in those days who had not read it', and long after the resident magistrates had been swept away by the new order in southern Ireland he found himself frequently compared to the stereotype Major Yeates RM. Lynch-Robinson explained in his memoirs, written in the early 1950s, that 'Even today, I cannot mention the fact that I was once an RM in Ireland without an immediate reference being made to that immortal work and without demands for stories of my own experiences in that capacity.'[19] Nearly fifty years later and almost a century after the stories were first published, new generations of readers are delighting in the comic universe created by Somerville and Ross and a wider audience has been introduced to the Major through the television series made during the 1980s. Yet although the stories are rooted in social realism, the 'angle of vision' in the *Irish RM* is narrow and somewhat distorting. The resident magistrates were not a monolithic group of Protestant upper-class unionists.

Nonetheless, the account the Major gives of his progress from army captain to resident magistrate would have been familiar to many RMs. He tells us that 'A resident magistracy in Ireland is not an easy thing to come by nowadays; nor is it a very attractive job.' We learn that he decided to apply for the post when Philippa accepted his proposal of marriage, and that his ambition was sustained by 'an ingenuous belief in the omnipotence of a godfather of Philippa's . . . who had once been a member of the Government'.

He has evidently waited a long time for the appointment, having meanwhile risen to the rank of major and 'spent a good deal on postage stamps and on railway fares to interview people of influence' before finding himself in the hotel at Skebawn, opening letters addressed to 'Major Yeates, RM'.[20] In his motive for applying for the post, in his pursuit of family and friends with influence, and in his long wait before getting a post he is quite typical of many resident magistrates, and his education and career background were also shared by some of his real-life contemporaries. There were, however, few army officers appointed in the late nineteenth and early twentieth centuries and university graduates were always a minority among the RMs. Although the institution remained predominantly Protestant, and therefore unionist, growing numbers of Catholics were appointed during the period 1890-1921. Some of these resident magistrates were constitutional nationalists, supporters of the Irish Party and Home Rule.

The structural change that took place in the resident magistracy after 1890 was part of the wider process known as 'the Greening of Dublin Castle', whereby the role of the old ascendancy in running the country was diminished. Conservative governments sought to incorporate more Catholics as a means of placating nationalists, while Liberal executives tried to prepare the civil service for a smooth transfer of power when Home Rule was eventually implemented. In 1892 the administration and judiciary were dominated by those who were unionist in politics and Protestant in religion. By 1921 both the administration and the court system were largely controlled by nationalists and Catholics.[21]

These changes in the resident magistracy were accompanied by marked fluctuations in its strength. Numbers declined from seventy in 1891 to only forty in 1907 but increased thereafter to sixty-six by 1911. Those in office in 1890 were mainly upper class and included three sons of the aristocracy, the 'Honourables' William F. Forbes and Harry de Vere Pery (younger sons of the earl of Granard and the earl of Limerick, respectively) and S.F. Carew, second son of the first Baron Carew. Close family connections with the landowning upper classes persisted and this was criticised as sharply as it had been during the 1880s, even though redistribution under the Land Acts was undermining the power of the landowners. The appointment of resident magistrates had been seen by successive administrations as, in part, a means of reducing the power of landowners who in the earlier nineteenth century had dominated the lives of their tenantry as JPs and members of the grand juries as well as employers and landlords. Yet until the 1890s this was the social class background of most resident magistrates, some of whom were actually the owners of landed estates. No such individual was appointed to any district in the county where he held land but, as nationalist critics always argued, a landowner was likely to share the attitudes and sympathies of his class no matter where he served as resident magistrate. An appointment that affronted nationalist opinion in 1892 was that of Robert Olphert. Olphert was a barrister and had been a crown prosecutor but he was also a son of the owner of the Olphert estate at Gweedore in Co. Donegal. As Tim Healy reminded the Commons, there had been much violence and many evictions at Gweedore during the Plan of Campaign, and Robert Olphert had acted as his father's agent as well as representing him in negotiations with Campaign leaders.[22] Olphert's social origins were not apparent from official documents, where his former vocation was given as the legal profession, but he was typical of many others and the landed interest continued to be well represented in the resident magistracy. In the early twentieth century, to give just one example, the former police officer John E. St George was appointed RM in September 1908. He was the son of Lt.-Col. St George of Kilrush House, Freshford, Co. Kilkenny.[23] The family estate was of several thousand acres in the late 1870s[24] and although the acreage had probably been substantially reduced by 1908, under the various land acts, such appointments were never popular.

It was not unusual for men from a landed-gentry background to join the RIC. Its officer-cadet entry system attracted recruits from higher social classes than those from which the English police force were drawn. Nonetheless, the resident magistrates who had served in the constabulary were not all of them sons of landowners. A small minority of police officers who went on to become RMs had worked in other employment before becoming RIC cadets at the minimum age of twenty-one. This in itself suggests that they came from families unable to support them into early manhood. Some had served in the army and one had been ranching in America but others had worked in areas of middle or even lower middle class status, such as school teaching and clerical jobs. William Rice, appointed RM in 1905, was unusual in being a Protestant who had joined the RIC as a constable and been promoted from the ranks. Recruits to the constabulary at this level were mainly Catholics, often the sons of farmers or shopkeepers, and although their level of education was generally higher than that of the bulk of the population their social status was in the lower strata of the middle classes. In general the resident magistracy became less closely associated with the upper class during this period. The increasing incorporation of the middle class is reflected in the presence of eight solicitors by 1911 whereas in the early 1890s RMs with legal qualifications were, with one exception, barristers and therefore of higher social status.

An important unifying factor between the upper and upper-middle classes was their shared experience of the British public school system, whose aims and methods were widely imitated in many private schools that were not among the top group of 150 or so. The system, with its emphasis on the classics and the sports field, fostered a cult of the amateur and the all-rounder while encouraging ideals of team spirit and loyalty to school, country, and empire. It is highly likely, given their social origins, that many of the resident magistrates were exposed to this ethos. The educational patterns of only a minority of them can be reconstructed but some were educated in England at prestigious schools such as Eton and Wellington or at similar Catholic establishments, like Stoneyhurst and Ampleforth, or at minor public schools. Others attended schools in Ireland, ranging from day schools in Dublin and small boarding schools in the provinces to St Columba's College at Rathfarnham, which was the chief Protestant school of its type and known as 'the Eton of Ireland'. One or two were privately tutored at home. Andrew Newton Brady was exceptional in having been educated in France, and David Harrel underwent the rigours of the Royal Naval School at Gosport in Hampshire. As for higher education, the official returns show that graduates were not numerous among resident magistrates in office during this period but evidence from other sources indicates that not all university-educated men stated their academic qualifications, so the proportion of graduates may have been higher than the 18.5 per cent and 30 per cent shown in the returns for 1892 and 1911 respectively. Opportunities for higher education were still limited at this time and the number of graduates among the resident magistrates is, although not large, a reflection of their privileged social origins. At both dates most of those with university degrees had studied at Trinity College, Dublin (a bastion of the Protestant ascendancy), followed by Oxford and Cambridge. By 1911 there were also graduates of the Queen's Colleges and the Catholic University of Ireland.

The sons of the upper and upper-middle classes traditionally went into the army or overseas administration or, to a lesser extent, the law. In Ireland, as we have seen, the RIC was also a socially acceptable career choice. These traditional vocations feature strongly in the returns made to the Commons between 1892 and 1911 but the source material does not lend itself to detailed statistical analysis of the early careers of resident magistrates. The 'former vocation' of the nationalist journalist and barrister P.J. Kelly is shown merely as 'barrister' while Christopher Lynch-Robinson is shown with no previous employment, although he had been an army officer and a temporary civil servant. Under-recording and partial recording such as these instances are further complicated by the overlap between categories as, for example, in the case of former police officers who read for the bar after joining the resident magistracy. What does emerge clearly from the returns is a marked decline over time in the proportion of ex-army RMs and an increase in the numbers of resident magistrates with legal qualifications. As the resident magistracy was 'demilitarised' it became a more professional body.

These changes reflected the response of successive administrations to continued criticism of the institution. Nationalist MPs, journalists and commentators not only continued to complain about the lingering influence of the landowning class but they also raised questions about the numbers of military men and RIC officers appointed, and about the legal knowledge of the RMs. Another concern was the religious affiliation and, by implication, the political allegiance of those appointed. At the beginning of the 1890s, only ten (14 per cent) of the total seventy-seven RMs had legal qualifications and of those only four had practised their profession. The composition of the resident magistracy at this time was a result of appointments made during the disturbed 1880s, when army officers were regarded as particularly suited to the post and the proportion of former RIC officers was allowed to rise to 34 per cent, somewhat above the customary maximum of one third. The official view was that such men were suitably qualified by their previous experience. It was argued that RIC men would have neccessarily acquired knowledge of the law, and it was assumed that army or naval officers would be familiar with legal procedures from attending courts martial. This sort of argument did not satisfy the Nationalist MP who complained to the Commons in 1905 about the appointment of 'English naval and military officers' rather than 'duly qualified Irish lawyers'.[25] An attempt had been made in the late nineteenth century to prohibit the employment of former officers in the Irish civil service but although no legislation to this effect was passed there was little justification for complaint because very few military men had been appointed to the resident magistracy since 1890, none of them English. There was, however, growing pressure on government over the matter of legal qualifications. The legal profession attracted many of the expanding Catholic middle class and as the numbers of solicitors and barristers rose so many of them, of both religions, hoped for public employment to give them a career in Ireland. They pursued their vested interests collectively through the Incorporated Law Society of Ireland, which in the early twentieth century urged repeatedly that all RMs should have professional qualifications. In March 1908 the government of the day was said to be 'fully alive to the desirability of appointing gentlemen who have sufficient legal training',[26] but what was 'sufficient' from an official perspective was considered barely adequate from other points of view.

Yet there were significant changes in the composition of the resident magistracy. By 1911 there were only five military men in office (7.5 per cent of the total sixty-six) and the proportion of former RIC officers was at the customary maximum of one-third. The largest single group, accounting for

40 per cent of the total, was made up of individuals with legal qualifications. Of those with other miscellaneous backgrounds, five had previously held the commission of the peace as ordinary magistrates and two had relevant experience in administering the overseas empire. Critics of the system pointed to the fact that less than half of those with law degrees had actually practised as barristers and the relevance of experience in remote parts of the empire was also questioned, with its reminder of the imposition of British imperial rule on native populations. Vesey V.S. Fitzgerald had been a divisional magistrate and political officer in India before his appointment as RM in 1882, and men with similar experience were joining the resident magistracy throughout the decades after 1890. G.H.P. Colley (a cousin of the Anglo-Irish writer, Elizabeth Bowen) was a resident magistrate in the Transvaal before becoming an Irish RM in 1909 while Major James Meldon, appointed in March 1914, had been chief of police in St Vincent and Grenada before acting as 'civil and military officer' in Uganda. Meldon's appointment in 1914 was raised in the Commons by the Irish Party MP, Mr O'Shee, who questioned the Major's qualifications and referred the Chief Secretary, Augustine Birrell, to a letter of protest about this matter, which the Incorporated Law Society had recently sent to the Lord Lieutenant at Dublin Castle. O'Shee pertinently asked Birrell, 'Is the law in Uganda the same as the law in Ireland', to which the Chief Secretary replied facetiously 'No, I understand there is some slight variation'.[27]

The religion and politics of resident magistrates and others were increasingly a focus of nationalist concern. No official documents recorded the religion of individuals in the judiciary or the administration but Irish Party MPs and several journals kept a close watch on this, arguing that religious prejudice accounted for the predominance of Protestants in positions to which direct appointments were made. The *Irish Figaro* took a keen interest in political appointments made by the Liberal Chief Secretary John Morley in 1895, and in the early twentieth century both the *Irish Catholic* and the *Leader* regularly publicised the proportions of Catholics and Protestants in various branches of the public service. Members of the Irish Party pledged themselves not to accept positions in the Irish administration and although they nominated candidates for appointment as JPs they generally held that it would be improper to use their influence to secure the appointment of any person to a paid government position. This made John Redmond reluctant to cooperate fully with Morley's attempts to make the resident magistracy more representative. Redmond noted in a memorandum of February 1894 that Morley 'said he was going to appoint a batch of RMs and said he would appoint one Parnellite barrister if I would name one. I said I could not do so. He asked me if I knew Miles and Dan Kehoe and were they Parnellites? I said yes'.[28] In the event, neither Kehoe was appointed but an anti-Parnellite Catholic barrister, P.J. Kelly, was made RM in 1895. Kelly had been editor of the *Belfast Morning News*, which strongly supported Parnell until the O'Shea divorce at the end of 1890. On his own initiative Kelly thereafter took an anti-Parnellite line in his editorials, which led to his dismissal by the paper's proprietor. It was not the end of his journalistic career for he went on to edit the *Irish News* which was established in 1891, with clerical support, as an anti-Parnellite Belfast daily paper.[29]

As a growing number of Catholics became RMs, the intermingling of religion and politics made this a sensitive issue even though the Irish Party did not directly nominate candidates for office. Unionists were suspicious of the politics of Catholics while any hint of religious bias in favour of Protestants was quickly seized upon by nationalists. It was this attitude that underlay the observations of an Irish Party MP who, in March 1901, brought to the attention of the Commons the recent appointment of five solicitors. Far from welcoming unreservedly these legally qualified RMs, the MP told the House that four of the five were 'gentlemen carrying on business in the North of Ireland' and he went on to ask the Chief Secretary if the names of 'any Dublin solicitors' had been considered.[30] Without a mention of religion, the MP was clearly highlighting the appointment of individuals likely to be Protestant-unionists. Even the rumour of an appointment was enough to provoke parliamentary questions the following year when there was talk in nationalist circles of a Mr Johnstone having applied or been recommended for a post as RM. Concern over this was understandable as Johnstone was allegedly 'Grandmaster of the Orangemen of the County of Cavan and City of Dublin'.[31] The rumour was, it seems, no more than that. Mr Johnstone did not become an RM, but the resident magistracy remained predominantly Protestant. By the spring of 1907, seventeen Catholics accounted for about a quarter of the sixty-seven RMs in office.[32] Two years later there were twenty-two Catholic RMs, just over one third of the total sixty-five.[33] This was a modest proportion in relation to the size of the Catholic population and, indeed, to the ratio of Catholics to Protestants who were county JPs, but it was enough to offend those unionists who equated Catholicism with nationalism. The issue prompted a question to the Chief Secretary from James Craig in June 1910. Craig was the unionist MP for East County Down (and later, with Sir Edward Carson, a major figure in events that led to partition; Craig became the first Prime Minister (1921-40) of the province of Northern Ireland). He began innocuously by inquiring about the number of vacancies for RMs but went on to ask whether Birrell 'proposed to limit the appointments to members of the staff of the *Freeman's Journal*', the nationalist newspaper with a wide circulation in Ireland. The exchange concluded with Birrell telling Craig that 'up to the

present' no member of the *Freeman's* staff had ever been appointed, to which
Craig responded 'The right hon. Gentleman has not fallen out with the
Freeman's Journal, has he?'.[34] Serious political concerns underlay Craig's questions for by now, with the Liberals in office but the Irish Party holding the
balance of power, it seemed to be only a matter of time before a Home Rule
Bill was passed. Unionist opposition to such a prospect was hardening into a
determination to resist it by whatever means seemed necessary.

Meanwhile, changes under-way in the resident magistracy were accompanied by continuities from the past, such as the continued importance of
patronage in obtaining a post. Many aspiring candidates looked for the support of influential connections. The fictional Major Yeates had based his
hopes on Philippa's godfather, who had once been something in the government, but some applicants had more powerful patrons. In January 1902
Frederick Fitzpatrick was appointed despite being five years over the official
upper age limit of forty, but it was his relationship to Chief Secretary George
Wyndham, rather than his age, that provoked criticism and charges of nepotism. Fitzpatrick had apparently first applied unsuccessfully some fourteen
years earlier. This had come to the notice of the MP for Donegal South,
Swift McNeil, who had somehow obtained Fitzpatrick's original letter – perhaps from a nationalist clerk employed at the Castle. He described the document as 'a begging letter . . . soliciting, on purely personal grounds' a post as
RM. Having read the letter to the House, the MP went on to complain about
'such individuals' as Fitzpatrick being 'put in a position to consign more
respectable gentlemen than themselves to prison cells for political reasons'.
The resident magistracy, he declared, was nothing other than 'a means of
providing out of public funds for the out-at-elbow protogees of the landlord
class'. Wyndham responded by merely stating that Fitzpatrick's local knowledge and experience had satisfied the Lord Lieutenant of his fitness for the
post. The Chief Secretary declined to answer when asked directly by McNeil
if the RM was 'a poor relation of the right honourable Gentleman?'[35]

There was no long wait on the list for Christopher Lynch-Robinson
when he decided to enter public service in Ireland, for he was a particularly
well-connected young man. His father was the Privy Counsellor, Sir Henry
Robinson, who was vice-president of the Local Government Board. (As *his*
father had been before him – it was one of the many 'hereditary' posts in
Ireland, according to the last Treasury Remembrancer, Maurice Headlam.)[36]
When Lynch-Robinson resigned his commission and came home from the
army his father gave him a 'temporary job' in the old age pensions department of the LGB, but after his marriage Lynch-Robinson found the 'meagre'
salary impossible to manage on unless he and his wife lived with his parents.
The Chief Secretary, Augustine Birrell, was therefore asked to help in return

for past favours: 'Some time before, my father had given Birrell's step-son an inspectorship in the Local Government Board and Birrell immediately responded with the promise of the first vacant Resident Magistracy for me.'[37] Christopher Lynch-Robinson was appointed at the age of twenty-seven, in May 1912, and served until the British withdrawal from the twenty-six counties of the Irish Free State.

Lynch-Robinson was by common definition Anglo-Irish but he regarded himself as indisputably 'Irish'. Of Anglo-Norman origins on his mother's side, he could trace his paternal ancestors to 'new English' settlers who came to Ireland in the seventeenth century. His early childhood was spent in Westport, Co. Mayo, before the family moved to Foxrock in Dublin. He had many relatives in England, where he was educated at Wellington and Sandhurst before taking a commission in the Royal Irish Fusiliers. Ireland was always 'home' to Lynch-Robinson but, like others of his kind, he found his indentity challenged by the cultural nationalism of the period, when a search for cultural identity found a place in Irish politics as it did in the politics of other European dependent countries.[38]

The exclusiveness of cultural nationalism was exemplified in the Gaelic Athletic Association, which was formed in 1884 with the Catholic Archbishop of Cashel as its patron. The GAA, which barred members of the RIC and the armed forces, aimed to encourage native Irish sports such as hurling while discouraging 'foreign' English games like soccer, rugby, hockey and cricket. The Gaelic League, founded in 1893, also sought to promote Irish sports and, indeed, all things Irish but it was more inclusive in its purpose than the GAA. The leading figures in the League were the middle-class Protestant Douglas Hyde (son of a Church of Ireland minister), the Catholic Ulsterman Eoin MacNeill, and Father Eugene O'Growney. The primary concern of the organisation was to revitalise the Gaelic language but Hyde, in particular, looked back to a pre-Christian Gaelic past and held 'a vision of a traditional Ireland in which the continuity of an idealised community had been broken by the abandonment of the language after the famine of the late 1840s'.[39] Hyde hoped to define an Irish 'race' in which there would be a place for the Protestant ascendancy, in an Ireland free of the taint of 'anglicization' and unified by the Gaelic language. Such notions were challenged by the editor of the *Leader*, D.P. Moran, who dismissed the idea that the Anglo-Irish were in any way Irish, arguing that the Gaelic and Catholic identities were inseparable and that Anglo-Ireland was irredeemably British, Protestant, and Unionist.[40] He also detected the anti-modernist strain in Hyde's Gaelic League philosophy. The glorification of the peasant and the tendancy to locate the 'real' Ireland west of the Shannon had no appeal for Moran or others who looked to a Gaelic and Catholic urban middle class to regenerate Ireland.

The Irish, like the English, were a mongrel ethnic mix with no sustainable claim to 'racial purity'. The case for a distinct cultural identity was easier to make, and 'anglicization' could be blamed for any discrepencies between the ideal Irish Ireland and uncomfortable reality. Yet the extent of anglicization is debatable. O'Tuathaigh suggests that there is some validity in the argument that a language-bound Celtic consciousness or *mentalité* persisted over time, but he goes on to assert that by the later nineteenth century the standards to which the Irish middle classes aspired were essentially the same as those of the British middle class in general, and he adds that: 'With the significant exception of religious belief and practice, the more prosperous, or even comfortable, elements throughout most of Ireland had achieved or accommodated to a substantial measure of "anglicization", or to put it another way, of incorporation into the cultural fabric of the larger (English-dominated) society'.[41]

The crusade to de-anglicize Ireland was likely to be a formidable task if not only the Anglo-Irish and other upper classes had become West Britons, but also the middle classes and even those who were only modestly 'comfortable'. Joseph Lee, however, has argued that, with the exception of language, Ireland 'was no more anglicized in 1892 than in 1848'. Lee sees the triumph of native values in such concessions from governments as the disestablishment of the Church of Ireland and the land acts, and he suggests that Hyde and others simply confused modernisation with anglicization.[42] The historical debate continues,[43] but the Gaelic Revival barely touched the old ascendancy,[44] with some notable individual exceptions. The Anglo-Irish literature of the time is concerned with questions of national or cultural identity in relation to the adjustments and attitudes of a ruling class in decline, and 'identity' is touched upon directly in several memoirs of this period, often with some irritation at the temerity of others in challenging the writers' self-definition. Not that this was a new experience for the Anglo-Irish, who were traditionally regarded as 'English' in Ireland and as 'Irish' in England. Most, it seems, were perfectly comfortable with the idea of themselves as a group distinct from both the 'mere Irish' and the English, with a hierarchy of loyalties to the family estate, Ireland and Britain. A definition such as this was suggested by John Eglinton in his *Anglo-Irish Essays* of 1917. 'A less invidious name for the Anglo-Irishman', he wrote, 'would now perhaps be the Modern Irishman, the Irishman, namely, who accepts as a good European the connection with Great Britain and yet feels himself to be far more distinct from the Anglo-Saxon than he is from the mere Irishman'.[45] This evaded the difficulties of religious differences by looking forward to a modern world rather than back to a Gaelic past. The resident magistrate, Christopher Lynch-Robinson, based his claim to Irish identity largely on the accident of birth and prolonged exposure to the climate. 'What is an Irishman?' he asked rhetorically in his memoirs, 'the Irishman of today is simply a person that has been born and brought up in Ireland and that has been subjected over the greater part of his life to the influence of the Irish climate and to the impact of the Irish environment. The result has been a type of individual which Kent and Sussex cannot produce . . .'.[46] He went on to suggest that the greatest difference between the two was that 'the Irish are more sensitive and have a much more subtle imagination than the English', which is perhaps some indication that his choice of identity was influenced by the romantic impulse behind the flattering stereotype of the Irish, which contrasted them favourably with the materialistic, philistine and slow-witted English.

Most of the resident magistrates were Irish, by Lynch-Robinson's definition. Only three in office during this period can be positively identified as non-Irish by birth, parentage or upbringing[47] but all of them would have been set apart from the 'mere Irish' by their speech, manner, dress and cultural preferences. This was not because of their 'identity' but a product of the social-class system. Those of upper-class origin included some who were Anglo-Gaelic, who could rightly claim descent from Celtic chieftains or old Irish families, but in many such families one generation or branch had at some time 'turned' to save their lands or escape the penal laws by converting to Protestantism, and there were few that had no record of intermarriage with the Anglo-Irish or the English aristocracy and gentry. Their Catholic faith was shared with the mass of the people but there was little else to distinguish them from Protestant Anglo-Irish members of the upper classes. As for the middle-class resident magistrates, they largely shared the values and attitudes of their socially superior colleagues. Although a hierarchy of status and wealth existed within the resident magistracy, all the RMs were 'gentlemen', drawn from the social groups which were regarded as being especially capable of carrying responsibility and deserving the automatic respect of their social inferiors.

It was their social class and gentlemanly status that primarily unified them as a group, but not all of them matched the image of the fictional Irish RM. A resident magistrate on the eve of the Great War was more likely to be a barrister than a former army officer. He might well be a Catholic and also a nationalist, although where evidence is available it indicates that the Catholic-nationalist and Protestant-unionist equation did not always hold true. A range of attitudes towards Home Rule and the union clearly existed among the resident magistrates and it seems likely that this diversity of opinion increased over time, particularly after the Liberals returned to power in 1906. There were Catholic-nationalist RMs such as the barrister and writer Henry Hinkson and Catholic-unionist RMs like James Woulfe Flanagan. Charles

Paston Crane, a Protestant, Yorkshire-born former RIC officer appointed RM
in 1897, is revealed in his memoirs as a predictably 'true-blue' Conservative-
unionist who feared that Home Rule was a threat not merely to the United
Kingdom but to the survival of the empire itself.[48] More surprisingly,
Christopher Lynch-Robinson had liberal and probably Liberal sympathies far
removed from the unionism of his civil-servant father, Sir Henry Robinson.
Looking back on the feudal paternalism of his grandfather's estate at Athavaille,
in Co. Mayo, Lynch-Robinson commented that 'The whole thing was an
insult to the dignity of man . . . Ireland was these people's country too, and
they were nothing but a pack of serfs in their own land.' His political education owed much to the influence of Sir Sydney Olivier, a one-time secretary
to the Fabian Society. Lynch-Robinson's army career culminated in a period
as private secretary to Olivier when he was governor of Jamaica, and two
years' exposure to quasi-socialist ideas gave Lynch-Robinson 'a decided political push to the left'.[49] His memoirs, written many years later with all the
benefits of hindsight, suggest that he was probably a mild constitutional
nationalist when he became an RM in 1912.

These were the Irish RMs of the late nineteenth and early twentieth
centuries. They had much in common with Major Yeates of the *Irish RM* but
the social reality was more complex and of greater historical interest than the
image presented in the comic stories of Somerville and Ross. In the comic
universe that they created the focus of attention is not on the work of a
resident magistrate but on the social activities of the Major, in 'a life pastorally
compounded of Petty Sessions and lawn-tennis parties'. We are given occasional glimpses of sessions day in Skebawn, with the court house full of 'the
bellowings of the attorneys and the smell of their clients', where the proceedings provided opportunities for 'studying perjury as a fine art'. We also know
that on some mornings the Major is occupied in writing letters but his duties
seem to take up little of his time. The image of the RM and his fictional
experiences would seem to support those nationalist critics who claimed that
the job was a sinecure but the reader would be well advised to ponder on the
hints of realism on which the body of the comedy rests. Somerville and Ross
were deeply familiar with the world of the Irish RM. Within their own
families, male relatives were JPs who no doubt recounted tales of the court
house to the cousins and they were themselves frequent attenders at the petty
sessions court in Skibbereen, where they gathered much material for their
writings.[50] Moreover, the RM for the districts of west Cork and Galway
would have moved in the same social circles as the literary cousins, and both
of them were fully aware of the contrast between the experiences of the RMs
during the land war of the 1880s and the jolly exploits of their fictional RM.
They portrayed only one side of the life of a resident magistrate but they

knew that the experiences of an Irish RM encompassed tragedy as well as humour, and that days of drama were set within a mundane context of routine work.

4

Public Duties: The World of Work

The post of resident magistrate offered the security of salaried and pensionable public employment in a role that carried considerable social status. Despite some unpleasant aspects to the job, and a steady decline in the real value of the income it provided, numerous applicants continued to write up to the Castle in hope of an appointment. This was no sinecure, although the work itself was not particularly onerous in normal times. The responsibilities of the RMs increased as the body of legislation was expanded and there was a corresponding growth in numbers and frequency of petty sessions courts. Attendance at these courts was the main duty of the resident magistrates, but not the only one, and during the period from 1890 the administrative division of the civil service kept a close watch on their performance. Their public duties brought the resident magistrates into contact with the whole range of Irish society. In the world of work they encountered petty sessions clerks, Castle officials, RIC officers and other ranks, members of the legal profession, county JPs, dispensary doctors, Protestant ministers and Catholic priests. At the petty sessions courts they gained many insights into human nature, and the experiences of an RM gave him considerable knowledge and understanding about the lives of the mass of the people. This chapter explores the work of the resident magistrates, beginning with some general comments on pay and conditions, length of service and other matters before moving on to identify various factors that differed from district to district. Thereafter, consideration is given to the duties and responsibilities of the RMs, and the focus then shifts to their relations with the officials and people they met in the course of their work.

One consequence of the structural changes described in chapter three was that as the middle classes were increasingly incorporated into the resident magistracy the RMs became somewhat less likely to be men of private means. At the beginning of the 1890s a resident magistrate was 'socially, only less inferior than the local magnate, to whose class he often belonged' and he 'usually had a few hundreds a year to eke out [his] salary'.[1] Until 1920 salaries remained at the levels set in the 1870s (starting at £425 for third class RMs, increasing by £125 per annum on promotion to second and the first class), although the Resident Magistrates (Belfast) Act of 1904 raised salaries for the Belfast resident magistrates to £1,000 a year.[2] The middle-class men appointed in this period were comparatively 'poor', according to Katherine Tynan.[3] The material circumstances of the resident magistrates became worse during the Great War but financial considerations did not deter candidates from applying for the post. The 'list' continued to exist because, as the Under-Secretary told the 1913 Royal Commission on the civil service, 'in the case of the resident magistrates vacancies occur pretty frequently, and there is a great competition for these posts'.[4] The 'department of resident magistrates' was the only one for which the administrative division kept a register of applicants. In some years no appointments were made, the average per year being about two. Once in office RMs tended to serve until retirement unless death cut short their careers. Resignations were few, although several RMs went on to higher office in the overseas administration or to other branches of the administration in Ireland. Sir Henry Blake was an RM and SRM before becoming governor of the Bahamas, Cecil Roche left the resident magistracy in 1892 to join the Fisheries Department, and there are other examples such as Walter Edgeworth-Johnstone, RM from 1907 until around January 1915, when he was appointed chief of the Dublin Metropolitan Police. There were temporary disruptions in their periods of office for resident magistrates like C.P. Crane, who went off to the Boer War in 1900-1,[5] and W.E. Callan, who while listed as an Irish RM was employed as private secretary to the Governor-General of Australia. Callan, a barrister and civil servant, was appointed RM in December 1905 but in a return to the Commons dated August 1911 his overseas posting was recorded with a note to the effect that his salary as a resident magistrate was 'in suspense' for the duration.[6] Some resident magistrates were called upon to assist the administration in other capacities, as in 1913 when Robert Starkie served on the Committee of Inquiry into the RIC and DMP.[7]

Notions of 'duty' and ideals of public service may have motivated many of the RMs but Christopher Lynch-Robinson regarded the salary as 'good for those days' and it was partly this that lured him away from the Local Government Board. He would have preferred to stay with the LGB but doubted his ability to make a successful career in local government, as the work was 'fearfully technical, and required a lot of legal knowledge and training'. A lack of legal expertise was, of course, no bar to becoming a resident magistrate. Yet Lynch-Robinson 'did not particularly like the idea of being an RM; punishing grown men did not appeal to me as an exactly interesting career'. He took up his first post in Donegal full of doubts about the future and later he 'pulled every string within reach' to get a transfer to a district near Dublin, so that he could read for the Bar.[8]

No maps of the districts to which the resident magistrates were appointed have been located but the RMs were responsible for the administrative areas in which their petty sessions were located and a district often encompassed parts of adjoining counties. The petty sessions for each district were listed in the annual RIC handbooks, which show that the districts were subject to some minor changes over time, in terms of the geographical area they covered, the number of petty sessions in each area, and the location of headquarters. There were also other variables that impinged on the working lives of the RMs. Local climate and topography made life more difficult in the far west than on the east coast, for example, while the condition of the roads and the availability of rail services differed from region to region. The size of a district and the number and location of petty sessions was determined chiefly by the density and distribution of population but districts tended to become larger with the advent of railways and motorised transport. These technological developments played some part in the reduction in the strength of the resident magistracy.

A district headquarters was usually in the principle town or centrally located, but the Castle was sympathetic to individual preferences over this matter. Requests to reside outside the designated district were invariably refused but there are examples of resident magistrates living, with official permission, in places other than the headquarters and in some instances the location of headquarters was changed to suit the incoming resident magistrate. On occasion nationalist MPs questioned this, as they did in August 1894 with reference to permission given to Colonel Longbourne to live at Portumna instead of Loughrea, which was the usual headquarters of the RM for that district of east Galway. It was alleged that Colonel Longbourne had a close association with the agent for Lord Clanricarde, on whose estates evictions were underway, and that the RM was intending to 'reside in the immediate vicinity of Portumna Castle'. The Chief Secretary's explanation that there was no suitable house available in Loughrea was countered by MPs suggestions that this was not so but that Lord Clanricarde owned an appropriate residence and refused to carry out necessary repairs.[9] The implication was that the RM would be conveniently on hand as some protection for Clanricarde's agent.

Another area in which the RMs had some choice was over where they served and the timing of transfers, which were sometimes made on request for family or other reasons. The idea of limiting the period that a resident magistrate stayed in one district was rejected in 1894, when a considerable number had been 'five years and upwards at their present stations'.[10] There was no clear pattern to length of postings but in general newly appointed junior RMs tended to move more frequently than their senior colleagues.

Some moved from place to place several times in a few years while others stayed in the same district for twenty years or more.

The workload varied between districts although not to the extent suggested by differences in numbers of courts held. Throughout the period 1890 -1921 daily petty sessions or police courts were held in Belfast and Cork city and, at various times, in other large places such as Limerick, Portarlington and Queenstown (Cobh). Belmullet, in north-west Mayo, was the district with the fewest petty sessions. Only five courts were held in that district, sitting six times a month, whereas at the other extreme there were twenty-one courts or twenty-five sittings each month in the Ballymena district of Co. Antrim. The Bantry district of west Cork (which included Skibbereen, the 'Skebawn' of the *Irish RM*) came somewhere in the middle, with ten courts sitting sixteen times a month. In assessing the workload, however, distances to be travelled and other factors need to be considered. The majority of RMs across the country had to attend at least one court at a distance of twenty miles or more from their headquarters and in the provinces of Ulster, Connacht and Munster a minority were responsible for courts from thirty to over forty miles distant. In this respect the RM for Clonmel district, Co. Tipperary, was best placed as his most remote court was only thirteen miles from Clonmel. In north-west Mayo, in contrast, the RM at Belmullet had a monthly court in the town itself but his other four petty sessions were from twenty-five to over forty-eight miles from his headquarters. Courts in such large, scattered districts as Belmullet were usually scheduled so as to make it possible for the RM to be away on a tour of the outposts for perhaps one or more weeks at a time. The frequency of petty sessions ranged from daily to weekly, fortnightly or monthly, and where the day or time coincided or otherwise precluded the RM attending he was urged to pursuade the JPs to alter the sittings, which could be done without reference to any higher authority. The distances to travel to court were only a part of the problem that some resident magistrates had to contend with in carrying out their duties. Mountainous parts of the south-west provided their own particular challenge and so too did the storm-lashed districts of the western coast. The RM for Galway had to travel no more than twenty-three miles to his furthest petty sessions but that court was on the Aran Islands. Bad weather sometimes prevented a crossing from the mainland and there was always the possibility of a gale blowing up and stranding the RM off-shore for several days.

Transport costs were covered by the commuted forage allowance but horses were still the best means of getting about in some circumstances. Major Yeates of the *Irish RM* noted ruefully that 'the man who accepts a resident magistracy in the south-west of Ireland voluntarily retires into the prehistoric age', and although he believed that the horse was 'obsolete as a mode of transport' he nonetheless recognised that to 'institute a stable' was inevitable.[11] Over the course of the stories the Major took to riding a bicycle and eventually bought a motor car. This was typical of the times and whereas horseback, side-cars and trains were the usual modes of transport for the resident magistrates of the early 1890s, by the turn of the century and later bicycles, motor cycles and cars were commonplace. When Lynch-Robinson took up his post in Donegal he found that most of his petty sessions courts 'lay at the back of wild, mountainous regions'. Stationed there from 1912 to 1918, he found the place 'delightful' in summer but 'the winters on that Atlantic sea-board were frightful'. His district was sparsely populated and there was little chance of rescue if his motor cycle broke down on 'the terrible roads, bleak and desolate and exposed to wind, rain and snow'. He later bought a second-hand Ford car and, 'as there were no garages within miles of Donegal', he studied motor mechanics in his spare time and fitted up a workshop, eventually becoming so proficient that he could 'undertake the most complicated repairs'.[12] The horse was not quite obsolete, however. Henry Hinkson, in the Claremorris district of Co. Mayo, made a gallant effort to reach Ballyglass petty sessions on horseback in February 1916, when heavy snow falls had made the road impassable to other traffic.[13] He was perhaps encouraged to keep faith with the horse by his experiences of motoring on the rough roads of Mayo. Among several tiresome experiences, the RM had a particularly trying journey in the autumn of 1915 when he was directed to attend the Crossmolina petty sessions in north Mayo, some considerable distance from his station at Claremorris. He explained his late arrival at court to officials in Dublin in a note attached to his monthly summary of duty: 'Left station at 9.45 by motor. Delayed near Foxford by a bad puncture and later passing through Newtown by a horse and cattle fair, which blocked the road for ¼ mile. Arrived at Court fifteen minutes late in consequence but in time to adjudicate on the important cases. On the return journey was again delayed by a punctured tyre.'[14]

When Lynch-Robinson moved on to Collon, Co. Louth, he was greatly impressed by the ease with which he could get to his courts, after years of travel on mountain roads in Donegal. In Co. Louth he could enjoy the comforts of the dining car on the Dublin-Belfast express when he attended courts in Drogheda or Dundalk and 'other Petty Sessions were easily accessible, at no great distance along fine steam-rolled roads bristling with petrol stations, garages and hotels'.[15] Louth was far from typical and it was not only in remote districts west of the Shannon that the state of the roads impinged on the routine of a resident magistrate. In the summer of 1914 Major Herries-Crosbie, RM for the Wexford district, was taken to task by the administrative division for having missed two petty sessions sittings in April. Herries-Crosbie had been using a car for two years and had seldom failed to reach his courts, which he considered a matter for congratulation as the roads in his district were 'mended' from November through to March by having small quarry stones spread over them, with 'no rolling or fine crushing'. This rough surface made it difficult to drive at more than walking pace and it did untold damage to the RMs car. Explaining all this in June he added that 'even now', in midsummer, the only road into Oulart was 'beyond description. . . . I have never seen such a road in the wildest parts of the United Kingdom.'[16]

The petty sessions were held on any day of the week including Saturdays and in some districts the resident magistrate was in court four or five days in most weeks, although the court schedules often left either a Monday or Friday (or both) free to make a long weekend once or twice a month. The RMs were, nonetheless, on duty at all times unless leave of absence had been granted. They recorded their movements in detail in the official diaries issued every year and the monthly summaries of duty sent up to the Castle showed their day to day whereabouts, 'at station' or attending a named petty sessions. Time of arrival at the court, and of departure, were recorded as was the number of miles travelled. Information about the 'exact nature of duties performed' when not in court was requested but rarely given, although some RMs were more conscientious than others about filling in the details asked for in their returns. The summaries were cross-checked at the Castle against those of the petty sessions clerks and an explanation was asked for if any discrepencies were found. In the courts it continued to be customary for the RM to preside and his role remained unchanged, as guide and influence on the unpaid JPs, who generally deferred to the resident magistrate but whose findings could not be over-ruled by the resident magistrate. If a resident magistrate did exceed his powers in any way his adjudication was usually set aside on appeal to the Castle, or challenged in a higher court.[17] The RMs dealt alone with the taking of depositions in indictable offences of a serious nature. This entailed taking and recording evidence submitted by the prosecution and deciding if a *prima facia* case existed. If so, the defendent was returned for trial but if no case was made then he or she was discharged. Every JP was empowered to take depositions but by customary practice it was left to the resident magistrates and, according to Lynch-Robinson, 'the difficulty of confining such duties to the RM was very easily overcome by the simple method of conducting the proceedings in a police barrack and putting a constable on the door to keep out the local Justices'.[18] 'Special Duty' is a recurring term in the monthly summaries, which covered all duties undertaken outside a resident magistrate's own district. It included covering for absent colleagues in adjoining districts, and attending courts where two magistrates were required for some cases but the attendance of local JPs could not be relied upon. It was also used when a resident magistrate was sent to investigate political or quasi-criminal political activity in a disturbed area.

The RMs were asked for a special report on their districts in the autumn of 1890, when famine threatened after a poor harvest and partial failure of the potato crop. These reports[19] provided information on the potato crop, on the usual diet of the people, on food prices, fuel supplies and costs, local employment and wages, and the health of the population. Most of the surviving reports are in the form of typed summaries, annotated by a Castle official, and they were clearly intended to supply evidence on which an informed decision could be taken about implementing relief measures. The cry of famine was often met with suspicion in Dublin and London, for there was a widespread and persistant belief that distress was always much exaggerated in the hope of extracting money from a reluctant government. There was also immediate concern in 1890 that granting relief in a district might indirectly assist the Plan of Campaign. These attitudes are apparent in reports from counties Waterford and Donegal. The resident magistrates for Dungarven and Tramore districts reported that 'The farmers of the County Waterford are not in the least dependent on the potato . . . the labourers are exceedingly comfortable and healthily housed'. The potato harvest was down by about a third and although food prices were generally 'very moderate', potatoes had gone up from 5*d*. (about 2p) to 7*d*. per stone. The RMs concluded that this sudden increase was 'mainly attributable to the *political* cry of famine'. The emphasis on 'political' was that of the unknown annotator at the Castle, who underlined other similar points in the report from Donegal. There had been a general failure of the potato crop in some of the most congested parts of Co. Donegal. The RMs pointed out that during the winter months there was practically no employment for men: 'In that season the women, by sprigging and knitting, are the principal bread-winners' but the women's earnings were 'very small'.

It was anticipated that in parts of the county there would be 'absolute want in very many cases . . . unless relieved by charity or employment' but Ulick Bourke, the resident magistrate for Dunfanaghy district, gave a different opinion about his area. Bourke was a barrister who had been a legal assistant to the Land Commissioner before his appointment in 1887 and he perhaps took a particular interest in events on the Olphert estate at Falcarragh, where the Plan of Campaign was operating.[20] He observed that 250 evicted families (1,150 people) were being supported by what he referred to as 'the Dillon Fund'. He did not foresee 'the slightest chance of famine or serious distress arising' unless support for the evicted tenants was withdrawn but he noted that a further 100 families were to be evicted later in the month. If relief works were started he believed that 'all the evicted tenants would be put on', although he added that works could be started in Gweedore and Glenties, 'which would not touch the Falcarragh end'.

This concern that relief might effectively subsidise the Campaign at government expense was also acknowledged by the RM for Bantry district in west Cork, an area that had been disturbed throughout the summer months. In July over one hundred policemen were drafted into Bantry when Captain Welch RM and another resident magistrate held a special court under the Crimes Act. While the court was in session, two companies of the Cameronian Rifles were held in readiness at Skibbereen in case of emergency. Eleven men 'of the agricultural class', from Goleen, were charged with unlawful assembly on a date in May. They were further charged with intimidating the Church of Ireland rector of Toomore and disturbing public worship at the Protestant church. Eight of the defendents were found guilty and sentenced to one month with hard labour, and they were ordered to find sureties for their good behaviour thereafter or serve another six months in default of bail.[21] It was against this background of unrest that the RM wrote from Skibbereen on 26 October 1890 to report on his district. He gave a mass of detailed information about the small farmers ('say with two cows and a pig'), the labourers and sand boatmen of the district, and the fishermen concentrated at Baltimore and Castletownberehaven. He noted that competition in the bakery trade might benefit those of the poor who bought in bread, he estimated what credit a family might get over the winter at the shop they dealt with for provisions, and described 'A new venture "The Tea Van" [which] plies its trade everywhere in this district'. A van driver, he explained, would leave ½lb tea at a poor man's cottage and not ask for payment until his next round, when he might repeat the offer, but then for every ½lb delivery he would charge 3*s.* (15p) a pound, leaving the labourer always in debt for what Welch claimed was tea inferior to that 'sold in Military Canteens at 1*s.* 3*d.*' (or about 7½p) . The RM feared that 'The outlook for the coming winter is bad' but he described the population as currently healthy. 'The children of the very poor, tho' clothed in rags and as dirty as human beings can be, are fine children and splendidly healthy', he commented, and the district was 'as healthy as any spot on the globe. People die of Old Age, Whiskey, Colds. . . . Occasionally of Fever, nearly always attributable to contaminated drinking water.' The people were likely to need relief before the winter was over but the Captain hinted at the need for forethought about how this should be managed. He remarked that 'Any extra relief given thro' the poor law Guardians would be relief to the Plan of Campaign and other aids to Boycotting'.[22] By mid November the priests and people of the district were putting pressure on the authorities to relieve distress. A crowd of about 800 small farmers and labourers, bearing black flags and demanding relief or employment, 'beseiged' the

Guardians of the Schull Poor Law Union at their meeting. Four priests led the demonstrators. Father Forrest, of Goleen, stated that his parishioners would starve unless they were relieved immediately and added that they would give up their holdings to enter the workhouse if no alternative aid was given. A deputation of directors from the Skibbereen and Schull Railway also attended the Board meeting and pursuaded the Guardians to pass a resolution calling on the government to grant money for extending the railway line to Crookhaven, so as to provide employment for the people[23] and, of course, cheap labour for the Company. There were always political implications in granting relief when land agitation was rife but inevitably mounting rural distress acted as a spur to political protest over the land question, as it did again later in the period when William O'Brien's United Irish League was formed.

The UIL was founded at Westport, Co. Mayo, in January 1898. With its slogan 'the land for the people', the organisation had a particular appeal for the smallholders of the west where opposition to graziers or 'ranchers' was growing, although the process of land redistribution was actually already underway through the activities of the Congested Districts Board. The League was from the outset a nationalist political organisation, not solely concerned with argrarian agitation, and it rapidly gathered considerable popular support throughout most of the country outside Dublin but it failed to establish itself in Ulster.[24] Its strength alarmed the parliamentarian factions, who feared losing the political initiative to O'Brien. Encouraged by the Church, the party reconciled its differences and was reunited in January 1900 under the leadership of John Redmond. Thereafter the UIL became the constituency organisation of the party, as had the Land League of the 1880s.

The significance of the UIL in the history of the resident magistrates is that once again special courts were constituted and certain counties proclaimed, and the conduct of the RMs again came under nationalist scrutiny. UIL activists were involved in cattle driving, in attacks on 'land grabbers' who took evicted holdings, and in the type of agrarian 'outrage' familiar from the past. UIL 'courts' were held to settle agrarian cases, opponents were villified in newspapers sympathetic to the League, and intimidation and boycotting were widespread in the most disturbed areas. There were numerous prosecutions for these and other offences, particularly that of illegal assembly. Agitation was not on the scale of the land war of the 1880s but the police were hard pressed in the worst districts, in parts of Clare, East Cork, Fermanagh, Galway, Roscommon, Sligo and Tipperary. The League achieved political success in the sweeping victory of nationalist candidates in the elections under the Local Government Act of 1898 but as a popular movement it was at its peak in the first years of the twentieth century, until its aims were largely realised in the Wyndham Land Act of 1903.

During 1901 and 1902 Irish MPs asked questions in the House about methods of taking depositions, about the powers of resident magistrates' in special courts, and about their relationship with the executive. Charles Paston Crane, home from the Boer War, turned down the offer of reinstatement in Donegal and was temporarily posted to Co. Sligo to deal with boycotting and intimidation: 'Bands of men marched through the town at nightfall, booing and hooting and occasionally throwing stones at houses of obnoxious persons' and police guarding a boycotted landed gentleman had to set up their own canteen because the RIC was also ostracised. It was difficult to get convictions at petty sessions, with the bench 'packed with sympathisers', so the RM adopted a more effective method of dealing with demonstrators. He had informations sworn and the defendants arrested, then brought before him out of petty sessions, and there bound them over 'in solvent sureties' to keep the peace and be of good behaviour for various periods or, in default of the bail, to go to prison.[25] The commission of the peace gave all JPs powers to act in this way but few chose to do so and Crane's methods were understandably unpopular. He was particularly criticized about a 'mid-night Court' held in the police barracks at Ballymote in July 1901, from which the defendants were said to have been bundled off to Sligo jail without being given time to raise bail.[26]

At the end of 1901 there was a sudden increase in the number of resident magistrates' certified as qualified to hear cases under the coercion acts, in anticipation of measures being taken to deal with the increase of offences of unlawful assembly. By July 1902 the *Dublin Gazette* listed twenty-two RMs as qualified to adjudicate in special courts under the Criminal Law and Procedure (Ireland) Act, twenty of whom had been declared so qualified between 6 December 1901 and 8 May 1902. The Chief Secretary told the Commons that of the twenty, 'fourteen were certified before the issue of proclamations, and six since'.[27] The resident magistrates R.L. Brown (appointed in 1894) and Alfred Harrell (appointed in 1900) adjudicated in a number of special courts from January to mid-July 1902, and convicted eighteen individuals during that period.[28] Harrell (a former RIC officer) was an easy target for criticism because of his relationship to the Under-Secretary, Sir David Harrell, an issue raised by the MP for Kilkenny, who asked if 'Mr Harrel [was] directed to act in nearly all of these cases by his father?'[28] The case that attracted most hostility involved the MP for Leitrim North, a Mr McHugh, who was sentenced by Harrell and Brown to three months imprisonmenmt for contempt of court. McHugh was a newspaper proprietor who had frequently attacked F.B. Henn, the resident magistrate for Sligo district, in the columns of his paper. Henn would usually have heard the case, as the alleged offence took place in his district, but 'Mr Henn's relations with the hon.

Member have, for some time past, been such as to make it undesirable that he should act as one of the Court'.[29] John Redmond took up the matter by reminding the House that some fifty to sixty persons, including several MPs, had been convicted and imprisoned since January by resident magistrates who were 'paid servants of the prosecutor . . . and removable at a moment's notice.' The special courts were a 'ludicrous' system of tribunals, he told the Chief Secretary, in which 'the right hon. Gentleman makes up his mind to prosecute some man for a speech which does not fit in with his view of how public controversy should be carried on, and he tells his Under-Secretary, Sir David Harrell, to institute a prosecution, and Sir David Harrell sends a note to his son who is one of these removable magistrates, and he tells his son to go down and give an impartial trial to the prisoner'.[30] The Chief Secretary pointed out in response that 'far from seeking a bench likely to be hostile to the hon. Member for North Leitrim' the government had 'avoided purposely including on that bench a man who had been outrageously attacked' in the newspaper owned by the defendant on trial. Wyndham went on to deplore allusions to the fact that Alfred Harrell was the son of Sir David Harrell, and in a noisy Commons' exchange he declared that the Under-Secretary had acted as any civil servant must, 'as the instrument merely of the Executive Government to carry out the orders and discharge all that is needed to effect the policy of the Government of the day'. This was greeted with cries of 'And so did his son'.[31] The whole incident highlighted and reinforced long-standing criticisms of the resident magistracy. Not only did it raise renewed doubts about the impartiality of the resident magistrates but it seemed to confirm the belief that the institution was tainted with nepotism and that loyalty to the executive was often reinforced by family feeling. Wyndham was still defending the RMs in the Commons in October 1902 but the experiences of Harrell and the others directly involved in the conflicts of the early twentieth century were exceptional incidents in the mundane routine of a resident magistrate's working life over the period from 1890. The daily round of the petty sessions was more familiar to the RMs than the political dramas played out in the special courts at time of crisis and conflict.

The petty sessions of a country district were also familiar to Somerville and Ross for the court house at Skibbereen was one of their 'favourite haunts for the garnering of dramatic flights of speech'.[32] The cousins were often among the spectators, as the Bantry lawyer and later QC, Sergeant A.M. Sullivan, recalled in his memoirs. In his young days, 'going to the courts' was 'something between national pastime and national education' and the entertainment was 'far superior' to that found in the later pastime of going to the pictures, because 'the tragedies and comedies were real and the actors living, and there was unfolded day after day the true and intimate life of the people of Ireland'.[33] In similar vein, Edith Somerville wrote in her Introduction to the Faber and Faber edition of the *Irish RM* (1928) that 'an Irish RM had his compensations. A southern or western Irish Petty Sessions Court can teach many things, often useful, more often entertaining'.[34] Courts were generally well-attended and both C.P. Crane (RM 1897-1920) and Christopher Lynch-Robinson (RM 1912-22) recount various amusing anecdotes comparable to some of the experiences of Major Yeates. Crane observed that 'an hour's "law" could be good entertainment' if the solicitor for the defence tried to browbeat the RIC sergeant or made 'an impassioned appeal to the Bench on behalf of his client; "Squandering his carcase on the Bench", as one litigant put it',[35] in a phrase that would surely have delighted Somerville and Ross. The work of a resident magistrate had its lighter moments but Lynch-Robinson looked back on his time in Donegal as 'an inactive monotonous existence occasionally broken by disconnected and unrelated incidents provided at irregular intervals by my Petty Sessions Courts'. No 'epoch-making cases' were brought before him, the majority being 'minor police cases of drunkeness, with or without disorderly conduct, failure to have a light on the donkey cart at night, using obscene and threatening language to a neighbour . . . allowing cattle to wander on the public road [and] a lot of family squabbles'.[36]

Courts around the country varied in size and dignity, as they did in Co. Kerry where assizes, quarter sessions and petty sessions were held in the county town in a 'pretentious, Corinthian-pillared edifice guarded by two guns captured at Sebastopol', while other petty sessions took place in 'the little whitewashed, thatched cabin in the remote country district, with its mud floor and bare rafters and, in winter weather, the pungent smell of turf smoke mingled with wet frieze'.[37] Major Yeates of the *Irish RM* was familiar with 'the inevitable atmosphere of wet frieze and perjury'[38] and so it seems was C.P. Crane, who claimed that:

> The perjury committed in these courts beggared all description. It was flagrant. The fluency with which a man or woman would lie to gain the smallest advantage over an adversary was such that it bewildered the brain. Sometimes, when hearing a publican's case, I have wondered whether the whole thing – offence, prosecution and defence was not a dream; whether the door described as 'open, your Honour', by the police and 'closed' by the defendant, had really any existence in fact. Whether the man 'just after having a pint of porter' according to the police, and according to a witness, 'not a tint good nor bad', had any existence either.[39]

Crane's comments should not be read as merely the expression of prejudices against the Irish masses, common to many Englishmen of his class and time. It seems that there were somewhat different attitudes to the law in Ireland than there were in England. As Charles Townshend reminds us, 'Maria Edgworth distinguished the attitude of "an Englishman who expects justice" and used the phrase "I'll have the law on you", from that of "the Irishman who hopes for partiality", whose threat was "I'll have you up before his honour".'[40] Elsewhere, in an appreciation of *Some Experiences of an Irish RM*, Stephen Gwynn remarked of the Irish that 'There is no people in the world more willing to invoke justice between litigants, there is none less willing to further the arrest of a criminal'.[41]

The RMs dealt mainly with the most minor infringements of the law in the cases that came before the petty sessions, although some were serious enough to be sent on to higher courts. It was customary for the petty sessions clerk to send a list of scheduled hearings, a day or two before the court, and the clerk usually drew attention to any case of a serious nature or legal complexity. When the list was a catalogue of routine offences the clerk might add a note to the effect that the RMs presence did not seem neccessary, but he might specifically ask him to attend if the local JPs were unreliable, unwell, or otherwise known to be unlikely to be on the bench. Henry Hinkson was sent a list of cases to be heard at the Killala petty sessions, in north Co. Mayo, when he had been in office little more than a month and was sharing some experiences of the fictional Irish RM. Hinkson was quartered in a Castlebar hotel and trying to find a suitable house, while also settling into his new role. The barrister found himself adjudicating in thirty-three cases at Killala on 2 December 1914. They included three cases of drunkeness (one of them 'disorderly'), two assaults, two 'abusive and threatening language', and six charges of 'unlighted vehicle'. There was also a more serious charge, of 'cruelty to child', but the majority were cases in which the defendant had allegedly broken the current sheep-dipping order.[42] This was the reality of the working world of the RM for much of an average career. There were some who never sat in a special court, never put down a riot, and who were no more oppressors of the people than the ordinary JPs who sat on the bench with the RMs. The population of Ireland was generally law-abiding, apart from quasi-political crimes arising out of the land agitation or other nationalist activities, a fact which led Christopher Lynch-Robinson to remark that there were 'no criminal classes in the Irish countryside.' Only two cases stood out in his recollection of adjudicating in Co. Donegal. One was a Somerville and Ross sort of case, in which a man was charged with attempting to dynamite salmon out of the Owenea river. James Sweeny was brought before the court at Killybegs but his brother, Michael Sweeny, gave evidence that he had not seen James throw a dynamite cartridge into the river, as the RIC constable alleged. The RM was 'much impressed by Michael's evidence in the witness box' and believed him to be telling the truth, but he also knew the police constable as 'a good and reliable man, and the last person on earth to manufacture a case against anybody'. The case was dismissed but Lynch-Robinson later discovered from the defending solicitor that it was actually Michael Sweeny, the witness, who had thrown the dynamite charge. The arresting officer had mistaken the identities of the brothers and accused the wrong one and so, without committing perjury, they were able to outwit the law. The other memorable case was more serious, involving a man and a woman charged with conspiracy to murder in the aftermath of a premarital pregnancy. Having 'got into trouble', the woman took the boat to England to stay with friends until the baby was born but while there she and her partner exchanged letters in which 'they laid very definite plans for the murder of the baby as soon as possible after its birth'. The baby was still-born but somehow the letters had reached the police and the couple were eventually arrested. They were not professionally represented and sat before the RM in the Raphoe police barracks 'frightened and miserable', asking no questions, offering no defence. Lynch-Robinson was evidently troubled by the pair. His knowledge of the law at that time was limited to what he could 'mug up' from the four law books he possessed (one of which, O'Connor's *Irish Justice of the Peace*, he was in the habit of taking to petty sessions in the carrier of his motorcycle) but as he wrote out the depositions he recalled the seven essential preliminaries to support a murder charge. He 'refused informations' and discharged the prisoners after deciding that the still-born infant was not a victim 'in being' (essential preliminary five), as the evidence showed that the umbilical cord had not been cut and therefore the baby had no separate existence from the mother. The resident magistrate's ruling went up through the RIC to the law advisors to the Crown and was eventually ratified by the higher authorities in Dublin. Lynch-Robinson was not informed officially of the outcome but asked his friend Bobby Roberts, the RIC County Inspector in Sligo, 'to keep me posted'.[43]

Resident magistrates had close professional relationships with RIC officers but they also came into contact with a wider range of people, of both religions and with various political views. Lynch-Robinson's petty sessions clerk in Donegal town, a young man called Atty Dunlevy, was 'a typical example of the New Thought in Ireland' when the RM knew him between 1912 and 1918, in the period when nationalism was growing ever stronger.[44] Informal friendliness clearly existed between some resident magistrates and the clerks to their petty sessions courts. Notes about forthcoming courts not infrequently touched on unofficial matters, as in early 1919 when the clerk to Croom petty sessions wrote to P.J. Kelly at Limerick to inform the RM that there was only one summons for 9 January, 'and that a case of trespass of goats which is likely to be settled before hearing'. It would not, he suggested, be necessary for Kelly to attend as he was sure of one the local JPs, and he added 'I am not forgetting the potatoes which I hope to have ready shortly'.[45] A good relationship between the resident magistrates and petty sessions clerks helped the smooth running of the courts and was also important because the resident magistrates' attendance recorded in his monthly summary of duty was checked at the Castle against the clerks' monthly returns.

Relations between the resident magistrates and the administration in Dublin were not always easy. Katherine Tynan remembered Arthur Balfour as their particular champion but noted that all too often 'Dublin Castle used to be contemptuous' of the RMs.[46] The magistrates in turn were often irritated by the bureaucracy of the administration. Many of them were in a position to take up their grievances with senior officials or members of the executive with whom they had personal contacts but in routine matters they were subject to the administrative division and the rulings of the assistant under-secretary or the under-secretary. An exchange of letters in 1912 between Andrew Newton Brady, one of the Belfast resident magistrates, and the Assistant Under-Secretary, Edward O'Farrell, reveals considerable resentment on the part of the RM. Newton Brady's essential complaint was about the tone of communications from the Castle and what he regarded as undue recognition of the special nature of the resident magistrates' work in Belfast. Among other topics, he raised issues relating to leave and reminded O'Farrell that his four days in London 'at the Royal Command', to receive his knighthood, had been counted against annual leave. It clearly annoyed Newton Brady that when he queried this ruling he was told the matter was closed. 'Now, if I were a prisoner in one of H.M. Prisons', he wrote, 'I would be entitled to present my memorial to Government for a consideration of my case; am I, as RM of Belfast, entitled to less consideration? I thought not, and think so still.' He had been more recently offended by the imputation of 'neglect' in not sending in monthly summaries of duty, reports and other paperwork, which 'was at most "an omission" owing to the great demands on my time'. He elaborated on the heavy work-load of himself and Mr Nagle in Belfast and declared that 'our attention ought not to be concentrated upon such trivialities as reporting our return from leave, or returning an unimportant paper at a particular time'. Newton Brady had himself once worked at the Castle, dealing with the resident magistracy, and he claimed to have 'performed that duty efficiently, with courtesy and without friction'. O'Farrell replied in a cool, even dismissive tone, set in the opening paragraph in which he restated that on the question of leave the government must ultimately decide, 'and it would be convenient if you would accept their decision with a good grace'. As to official communications, O'Farrell remarked that 'it appears to me that anything unusual in the tone of the Government minutes has been consequent on the manner in which you have replied to minutes addressed by the office to you in the same form as those sent to all other RMs. This is unfortunate and could easily be avoided with advantage.' The RM had written directly to O'Farrell, who intimated in his reply that he was treating the letter as unofficial but told Newton Brady that if he and Garret Nagle, the other Belfast RM, decided to raise the question of the general regulations formally, 'it would be well to confine your representations to that question and to the considerations bearing on it'.[47]

Edward O'Farrell was a Catholic official who had served on both the Land and Estates Commissions and was registrar in the Chancery Division of the supreme court immediately prior to his appointment as assistant under-secretary in 1908. He was a part of the transformation of personnel as the 'greening of Dublin Castle' progressed, and it may well be that as more Catholics (who were likely to be unsympathetic to the remnants of the old ascendancy) were brought into all levels of the administration so the resident magistrates were treated with less deference than they had been accustomed to expect. O'Farrell was 'a pleasant and kindly old gentleman in his private life', according to Lynch-Robinson, but in his official duties he 'seemed to have a delight in taking it out of the RMs on every possible occasion'.[48]

The RMs were 'increasingly worried and harassed by staff at the Castle', or so thought Sir Henry Robinson.[49] The administration was notoriously slow-moving and bureaucratic but it eventually caught up with many resident magistrates who were in some way at fault. In April 1914 Joseph Kilbride, stationed in the Galway district, was asked why he had reported that his attendance at Derrynane petty sessions on 1 January was not required, when the clerk's report showed that he had telegraphed the RM on 31 December that a case of malicious injury to property had been entered for hearing. The court was cancelled because no magistrates attended, and Kilbride was held responsible. Kilbride had arranged to attend 'a social function' at the home of Colonel Kilkelly in Drumcong on New Year's Day and as this was in his district, and he would not be away from home overnight, he was entitled to do so without permission if there were no cases for the petty sessions. He had written his report early in the day but, having later received the telegraph, he wired to Dublin for official leave to miss the court but apparently assumed that local JPs would attend. He was rebuked for this and reminded that it was his duty in such circumstances to inform the administration of the need for another resident magistrate to attend court in his place.[50]

Kilbride sent up to Dublin a lengthy explanation and justification of his conduct and so did Major C.H. Herries-Crosbie, RM for Wexford, when in

June 1914 he recounted his difficulties with poor roads, broken down cars, unreliable garages and incompetant mechanics, which accounted for him missing two courts in April. The reprimand from the Castle was brief and to the point: 'it is to be hoped that the fact that roads are bad or a motor is out of repair will not be considered as of themselves a sufficient reason for non-attendance at Petty Sessions'.[51] Such was the petty bureaucracy that even minor matters were picked up and some were pursued to great lengths. Early in 1915 Lynch-Robinson received a memorandum from O'Farrell that 'It has been observed that your last twenty-five reports have been written upon official notepaper bearing the Royal Arms', and asking for an immediate explanation. The RM assumed that what concerned O'Farrell was that the paper was not the standard issue to resident magistrates and had obviously not been paid for out of the official stationery allowance.[52] Later that year the RM for Letterkenny district in Co. Donegal, R. Sparrow, was contacted about his 'travelling account' for the previous November. He was asked to explain his absence from headquarters for more than seven hours on three days at petty sessions, which, having regard to the distances travelled and the duration of the courts, seemed excessive to the Castle. Sparrow returned the usual harrowing description of the Donegal roads in winter, on which it was 'impossible to travel . . . with horse-car or bicycle at the ordinary pace', and added somewhat plaintively that if he was to get any luncheon after court he could not avoid being away from his station for seven hours or more.[53]

Between the Castle and the courthouse the RMs most frequent professional encounters were with the RIC, with members of the legal profession, and with local Justices of the Peace. The resident magistracy and the RIC were always closely associated and relations between the two often went beyond the merely professional. Nonetheless, loyalty did not outweigh the impartiality of Lynch-Robinson when a defendant charged with being drunk and disorderly, resisting arrest, and assaulting the police issued a cross-summons for assault by a constable. The bench was 'packed' and the constable's solicitor (the nationalist J. Dunlevy) offered no real defence but hinted that 'the less said the soonest mended'. The RM believed the accused man's story that he had been beaten up in his cell, and that the police account of his 'accidental' injuries was false. The local JPs dismissed both charges but Lynch-Robinson recorded his dissent and in announcing the findings of the bench he added that personally he would have found the constable guilty and imprisoned him for assault.[54]

Solicitors appearing for the defendants in the petty sessions courts were, in many cases, Catholics and nationalists but religious and political differences did not preclude either amicable professional relations or personal friendships. As Katherine Tynan recalled, there were occasions when her husband shared a car to the courts with Sinn Fein solicitors and it was not unusual for Henry Hinkson to spend an evening with one or other of them, when he was away from home. It was with the JPs that friction was most likely to occur, because the local magistracy changed more radically than the resident magistracy did from the early 1890s to the 1920s. When John Morley was Liberal Chief Secretary (1892–5) he began the process of changing the overall religious and political character of the local magistrates, by appointing 554 Catholics in the total of 637 JPs appointed.[55] In many instances the lord lieutenants of the counties were not willing to recommend Catholic persons the government wanted to appoint but, at the cost of offending the old ascendancy, Morley simply made the appointments directly. They became known derisively in unionist circles as 'Morley Magistrates'. Unionists argued that these magistrates were inferior in ability and respectability, a view shared by Charles Paston Crane RM, who considered them likely to be under-educated and lacking awareness of the importance of administering justice impartially. Yet if the 'Morley Magistrates' were weak, partial or unjust, they should not be judged too harshly, Crane thought, for he blamed the government for appointing 'men dependent on the people for their living – shopkeepers, farmers, publicans and the like – and independent action was well-nigh impossible for these with the shadow of boycotting hanging over them on the one hand, and the shadow of bribery and corruption on the other'.[56] Further change came with the reforms of the Local Government Act of 1898, when the local elections returned nationalists in great numbers to the newly-created councils, the chairmen of which were *ex officio* JPs.

Matters arising from the licensing petty sessions were often contentious issues for the RMs, as they were for Major Yeates. In the *Irish RM* story 'Occasional Licences' it was a 'Morley Magistrate' who broke ranks by granting a license to the publican Sheehy, for the sports in Skebawn on 'Pether and Paul's day' and Flurry commented that the license was 'as good as a fivepound note' in the JPs pocket, adding that Moriarty had told him that 'his Commission of the Peace was worth a hundred and fifty a year to him in turkeys and whiskey, and he was telling the truth for once'.[57] There is little evidence of specific complaints from the RMs about individual JPs, but in June 1916 the resident magistrate for Dunfanaghy district of Co. Donegal asked for advice from the Castle when a Mr McNulty presented himself to take the necessary oaths to become a JP. McNulty had recently been appointed chairman of the district council and thus became an *ex officio* Justice of the Peace but the RM was unhappy about this and similar appointments. He explained that, 'I might say that this man is a Publican and Farmer, and was convicted and fined 1s. [5p] and costs at Dunfanaghy Petty Sessions on 1 April last, for a breach of the Licensing Acts. This is the second publican

who has been recently appointed a magistrate here . . .'.[58] The democratisa-
tion of the bench went ahead in the face of misgivings from Mr Sparrow and
some other resident magistrates but later the unseemly behaviour of Mr
Patrick Rice at the Dundalk petty sessions, on 19 July 1918, was reported by
the RIC District Inspector. The officer would not commit himself to saying
that the JP was 'actually drunk, but he had been drinking and he periodically
is known to indulge in bouts of drinking'. He added that 'Mr Rice is not an
impartial magistrate and is a man who from his standing and habits ought not
to have been appointed.' William O'Reilly from Navan district, Co. Meath,
and Alan Bell from Portadown, Co. Armagh, were the resident magistrates on
the bench at Dundalk petty sessions with Mr Rice and other local magistrates. Both the RMs confirmed the District Inspector's report. Rice was
'unquestionably' under the influence of drink when the court commenced
and Bell asserted that at an early stage in the proceedings Rice suggested an
adjournment for lunch until 3 p.m., despite there being a long list of 200
cases to hear. O'Reilly described the JP as becoming extremely belligerent
towards police witnesses in cases of assault upon the police by John McGuill
and cross-summons of assault by the police on McGuill. When the magistrates retired to consider their findings Patrick Rice was 'blustering and ag-
gressive' to Alan Bell, accusing him of 'dictating' to the bench and, according
to O'Reilly, he soon became 'more violent; thumping the desk and declaring
he would not be dictated to by any RM'. Rice then left the court, saying 'the
whole business was a [blank] farce'. He later apologised for his behaviour and
he was not dismissed from the Commission of the Peace.[59]

Other encounters in the world of work were with the counterparts of Dr
Hickey and Father Scanlan of the *Irish RM*. Like Major Yeates, the resident
magistrates met the doctors in their districts out hunting or at social events
but they also relied upon them for information about the general health of the
population and were professionally involved in some areas of a doctor's work.
The commital of 'lunatics', for example, required the signature of a magistrate. When epidemic disease broke out the RM and the doctor would cooperate in efforts to contain its spread, as happened during the post-war influenza
epidemic of 1919. C.P. Crane cancelled the petty sessions at Coolmagort, near
Killarney, on the advice of Dr O'Sullivan who considered that it would be
'dangerous to public health' to bring many people into close contact at the
court.[60] The RM might also meet the priest socially, and he was very likely to
appeal to him for help in restraining popular protest when a district was
disturbed – unless the priest himself was a leading participant in protest, as
was not infrequently the case. Resident magistrates consulted the priest about
various matters in which the priest's local knowledge was likely to be greater
than that of the RM, and they were sometimes in agreement as to the causes

of a problem. For example, when W.M. Scott Moore noticed an 'outbreak of petty pilfering' among the children of his Mullingar district, he suggested that the popularity of 'the pictures' was to blame, as children were tempted to steal to get the price of admission to the cinema, and he added that he had discussed this with the local priest who agreed with the opinion of the RM.[61]

As for their relations with the mass of the people in their world of work, it was inevitable that the resident magistrates should become a focus of hostility at times. Yet not all encounters between the RMs and those opposed to British rule took place in the special courts, or involved violent confrontation on the streets. On occasion the people managed to outwit the law enforcers, as did the members of the Thomastown Brass Band on 22–23 November 1890. It was the usual custom for nationalists at Thomastown and Inistioge to commemorate the Manchester Martyrs (three men executed for murder after a policeman was killed during the rescue of Fenian leaders in Manchester, in September 1867) by parading in torchlight procession, accompanied by the band, and for political speeches to be made. This custom was challenged in 1890 when Henry Bruen RM arrived by train from Kilkenny with a force of some twenty RIC men. Bruen signed proclamations prohibiting the planned events, a measure which the local *Journal* condemned as likely to provoke what it 'was ostensibly intended to suppress – a riot'. There was no riot, but the band-members and others outwitted the law by various diversionary tactics and changing the location of the celebrations. 'Mr Bruen RM, one of the most unwarlike personages you could see, was walking about all day armed with an umbrella,' the *Journal* reported, but the proclamation was 'set at naught' and the authorities 'were "fooled to the top of their bent"'.[62] Yet among the poorer classes in general, many 'looked up' to the resident magistrate and from day to day 'there would often be a queue waiting for him outside his little room so that he might settle their quarrels unofficially'.[63]

The resident magistrates themselves were a small but cohesive group within the British administration of Ireland. Stationed many miles apart in their districts they nonetheless met quite frequently, in the petty sessions courts or when covering for colleagues on leave or in ill health. They were collectively represented in the Resident Magistrates' Association, which also brought them together socially at its annual dinner. 'They were', as Katherine Tynan expressed it, 'men and brothers to each other',[64] bound together by professional loyalties which were often reinforced by ties of kinship or friendship in their private lives.

5

Private Lives: Home, Family
and Community

The private lives of the RMs were not sharply separated from the world of work, for their occupational role was embedded in a network of personal relationships. In contact with the wider community the degree to which a resident magistrate was integrated into his district was determined by various factors. He had clearly defined functions and status within his local society but his everyday relationships were also shaped by his social class, his leisure interests, his religion and politics and, of course, his personality. These areas of interest are difficult to recapture, undocumented and largely unrecorded as they were, and the wives and children of the resident magistrates' are particularly shadowy figures in the source material. What follows is inevitably little more than a glimpse into the private lives of the RMs but it offers some insight into their experiences of home, family and community in the period from 1890.

Home and family meant different things to individual RMs. Some were unmarried or widowed, others married during the course of their service, but in many cases a newly-appointed resident magistrate had a wife and often children who shared in the changes that followed. A resident magistrate was expected to maintain a certain social position in his district and he, and his family, were also expected to conform to respectable notions of private conduct. Failings in this area were likely to be seized upon by critics of the system much as they were in the world of work but where there is evidence of unbecoming conduct on the part of resident magistrates it seems that their official position was unlikely to be threatened. Social deference and prevailing attitudes protected them from hostile press comment and the private affairs of a resident magistrate were not of concern to the administration, unless they had some direct bearing on his public duties. In February 1891, for example, the Chief Secretary was asked if the government intended to take any action with regard to John MacSheehy, RM for the Parsonstown district of King's County (Offaly), who had been sued for a debt of over £30 in the previous September. Balfour's attention was also drawn to earlier cases at Kildare quarter sessions in 1890, in which Colonel the Hon. W.F. Forbes had been sued by various tradesmen for the cost of goods supplied to his wife. The Chief Secretary's response was that these matters were 'solely personal, and the Government do not intend to interfere'.[1] There had been no particular press comment on the cases and it seems likely that Swift McNeil, the Donegal MP who put the Commons question, was merely pursuing his campaign against the resident magistrates. His further comments on the Forbes cases did, however, reveal a state of marital disharmony that was undoubtedly something of a local scandal and probably the topic of much gossip in Co. Kildare.

William F. Forbes was a resident magistrate of the early type, a son of the aristocracy who was appointed RM in his late twenties after an army career. Born in 1836, Forbes was a captain in the Grenadier Guards and later honorary colonel of the Leitrim Rifle Brigade. He was a JP for counties Longford (where his brother, the seventh earl of Granard, lived at Castle Forbes, Newtownforbes) and Leitrim and also a deputy lieutenant for Leitrim, where he owned almost 6,000 acres of land with an annual valuation, in the late 1870s, of £811.[2] In October 1863 he married Phyllis Gabriella Rowe, the second daughter of a gentry family from Ballycrow, Co. Wexford. Two years later, in August 1865, he was appointed to the resident magistracy. He was stationed for much of his career at the Curragh Camp, Co. Kildare, but during the early 1880s he was one of the Special Resident Magistrates and from 1885 to 1889 he served in Belfast.

The marriage produced seven children, aged from eight to twenty-four by the time the family moved back to the Curragh from Belfast. The relationship was by then deeply troubled. The Hon. Mrs Forbes attended the Kildare Hunt Ball of March 1890 unaccompanied by her husband,[3] and the following month a 'painful narrative of domestic disagreements' was disclosed at the Kildare Quarter Sessions. The Colonel acknowledged that his marriage had degenerated into 'a row [that] had been going on for years' and he told the court 'I gave her notice in Belfast when she ran up bills on me to £150 in a month'. From his annual income of about £1,000 he paid his wife an allowance of £200 'as regularly as I could', but he admitted that during 1889 he had paid her little more than a few pounds over some eight months. In April of that year Forbes' published notices in the *Freeman's Journal*, the *Irish Times*, and the Dublin *Daily Express* disclaiming responsibility for any of the Hon. Mrs Forbes' future debts. It had been his custom to deduct from her notional allowance any sums paid out on her behalf, but Phyllis Forbes was now refusing to accept money from him directly. She had recently returned, through her solicitor, a cheque for £132 and was demanding £297 to cover her allowance and outstanding bills from dressmakers and others. Matters

had been brought to a head in the summer of 1889 when, shortly after the
return from Belfast, Mrs Forbes took the four younger children off to Bray
against her husband's wishes. The RM paid for lodgings there but, because
'She left my house without my consent', he objected to settling other accounts. Tradesmen were now pressing to recover debts for bread, chickens,
lobsters, and boots supplied to the Hon. Mrs Forbes. She had 'a fortune of
her own' when she married Forbes, but when asked what had become of it
her husband explained that it was 'lent on security'. In reply to the question
'Who gets the interest?', he said 'It is lent on my estate.' Phyllis Forbes,
reduced to dependancy on a husband who was trying to control her behaviour
by exercising his economic power, showed considerable spirit in making a
public stand against him. In court she asked to make a statement, which the
judge allowed after telling her that he 'would like to avoid unpleasant and
angry discussions between husband and wife'. 'All this trouble and inconvenience', she stated, was caused by 'a threat' made by the Colonel some three
years previously and she 'would tell if they ask and if not she would reserve
it for a higher court'. The judge, wanting to hear no more of the intimacies of
the marriage, stopped her at this point and found for the claimants.[4] Further
details were revealed, however, at the October Quarter Sessions. The RM
was then sued by several Kildare shopkeepers for goods supplied to his wife
and children. His cook, Mary Grogan, was also suing for over £7 owed in
wages and for the sum of 6s. (30p) cash lent by her to her master. In referring
to this case in the Commons, Swift McNeil alleged that the press reported
that the Hon. Mrs Forbes had made a sworn statement that whenever she
went to her husband's study to discuss these bills 'the lamp was put out, and
sometimes she was struck and knocked down' by the Colonel.[5] The marriage
dragged on until the death of William Forbes in 1898, leaving his wife to
some five years of perhaps happier widowhood before her own death in 1904.

Family life was somewhat disrupted whenever the male head of household took up an appointment or was transferred to a new station. Like Major
Yeates of the *Irish RM*, most of the resident magistrates were familiar with
the experience of settling into a district while staying at a hotel before finding
a suitable house to rent. Not all of them moved into a 'big house' such as
Shreelane. The size and style of their homes varied according to individual
need, financial circumstances and what was available in any district. Charles
P. Crane was single until 1908 when, aged forty-one, he married Mary Alice
Caroline Skrine of Warleigh Manor, near Bath in Somerset. As a bachelor in
Donegal during the 1890s Crane lived in 'a little, common, newly-built cottage', with a 'diminutive' garden separated from the main Donegal-Killybegs
road by only an iron railing. The garden was often invaded by straying cattle
on fair days but the RM planted it up and made it quite colourful. He found

his 'small and ugly' cottage a cheerful place to live.[6] Down in Kerry in 1901 he took 'a fairly substantial habitation' at Day Place in Tralee, a house built over the river Lee which frequently flooded the basement, 'much to the annoyance of the cook'. An exceptionally severe storm left the streets of Tralee underwater on one occasion and the kitchen was flooded to a depth which made it impossible to get into the room, where the bread for breakfast was adrift on the floating kitchen table. Crane recalled with amusement the efforts of his manservant, wearing a pair of waders, to hook the table leg with a gaff and 'land' the breakfast.[7] When he moved on to Killarney in 1905 he found that there was very good hotel accommodation in the district, which was then as now a popular area for holidays. Crane lived for a year at the Great Southern Hotel near the railway station in the town until, 'feeling the want of a settled residence', he took Bridge House. This was about a mile from Killarney, with a pleasant outlook over the Flesk river to the bridge spanning the Killarney–Muckross road, but 'it had its disadvantages, as most small Irish houses have'.[8] Towards the end of his career, Crane and his wife lived at Danesfort, Killarney, a place which they were so attached to that they contemplated staying on in Ireland after his retirement, until events of 1919–20 made England seem a more attractive prospect.

What Mrs Crane (daughter of Colonel and Lady Mary Skrine and niece of Earl Temple, of Newton Park, Bath) thought of Ireland in her role as wife of the RM is not revealed in her husband's memoirs. Christopher Lynch-Robinson's wife is a similarly mute and fleeting figure in his reminiscences. Only the memoirs of Katherine Tynan offer a woman's perspective on the experience of moving to a strange area, finding a house, settling the family and adjusting to changed circumstances. Best remembered as a writer of prose, poetry and occasional journalism, Tynan was married to the writer and barrister Henry Hinkson, who was appointed to the resident magistracy in October 1914. She was unusual in having a public *persona* distinct from her role as Mrs Hinkson, in recognition of which she is referred to hereinafter by her own name and the term 'Tynan-Hinkson' is used when referring jointly to the married couple. Katherine Tynan was born in Dublin in 1861, the fourth daughter of Andrew Tynan of Whitehall, Clondalkin. She was educated at a Dominican convent in Drogheda until the age of fourteen, and thereafter at home. An early supporter of the Ladies Land League and a life-long devotee of Parnell, she was closely associated with W.B. Yeats and other prominent figures in the national literary revival of the late nineteenth century. The Tynan family home was a place where 'all sorts and conditions of men and women might be met. Here a Protestant Home Ruler hob-nobbed fraternally with an enthusiastic Conservative, or a Fenian leader. All politics were forgotten as well as were all creeds'.[9] Among the guests was likely to be

Henry Albert Hinkson, who had been born in Dublin, where he attended the Dublin High School. He went on to study at Trinity College and after a period in Germany he took MA in Classical Honours at the Royal University of Ireland, in 1890. A sometime senior classical tutor at Clongowes Wood College in Co. Kildare, he was a writer of modest reputation, and a member of the English Bar from 1904. He and Katherine Tynan married in 1893 and had two sons and a daughter.[10]

The Tynan-Hinksons were representative of the urban Catholic middle classes who were coming to the fore in many areas of Irish life during this period, but the couple lived in England for nearly nineteen years until just before the Great War. This did nothing to corrupt Tynan's romantic nationalism or, according to one commentator, to modify her 'Irish' way of speaking. Maurice Headlam, sitting next to her at a Dublin Castle dinner, noted a brogue in Tynan's rolling 'r's' and talk of 'me pomes'. He was unkind enough to suggest in his memoirs that this was an affectation.[11] Tynan had certainly cherished her 'Irishness' while living in England and the constitutional nationalism of the Tynan-Hinksons endeared the couple to the 'Home Rule Viceroy', Lord Aberdeen, and to his wife. When Aberdeen offered Hinkson a resident magistracy it was 'a fillip we badly needed', Tynan recalled, but the vacancy was in Co. Mayo and Lord Aberdeen expressed the hope that 'the place will not be too uncongenial for the present'. The Tynan-Hinksons' 'kind friend' was out of office within a few months of making the appointment and, lacking influence with the new administration in Dublin, they stayed on in Mayo until Hinkson's death in January 1919.

His first station was Castlebar, the county town of Mayo, but no suitable house could be found there and in December Hinkson took over the Claremorris district. It was a good three months after his appointment before domestic routine was properly established in the west. In the early autumn of 1914 the family was living at Shankill in Dublin, where the daughter, Pamela, attended a convent day-school. Seventeen-year old Toby had recently left school and was anxious to join the army, while the younger son was still at Shrewsbury public school in England. The new RM headed west at the beginning of October on the long journey from Dublin. Tynan travelled down to see her husband 'settled in' and later wrote that Mayo 'felt that it was the end of the world and beyond.' For a time Toby stayed with his Father to keep him company while Katherine and Pam remained in Dublin, as the lease on the Shankill house had not expired. At the end of December Henry Hinkson moved into a hotel at Claremorris for several weeks and eventually found a house nearby. When Katherine joined him the house was not ready for them but, resigning herself to 'the comforts of a West of Ireland hotel' in the short term, she set off with the RM and 'a blithe heart' to inspect their new home.

A 'churlish person' refused them admittance and, to make matters worse, the bright day turned to rain. Katherine developed a severe chill and she was to suffer from the 'damp cold' of Mayo for many months before becoming acclimatised to the local weather. The day after they finally moved in to Carradoyne, 'rain, hail, sleet, snow and a gale from the Atlantic' combined to flood the hall floor every time the door was opened, as the last of their furniture was carried in from the van. The Georgian house was 'very pleasant to look at outside, with its long rows of windows swathed in ivy' but it had the usual disadvantages of partly-furnished rented accommodation: 'I do not know', Katherine observed in her memoirs, 'what Carradoyne might have been if one had been permitted to choose one's wall-papers and dispense with the furniture that was not required.' There were some compensations, such as plentiful supplies of turf and wood for the fires, and in the spring the garden emerged as 'charming' but as summer advanced the charm of the garden was lessened by the advent of assorted insects. 'No one had thought of mentioning the insects' as one of the features of life in the west, which seems to have been as 'foreign' to the Dublin-born Tynan as Skewbawn was to the English wife of Major Yeates of the *Irish RM*. The Tynan-Hinksons lived at Carradoyne for eighteen months until the Congested Districts Board, which had taken over the estate, began harrassing them to move out. Letters from the Board's solicitor were becoming increasingly irascible when some old friends, the Lamberts, wrote to ask if the RM knew of a likely tenant for their property near Claremorris. This was Brookhill, 'a very desirable habitation'. The RM and his wife found it 'delightful' to be tenants of the Lamberts, whose agent 'could not have been kinder'. After some months at Brookhill they were pleased to hear that the agent had said to a neighbour that they were admirable tenants who never asked for anything to be done but then, as Katherine wryly recalled, 'I believe it was that very night – all the pipes burst and the roof sprang a leak.' The children, meanwhile, were growing up and a new stage in family life was developing. Pam stayed with friends in Dublin until her schooling was over, as it was thought that she would be lonely in Mayo, but she was living at home as the Great War drew to its end. Both her brothers were by then wearing the King's uniform and fighting in the Great War.[12]

The comradeship of other RMs was some comfort to the Tynan-Hinksons during their early and less than happy years in Mayo. They formed a friendship with 'Jack' Milling, who was RM for the adjoining district of Westport. Another personal friend was the barrister Jasper White, stationed at Loughrea in Co. Galway since his appointment in 1903. The RMs often had much in common with each other. Some had been at the same schools or served in the same regiments and so formed a part of the 'old boy' networks of those institutions. Former RIC officers and barristers had, in many cases, known each other in their careers before becoming resident magistrates. There were also blood relatives and kinsmen by marriage among the RMs, who were part of the great 'cousinhood' of Ireland, where almost every family of note seems to have been connected by some degree of kinship. As we have seen, there were also family relationships between resident magistrates and a chief secretary, an under-secretary, and one of the most powerful civil servants in Ireland. Other RMs were related to bishops and leading academics, some were the sons or grandsons of politicians, and all in all they were very well connected. Such connections were of importance in getting public employment, even without the improper exercise of influence. Men looked to their relatives for support in getting appointed to the resident magistracy and those with further aspirations, such as Robert Starkie, continued to do so once in office. While serving as RM, Starkie repeatedly pressed his claims to more prestigious posts with the support of his brother, W.J. Starkie, who was head of the Board of National Education.[13] Many resident magistrates were related to the aristocracy and gentry of England as well as those in Ireland; through family background and personal friendships they formed part of the social and ruling elite that not only ran the country but participated in the governance of the whole United Kingdom and the British empire. Some were far less integrated into those networks than others and family was more important than influence based merely on friendship, which could be a transitory thing as the Tynan-Hinksons found after a change in political climate left him without powerful patrons at the Castle. It might have seemed that Hinkson's appointment would have been a popular one, as the RM was a Catholic-nationalist barrister. There were, however, initial objections from local nationalists because he was a member of the English Bar. For a variety of reasons the Tynan-Hinksons did not find much pleasure in their new life but Tynan believed that for RMs in earlier times 'it was all easy and kindly, and there was plenty of social life'.[14]

The RMs continued to be representative of the higher ranks in Irish society, which barely acknowledged the existence of a middle class.[15] Their social origins were invariably in the categories indentified by Nora Robertson, herself a daughter of the ascendancy. To Row A she alloted peers who were lord or deputy lieutenants and high sheriffs of their counties, and Knights of St Patrick. If breeding was suitably buttressed by money, the sons of this group might join the Guards, the Hussars, or the Royal Navy. Row B comprised lesser peers with smaller seats, baronets, solvent country gentleman, and the younger sons of Row A. Service in the navy and less pretigious army regiments, such as Highland regiments, was typical of this group and 'Row A used them for marrying their younger children.' Row C accounted for the less solvent country gentry whose sons joined Irish regiments 'which were cheap' or the Indian army, but who were 'recognised' by Rows A and B and often belonged to the Kildare Street Club. Row D was made up of loyal professional people, gentlemen farmers, and substantial businessmen. They 'rarely cohabited' with Rows A or B but were often wealthier than those in Row C, and 'if really liked' they might achieve membership of the Kildare St Club.[16] The resident magistrates were drawn chiefly from Rows B and C during the period 1890 to 1921 but with increasing numbers from Row D. Only very few of those with service records had been in the navy, the Guards, the Hussars or a Highland regiment. Service in an Irish regiment was more common although the majority of former army officers had served in English regiments. By 1919, after the Great War, men were being appointed from the Royal Army Service Corps, the Royal Flying Corps and the Canadian Air Service Corps.

Some resident magistrates were members of the ascendancy clubs in Dublin, the Kildare Street and the Sackville Street, and also of the Royal St George Yacht Club at Kingstown (Dun Laoghaire) which was a 'marine extension to the Kildare St.'[17] The Kildare Street was the centre of unionist-ascendancy masculine life in Dublin and the leading club in the country. From the 1880s the Sackville, situated on the increasingly decaying north side of the Liffey, had declined in status although some of the elite retained membership of both these clubs. Membership of a club in London was not unusual. There were RMs who belonged to the Oxford and Cambridge club, or to the literary and artistic Savages club, and some were members of the Carlton club which was the Conservative equivalent in London to the Kildare Street in Dublin. In Ireland, the University and St Stephen's Green clubs also had members who were resident magistrates but the majority of those who can be identified as belonging to a club where members of the United Services in Dublin. Walter Edgeworth-Johnstone was an exceptionally keen club man who, in the early twentieth century, belonged to the National Sporting, the University, the Kildare Street, the Royal Irish Automobile and the United Services clubs. Club membership reflected individual interests and provided accommodation and congenial company on visits to Dublin or London.

It also provided entry into various social and political networks. The Kildare Street, with seven to eight hundred members drawn from the social and political elite, was particularly exclusive. Provincial clubs had a somewhat more mixed membership and there were RMs who joined a local club in preference or in addition to one in Dublin. Robert Starkie joined the Cork County Club in 1905, when he was transferred to Cork from a station in Co. Down, and the bachelor P.J. Kelly was not merely a member of the Junior

Club in Limerick but took up permanent residence there. He used the club as his headquarters while RM for the Limerick district from 1911 to 1919.

A resident magistrate's day to day relations with the people in his district were shaped by his official role, his social class, his religion and politics, and his personal interests. To the writer and nationalist MP Stephen Gwynn, the religious divide seemed to create an impassable gulf between Protestants of his class and the bulk of the Catholic population. In *Today and Tomorrow in Ireland* (1903) he recalled the crowds of country people hurrying to the Catholic chapel as he went to attend a Church of Ireland service somewhere in the west, and he wrote of the occasion:

> There were two or three coast-guards with their families, a policeman from Ulster, our own numerous party – and perhaps a score of other people, from the great house five miles off . . . After service, when there was the usual five minutes of assemblage outside the church-porch, the congregation was entirely innocent of brogue . . . the same kind of an assembly might be found, I should say, at any station in India, and it would be just about as much in touch with the worshippers at the adjoining temple.[18]

Gwynn perhaps overstated the alienation between the Protestant minority and the Catholic majority. The difference in religious belief and practice was a part of Irish life but in general Protestants and Catholics of the same social class mixed easily enough with each other, even if religion was avoided as a topic of conversation and mixed marriages were often a cause of dismay to families.[19] Within the resident magistracy Protestants had good professional relationships with Catholic colleagues and frequently encountered Catholics of all classes.

In their private lives the resident magistrates' were involved in a variety of sporting, creative and intellectual pursuits and some of these leisure activities took place in a wide social circle. In contrast to Major Yeates of the *Irish RM*, virtually none of the resident magistrates whose recreations can be identified actually rode to hounds. Shooting was the most popular and widely-shared activity. Fishing and golf came in second place but beyond these preferences individuals' engaged in tennis, cycling, sailing, mountain climbing and enthusiastic motoring. Rugby, polo and cricket had been youthful pastimes for many of them. Charles Crane enjoyed field sports but was also an amateur artist who took great pleasure in his hobby as a painter in water colours. He became fascinated by the history, flora and fauna of Co. Kerry and collected a mass of notes on the subject which he eventually wrote up for publication in 1907 as a *Little Guide to Kerry*. Crane was not unique in his literary efforts. Henry Hinkson was the author of numerous novels, collections of verse, professional studies such as his *Copyright Law* (1903), and many short stories. Other resident magistrates' wrote on subjects ranging from Walter Edgeworth-Johnstone's *Boxing: the Modern System of Glove Fighting* to Christopher Lynch-Robinson's short stories, based on his life as a Donegal RM, which were published in the *Queen* and *Country Life* magazines. The Tynan-Hinksons were fortunate in that both enjoyed writing and reading but, despite their shared interests, the couple felt 'rather lost' in their Mayo district where only the Claremorris doctor and his family 'had touch with literature'.[20]

It was primarily the official role of the RM that defined his place in the community of a district. It was work that took them to their stations and the length of time they were to stay was uncertain but it seems that most of them behaved much like any other gentleman moving into a neighbourhood, and soon established themselves within the gentry social circle. As resident magistrates, they met the whole range of local society and everyday relationships were normally quite amicable. An RM often showed a sympathetic attitude in court and the population in turn usually showed tolerance to a resident magistrate when he enforced the law to the letter. Legislation relating to popular pastimes such as gambling and drinking was often regarded by the mass of the people as an infringement of traditional liberties but the leniency of some of the RMs in cases relating to drink suggests that not all of them were eager to control the behaviour of the lower orders. At the Nenagh petty sessions in September 1890 Captain Holt Waring RM presided over a long list of cases which occupied most of the day. Five publicans were charged with breaches of the Sunday Closing Act. Paying customers had been found on the premises of a Mrs Maher during three separate raids during one Sunday but far from imposing a stiff sentence for this defiance of the law the bench, 'in mercy to her', struck out the third charge, which kept the set fine down to £3, although that was a not inconsiderable sum at the time. Mr McCreedy, who owned a public house in Queen's Street and an adjoining shoemaker's shop, had been the target for RIC attention over a long period but the police repeatedly found that 'parties going into the licensed premises mysteriously disappeared' at the approach of the constabulary. Eventually an alert constable noticed people 'suspiciously leaving the leather department' and investigations revealed a concealed door between the two buildings. The RM adjourned this case for a week, telling the court that he did not want to deprive McCreedy of his license and would give him time to block up the door as he had promised.[21] This may not have pleased the RIC but was probably a popular decision with the publican and his customers. Later in the period C.P. Crane, always a stickler for rigid law enforcement, imposed penalties on 'most people' in his Co. Donegal district for disregarding a muzzling of dogs order. The order was introduced in an attempt to stamp out canine rabies but it was widely ignored in Donegal where the RM fined everyone 'from the priest and parson and the local "gentry" to the peasant whose dog was his constant companion.' This 'never caused any estrangement', he claimed, and he added that he was always treated with 'kindness and hospitality' by his neighbours of every social class.[22]

It was a different matter when the RM adjudicated in special courts or in quasi-criminal cases of a political nature. In August of 1890 the Hon. W.F. Forbes made yet another appearance in the dock rather than on the bench. Henry O'Connor, sub-editor of the *Leinster News*, brought an action against Forbes and the RM for Tullamore, George Mercer, for damages of £2,000 in compensation for alleged assault, battery and false imprisonment. O'Connor had been prosecuted under the Crimes Act for publishing 'certain material'. Forbes and Mercer found him guilty and sentenced him to two months with hard labour but the conviction was quashed on appeal, after O'Connor had served four days.[23] The case against the resident magistrates was dismissed but the incident reflects the ill-feeling caused whenever politics came to the fore. C.P. Crane was later the focus for hostility while temporarily posted to Sligo to put down boycotting there in 1901-2, when his conduct provoked criticism at local level as well as questions in the Commons and he was lampooned and attacked in some Sligo newspapers.[24] There are scattered references in the press to petty vandalism directed at resident magistrates during the 1890s, as in Ballina, Co. Mayo, when the house of Richard Crotty RM was a principle target in a spate of window breaking, but there is other evidence to suggest that some of them were quite fully integrated into their communities. Subscription dinners were sometimes held to mark the RMs departure on transfer and when A.E. Horne left Westport, Co. Mayo, the Cycling Club made him a presentation to show their gratitude for his services as its president.[25] It was part of the expected social role of a resident magistrate to hold office in local organisations of a non-political nature, as it was to subscribe to charities and sponsor events such as sports days or horse shows.

A resident magistrate could sometimes find himself on the wrong side of the law, caught up in an exploit similar to those of Major Yeates when led astray by Flurry Knox. This happened to Henry Hinkson in the autumn of 1916, soon after he had instructed the RIC in Claremorris to crack down on motoring offences in the district. Vehicles being driven without lights or exceeding the speed limit were the particular targets of special police patrols. Katherine Tynan and a visiting friend went off to the Louisburg petty sessions with the RM in August, to combine his duties with a tour of the Clew Bay area, which culminated with them taking a late tea at Westport. As they

headed home in the evening the car broke down 'four Irish miles from anywhere' but after sitting hopefully at the roadside for three hours they were
rescued by a Claremorris man, who had recently been fined by Hinkson for a
motoring offence. Relishing the situation, the driver set off at breakneck
speed, ignoring the RMs pleas to 'go quietly'. The passengers soon realised
that there were no lights on the car but, scattering sheep and pursued by
mongrel dogs, it raced on to Claremorris where, Tynan recalled, 'we flashed
before the scandalised eyes of the District Inspector and one of his patrols,
and were gone before he could cry halt.' As the driver pulled up at the RMs
hall door he remarked with a chuckle, 'That was a near thing! If the tail light
had been on they'd have seen the number!'[26]

When Katherine Tynan wrote about her life in Co. Mayo she revealed
that her experiences were very different from those of Philippa Yeates, the
English wife of the RM in the Somerville and Ross short stories. Philippa
regarded the whole experience 'in the light of a gigantic picnic in a foreign
land' and was enchanted by Shreelane with its 'menage of incabables', as
Major Yeates' scathingly described his staff,[27] while at the Poundlick Races
she rejoiced in the 'Real Primitives' around her, declaring the country people
to be just the sort she loved.[28] Katherine Tynan, who frequently remarked
on her devotion to 'the people', could be as patronising as the English Mrs
Yeates but she was quickly disillusioned of her romantic expectations of life
in the west. In describing her first journey to Co. Mayo she wrote of everywhere beyond Athlone as being the 'Back o' Beyant'. 'There is a terrible
place called Manulla Junction, before you reach Castlebar,' she observed,
'where the train sits in the middle of the bogs as though it never meant to go
again'. She later wrote that she looked back to her first day in Mayo with 'a
sort of pity for myself. I had said to the children: "It may be ramshackle but
it will be, oh, *so* friendly!" It wasn't friendly except for one or two people, and
the priests and nuns, when I gave them a chance.'[29] It was not long before the
RMs wife gave up trying to engage the country people in conversation and,
apart from a few deferential 'old retainers' of the Lamberts at Brookhill, she
found the Mayo peasantry cold, secretive, and altogether not what she had
anticipated.

Two of their servants had followed the RM and his wife into 'exile' and
it was part of Tynan's routine to spend a few hours in the kitchen each
evening, reading to these 'faithful servants and friends.'[30] Tynan seems to
have had genuine affection for her servants, especially the parlourmaid, Ellen,
and it was not unusual in small households for close relationships to exist
between a mistress and her staff. Without Ellen and her colleague, Tynan
might have encountered local girls and women as scullery maids, parlour
maids or cooks as it is unlikely that she would have shared the prejudices of

some Anglo-Irish households where only Protestant servants were employed. In others the upper servants were Protestants even if the lower ranks were Catholic and nannies and governesses were often English, employed to guard against a child picking up the brogue.[31] The Lynch-Robinsons employed a nursemaid after the birth of their son but her nationality is not mentioned in the RMs memoirs. C.P. Crane has little to say about his domestic arrangements but it seems that his cook and other daily staff were local to his districts although he relied chiefly on his 'excellent man, Duff', until the servant's sudden death in the winter of 1899. Crane found it hard to replace his manservant. He admired what he perceived as the 'Scottish' characteristics of the Donegal people (especially their industriousness and lack of 'mawkish sentimentality', compared with what he considered typical of Kerry folk) but he wanted a true Scot to take Duff's place. He was about to take on a Scottish ex-soldier, whose qualifications included the ability to play the bag-pipes, when his plans were changed by an opportunity to join the Boer War.[32] On his return from South Africa, Crane recruited another manservant in England. This was Dugdale, who had never been in Ireland and whose introduction to the country was preceeded by the horrors of seasickness on the crossing to Belfast.[33] Domestic service still accounted for the majority of employed women and for large numbers of men in both Ireland and England but rates of pay and conditions of service were very varied. Jimmy Brogan, a Donegal boy employed by Christopher Lynch-Robinson, was fortunate in having an employer who gave him the chance to learn new skills. Jimmy had done merely 'odd jobs about the place, working in the garden, chopping wood and so forth' but the RM felt he owed it to the boy to 'start him off at something in life' after his years of good service. He took Jimmy with him in 1918 when he transferred to Collon, near Drogheda in Co. Louth, and there he bought the boy a second-hand Ford car. Having taught him to drive and do 'running repairs', Lynch-Robinson then let Jimmy Brogan hire out the car as a 'hackney vehicle', paying for the petrol and oil but keeping what was left of the takings.[34]

Beyond the petty sessions court and his immediate domestic circle, a resident magistrate was most likely to encounter the 'mere Irish' in his leisure pursuits. It was in the field of sports, Stephen Gwynn suggested, that Protestant and Catholic saw most of each other in Ireland but it was usually the case, he added, that 'the Protestant shoots, the Catholic carries the bag; the Protestant hooks the salmon, the Catholic gaffs it.'[35] There was some truth in this observation but the religious difference merely reflected the class structure and it was not unusual for both gentleman and ghillie or gamekeeper to be Catholic. Somewhat broader class encounters were a characteristic of the hunting field, as Somerville and Ross recognised and explored to comic effect in the *Irish RM*. Similar encounters were recalled by the civil servant, Maurice Headlam, who hunted frequently in Ireland. His horsemanship was not up to the high standards of the Meath hunt so, apart from a day with the Kildares, he confined his hunting to Kilkenny. The field was never larger than twenty to thirty except at the meet following the hunt ball but hunters, pedestrian followers and country people were on the best of terms and there were 'generally one or two priests out, as well as farmers and "gentry".'[36] Hunting was an expensive pastime, which may account for so few of the resident magistrates' riding to hounds by the early twentieth century. Lynch-Robinson never hunted, partly because he could not afford to but also because he had no interest in horses. Unlike Major Yeates of the *Irish RM*, he did not change his mind on the subject. When he was stationed in Co. Louth he attended many courts in neighbouring Co. Meath and he found that people there talked of little else but horses. Whenever he was invited to lunch by a local magistrate, the RM was invariably dragged round the stables to admire the hunters and found himself at a loss for a suitable remark. Every horse looked the same to him, and he soon found that jocular remarks about a hunter's 'nice paws' or somesuch rarely went down well.[37] Charles Crane makes no reference in his memoirs to hunting, although he kept several horses and took one of his ponies to South Africa during the Boer War, but much of his spare time was devoted to fishing and shooting. In Donegal and Kerry, salmon cutlets or snipe in season were often welcome additions to his larder. His memoirs offer descriptions of fishing expeditions and long days shooting on the bogs, and of friendships formed with counterparts of the fictional Slipper, albeit more sober in their habits. Crane was glad to have known picturesque characters like his 'old friend Mustagh Boland, the poacher, Timothy Breen, the fisherman and poacher, and Teigne na gire (Shade of the Dogs) the gamekeeper'[38] but these relationships were essentially those of an employer and employee. Real friendships could grow out of comradeship forged through shared interests, skills and experiences in field sports but social class differences would nonetheless have set clear boundaries between the RM and people like Boland or Breen. Those differences would have been just as marked even if Crane had not been a Protestant and an Englishman.

Religion and politics were always present as background influences on social relationships but they were private matters to a resident magistrate and there is no evidence of blatant sectarian or political bias among the RMs in this period. They were expected, as civil servants and part of the judiciary, to be aloof from politics and religious strife and, on the whole, they seem to have strived to attain the ideal as impartial administrators of justice. Both Crane and Lynch-Robinson served in Co. Donegal and there encountered the sectarianism of Ulster. Crane had one clash with Orangemen who were determined to march through Donegal town, which they had not done for many years. On that previous occasion there had been riot and bloodshed. Fearing a repeat, the Castle sent a squadron of dragoons from Belfast to aid the civil power and also reinforced the RIC. Orangemen came from Londonderry and elsewhere by special trains, while 'the other side flooded the town with wild-looking men from the glens, armed with thick sticks.' Trouble was averted by Crane taking a firm line. He agreed with the Orangemens' claim that they had right on their side in seeking to march were they pleased but, in the interest of public order, the authorities laid down the route to be followed. The event went off peacefully enough and when a truculent leader of the Orangemen told the RM that he was going to insist on his rights and take his followers back through the town, Crane simply replied that he would order the officers in charge of police and troops to 'take action', whereupon the Orangemen withdrew to the railway station in an orderly way along the approved route. During his years in Donegal, Crane formed friendships with some farmers who were Orangemen and with 'many Roman Catholics', whose friendship he valued equally. He found relations between the two traditions to be 'amicable' for the most part, 'except during the month of July.' He had no patience with sectarianism but showed little understanding of the under-lying socio-economic and political conflicts in which it had its origins. He dismissed it as 'childish and stupid' and commented, with smug confidence in the superiority of his nation, that it all seemed 'foreign to that spirit of toleration' which was the bedrock of English life as perceived by the RM. Crane worshipped in the Church of Ireland but he found the Protestantism of Donegal a more austere faith than the Anglicanism in which he was reared. The small church he attended there was bleak and unadorned, so much so that even the clergyman felt it needed something to brighten its appearance. The RM offered to donate a tapestry to hang behind the altar, a suggestion that quite pleased the vicar but when he put it to the congregation someone accused the resident magistrate of being 'papistically inclined', and the offer was refused.[39] Christopher Lynch-Robinson, stationed in Donegal more than ten years after Crane moved on, found that 'in local affairs the line up was pretty well always Catholic *v* Protestant' and 'neither had any use for the moderate or non-party man.' As the resident magistrate, he had to 'steer clear of both sides' and 'they did not expect the RM to do otherwise.'[40]

Resident magistrates had to be acceptable to the 'quality' if they were to enjoy all the privileges of a gentry life style. It seems that Charles Crane was accepted as the 'right sort' even before he married the niece of an English earl. In Co. Donegal Lord Conyngham rented his Mount Charles shooting rights to Crane, who shot alone with his manservant or with parties of friends. In the first season, the total bag was some 600 head of assorted game. When the best of the grouse shooting was over, the RM let the local solicitor and his friends course hares on the land. Poaching was widespread but preserving the game did not in itself cause conflict because 'grouse money' was paid to farmers on the Conyngham estate, which meant that for every bird taken on their stretch of mountain grazing they were given some rebate on their rent. The professional middle classes seem to have been the closest of Crane's friends in Donegal, men who included a retired naval commander and Dr Warnock (who was later a friend of Lynch-Robinson), as well as Mr Shea, the Church of Ireland rector at Mount Charles. In Kerry, too, Crane encountered the whole range of society from Lord Kenmare and Lord Ventry to their ghillies and gamekeepers. Moreover, in the big houses of his district he met many influential people, such as Chief Secretary George Wyndham.[41]

It was very different for Katherine Tynan and Henry Hinkson in Co. Mayo from late 1914 until the arrival of British troops in 1918, whose presence in the district greatly enhanced social life at Brookhill.[42] Not only did 'the people' prove disappointingly unfriendly but the RM and his wife were 'the objects of something like a social boycott by the Mayo "quality" '. Tynan thought her husband's official position might have influenced local attitudes although a priest told her that the Mayo peasantry were simply not used to being spoken to casually by their 'betters'. As for the gentry, the Tynan-Hinksons' religion and politics made them suspect to some Anglo-Irish unionists, many of whom refused to attend Dublin Castle functions while the Home Rule viceroy, Lord Aberdeen, was in office. Another factor was that it was widely believed in Mayo that Alan Bell had been transferred to a station in Co. Armagh to make way for Hinkson. Bell was popular with the unionist gentry and had 'very much objected to leaving Claremorris'. Tynan acknowledged that there were other 'personal' matters to account for their initial unpopularity, which was perhaps a reference to her earlier membership of the Ladies Land League and her much publicised devotion to the memory of Parnell. Neither would have endeared her to the Mayo gentry who were, in any case, 'the most exclusive in Ireland' according to the Under-Secretary, Sir David Harrell, who had himself been a resident magistrate in the county during the 1880s. Tynan recalled that: 'My husband passed by, week after week of the wild winters, the houses of his brother-magistrates of the Unionist class, without hospitality. The other Resident Magistrates, the ever-hospitable priests, a sprinkling of the "quality" opened their doors to him . . .' but it was only a 'handful' of the Anglo-Irish gentry who made them welcome.[43]

The first spring and summer were 'not so bad' for Katherine Tynan. Her daughter, Pam, was with her for a while and in February the two of them went up to Dublin for the 'going out' of the Aberdeens. They stayed at the Lodge in Phoenix Park and attended the farewell reception for the Lord

Lieutenant at Dublin Castle. She was again in Dublin in April, to meet up
with Lady Aberdeen who was making a return visit to Ireland. Thereafter the
thirty-six days' annual leave became especially precious, making it possible to
get up to Dublin at intervals. Katherine later wrote of how, when back in the
city, she and Hinkson used to 'plunge into life, we see all manner of interesting people, we pick up threads, we taste what would be ours if we were not
Mayo's, we live furiously'. There were the pleasures of the Dublin theatres
and art galleries to enjoy, friends to take tea with (people such as Sir Horace
Plunkett, and A.E., or Lady Esmonde out at Gorey) and a chance to see
Pamela after she had been sent back to school to avoid the loneliness of the
west but all too soon it was 'back again into the wilderness for another four or
five months'. In her memoirs Tynan rationalised her isolation in Mayo by
consoling herself that she was a woman with little time for social recreation.
There might have been plenty of company of the bridge-playing and tennis-
playing kind if she had lived near Castlebar or Westport, she thought, but no-
one played such games in Claremorris. If they had, she would have probably
offended her neighbours by being too busy to take part. She completed a
prodigious amount of writing in the space of a few years at Claremorris,
including nine novels, several volumes of reminiscences and verse, two 'school-
books', and a great number of short stories and articles but some of her time
was given to other matters while in Mayo. She was influential in inspiring a
campaign against 'baby farming', which was eventually taken up by the Society for the Prevention of Cruelty to Children, and she was actively involved
in raising money to endow beds at the Red Cross hospital set up in Dublin
Castle by Lady Aberdeen during her last months as wife of the Lord Lieutenant.[44]

Katherine Tynan was perhaps no more representative of the wives of the
RMs than was the fictional Philippa Yeates, but her experiences are a reminder that there were many discontented women languishing in the big
houses and gloomy rectories of rural Ireland and, indeed, elswhere. Tynan
had the inner resources of a creative person and the advantage of an established reputation but many of her generation were less fortunate. Although
educational opportunities had improved for women during the nineteenth
and early twentieth centuries it was still the case that only a minority had
careers, and the life history of the majority was of a childhood and youth
spent in a patriarchal family until marriage subsumed the mature woman into
another patriarchal family. It was difficult for those women, like Somerville
and Ross, who remained unmarried and tried to create a working life of real
worth and economic independence. The maiden aunts who crowd the pages
of Victorian fiction reflect contemporary concern about the 'problem' of so-
called surplus women, which was especially acute in Ireland where large

families were the norm, and it was intensified by the Boer War and then the Great War, which claimed disproportionate numbers of the marriageable sons of the gentry. A single woman of thirty or forty was forever a daughter of the house or dependant on her male relatives, as the sisters of the RM James Woulfe Flanagan were (discussed below). Marriage itself did not always fulfill expectations and motherhood, which almost invariably followed, was not accepted by every woman as the crowning peak of destiny. Edith Somerville's cousin, Lionel Fleming, remembered his Mother's life as a long 'revolt against the disorder and laziness of Ireland' in a big, damp rectory in west Cork. His Father was 'happy enough' but his Mother's discontent was obvious for she never made any secret of the fact that she did not want to be in Timoleague, 'did not, indeed, want to be in Ireland at all'. Mrs Fleming was a 'delightfully affectionate' mother, according to her son, but 'children bored her, and she had five of them'.[45] These asides from the history of the resident magistrates' merely hint at the obscure lives of the women in their families. All that can be said with certainty is that their experiences differed with individual circumstances but were shaped by class, culture, religion, and prevailing beliefs about the innate nature of women. In some of the biographical studies of Part III, below, women move closer to the foreground but in those chapters they still rarely speak for themselves and what is known of them is largely mediated through the perspectives of their male relatives.

The private lives of the RMs remain largely unknown but having offered some insights into this aspect of their history the narrative now moves on to the end of Philippa Yeates' 'gigantic picnic', to the experiences of the resident magistrates' in the period from 1912-13 to 1921. Storm clouds gathered over the sunny world created by Somerville and Ross when the Home Rule crisis erupted in 1912. Ireland moved inexorably, or so it seemed to many contemporaries, towards civil war but then the wider European conflict turned attention to the enemy without. The Easter Rising of 1916 and its aftermath was to bring about a substantial shift in public opinion in Ireland, which found political expression in the triumph of Sinn Féin at the first post-war general election, and the Irish RMs found themselves once again pushed into the front line of conflict between British rule and nationalist aspirations.

6

Troubled Times: War and the Triumph of Nationalism

The final phase of the history of the Irish RMs encompassed political crisis, world war, and armed rebellion in Dublin. By the time of the armistice in November 1918 most people in Ireland wanted full independence from Britain, not merely devolved government under a Home Rule Act. This change in attitudes was reflected in the results of the December 1918 election when Sinn Féin won the majority of Irish seats. The newly elected MPs disregarded the Westminster Parliament but met in Dublin to establish Dáil Éireann. Guerrilla war ravaged Ireland from January 1919 until the truce of midsummer 1921, which led to the Anglo-Irish Treaty and to British withdrawal from the twenty-six counties.

The return to power of the Liberals in 1906 meant that a third Home Rule bill was a future certainty but with the Lords veto still in place it was likely that, as in 1893, the upper House would reject any measure to give Ireland limited independence. The crisis over the 'People's Budget' of 1909 was therefore of great significance for the Irish cause. The Liberals' considered it unconstitutional that the Lords' had rejected the budget and, although the elections of January and December 1910 did not give them a clear mandate for reform of the upper House, they effectively strengthened the Commons by legislation under the 1911 Parliament Act. The Lords could no longer kill a bill but only delay its passage until it had been carried three times in the Commons. The third Home Rule bill was introduced to the Commons in April 1912; in January of 1913 and again in July of that year it was carried in the Commons but defeated in the Lords. On 25 May 1914 it was passed by the Commons for the third and final time.

Opposition to Home Rule hardened as it seemed increasingly likely to become a political reality. Some Ulster unionists started drilling in January 1912, several months before the Bill was introduced to the Commons, and in September 1912 many thousands of people signed Ulster's Solemn League and Covenant, thereby pledging themselves to resist Home Rule. A year later, in January 1913, the Ulster Volunteer Force (UVF) was formed in Belfast and in November the Irish Volunteers were founded in Dublin as a southern counterpart to the UVF. In the spring of 1914, large quantities of arms and ammunition were landed at Larne, Donaghdee and Bangor for the UVF. At about this time the fifty-eight resident magistrates were asked to report on the attitudes of people in their districts towards the law, and on the nature of relations between those of different religions and political views. They were also asked to assess the threat to public order posed by the UVF and the Volunteers and to recommend any special precautions they felt necessary to preserve the peace.[1] Those stationed in Ulster districts were broadly agreed that the population was essentially law-abiding and that relations between Catholics and Protestants were superficially satisfactory, although most of the resident magistrates commented on underlying tensions. One RM noted that the Home Rule issue touched upon religious and political sentiments, adding that when such feelings were aroused 'both parties become fanatics'. The consensus of opinion was that the UVF, described as 'fully armed', was a well-disciplined body under the firm control of its leaders; the Volunteers, on the other hand, were considered to be undisciplined, badly organised and lacking strong leadership. Many resident magistrates believed the UVF was no threat and some went further to suggest that it was an important factor in maintaining the peace, by chanelling and controlling what might have other-wise been disorganised and violent opposition to Home Rule. Sir Andrew Newton Brady, reporting from Belfast, was however in no doubt that the UVF constituted 'a very grave danger not alone to the peace of Belfast but to the interests of the State at large'. He predicted that civil war would follow if the Home Rule bill was passed 'without the amendments considered neces-sary', to exclude all or part of Ulster.

In Co. Cavan, where there were branches of the UVF and the Volun-teers, the Ancient Order of Hibernians (AOH, the Catholic counterpart of the Orange Order) was also well supported but the resident magistrate did not foresee any of these organisations initiating local disturbances. 'Aggres-sive activity' was not, in his opinion, 'a characteristic of the Cavan people' but he acknowledged that they were likely to be drawn into any 'general move-ment' that developed elsewhere. Christopher Lynch-Robinson stressed that in the eastern part of Co. Donegal there was 'a lack of confidence on the part of all creeds and classes in the ability of the Magistrates, the Police, and the Executive to preserve the peace and hold the scales of justice evenly between both parties'. He added that unpaid magistrates gave their decisions on party lines and that Protestants had no faith in the impartiality of the police, for which he believed there was some justification in the Raphoe area where the constabulary had 'been contaminated by the political atmosphere'. The RM urged that immediate steps should be taken to restore public confidence in the ability of government to protect life and property but he made no suggestions as to how this might be done.

Few of the resident magistrates in Ulster considered it necessary to take
any special precautions in the circumstances although many commented on
the need to enforce the ban on the importation of arms to Ireland, which had
been announced in December 1913 but flouted by the UVF in April 1914. It
was generally agreed that the military would be needed to aid the civil authorities if disturbances broke out, and the majority of RMs emphasised the
importance of preventing the Volunteers acquiring arms. Captain Gosselin,
resident magistrate for Omagh, Co. Tyrone (and son of Major Gosselin, the
RM seconded to special duties investigating Fenianism, from the 1880s until
his retirement in 1896) put this forward as the primary aim of the police,
arguing that 'so long as they are unarmed', the Volunteers would not 'interfere' with the UVF. Gosselin described the UVF as 'drawn from the best
classes' and being in 'a wonderful state of discipline' but he added that they
were 'a standing menace to Government'. As a second course of possible
action he proposed that an 'overwhelming force' should be sent to the province, 'to overawe the Ulster Volunteers, or if not overawed to wipe them out'.

Reports from the resident magistrates in Connaught, Munster, and Leinster
indicated that the strength of the Volunteers varied considerably from place
to place. The UIL and AOH were numerically stronger in many districts. In
Co. Galway disputes over land still accounted for most breaches of the peace,
while in Co. Cork disturbances often originated in conflict between the
O'Brienite and Redmondite factions of the Home Rule party. The Castlerea
district of Co. Roscommon was not untypical in being free of religious animosity or political discord. As the RM stationed there pointed out, 'the great
majority of the people are Nationalists and the small minority who are not
have no say in public affairs and never come into contact with the majority'.
In districts where Protestant-unionists were more numerous, fears were expressed about local retaliation or reprisals against individuals or property if
Catholics were injured in disturbances occuring in Ulster. It was suggested
by some resident magistrates that the Volunteer movement reduced the threat
of disorder by subsuming rival nationalist factions into one body. It was also
said to be beneficial in drawing young men away from the public houses.
Respectable shopkeepers and Catholic clergymen constituted many of the
organising committees, which inspired a vague optimism that the movement
might 'raise the moral tone' of the people. Differing views were expressed in
comments about 'undesirables' and 'the rowdy element of the population'
filling the ranks of the Volunteers. The RM for Sligo town was convinced
that all Volunteers were 'disloyal' and he asserted that 'if they become roused
[they] would get out of hand and become a dangerous rabble'.

The Volunteers were not regarded as any immediate menace to public order but most of the RMs were anxious about the future role of the movement, particularly if it obtained arms. The reports were not entirely objective, perhaps, but rather reflected the RMs personal outlooks to some extent, with Protestant-unionist former police officers being particularly inclined to emphasise the dangerous potential of the organisation. The general opinion was that the ordinary law administered firmly was sufficient in the circumstances although a variety of other measures was suggested, such as reinforcing the RIC and bringing in extra troops in readiness to meet any emergency. Restrictions on the carrying and possession of arms were also recommended and Captain the Hon. Harry de Vere Pery (one of the few RMs with a naval background) called for a coastal blockade to prevent large consignments of weapons being brought into Ireland. Arthur Harrell, stationed at Bandon in Co. Cork, was the only resident magistrate who anticipated the future role of the Volunteers in the struggle for independence. Internal nationalist disputes were breaking up or delaying organisation in the Bandon area but Harrell took the long view rather than concentrating on the immediate situation. 'Secret and semi-secret societies exist for the subversion of British rule in Ireland', he noted, and he went on to state unequivocally that 'the real object of the Volunteer movement is to establish an Irish Republic by force of arms.'

Political tension increased after the UVF arms were landed, without let or hindrance from the police or military. Guns for the southern Volunteers were later brought in to Howth, Co. Dublin, in July 1914. They were not impounded but troops returning to Phoenix Park killed four people and injured others when they opened fire on a crowd in Bachelor's Walk. External events then impinged on Irish affairs, with the commencement of the Great War. Britain declared war on Germany on 4 August. The Defence of the Realm Act (DORA) came into force immediately and in September the Home Rule Act was suspended for the duration of hostilities. John Redmond pledged Ireland's support for Britain and urged the Volunteers to aid the war effort. This caused a split in the movement, whereafter Redmond's followers used the title 'National Volunteers' and the breakaway group, who determined to resist any attempt to force Irishmen into service, were known as the 'Irish Volunteers'.

In the early spring of 1915 it was reported that fear of conscription was encouraging popular support for the Irish Volunteers. The RIC County Inspector for Monaghan was confident that 'cowardice and laziness rather than any pro-German feeling' were the causes of antipathy to military service.[2] It did not occur to him, it seems, that anti-British feeling might also be a factor. Although many thousands of Irishmen did join up, there was an unusually large number of male adolescents and young men in the country during the war years, when emigration was greatly reduced by the international conflict. This created a pool of potential recruits to the nationalist cause and as nationalism became more confrontational it was chiefly disaffected youths who appeared with increasing frequency in the courts. This was of some significance for the resident magistrates but they were affected more immediately by the impact of war. Under DORA the RMs were empowered to hear cases of possession of arms, the wearing of military uniforms, and the possession of seditious literature. Their duties were further increased by other emergency legislation such as the food regulations introduced later in the war, which were supervised by the resident magistrates in each administrative district. The geographical area of responsibility of many of them was also increased, to compensate for the shortage of manpower. A number of resident magistrates were seconded for military service and recruitment virtually ceased until 1919.

For Christopher Lynch-Robinson the outbreak of war brought sudden change to his quiet life. He recalled that he and his wife were lying in bed in their house on the edge of Donegal Bay when 'the First World War burst upon us from the front page of the *Belfast Telegraph*'.[3] The war brought new experiences and greater variety into the humdrum routine of the RM. He encountered a recruiting officer who proposed to 'stir up the fighting Irish spirit' by showing film of the front line in France, in a Derry cinema. This seemed a mad idea to Lynch-Robinson, who suggested that behind-the-lines scenes of soldiers drinking with French girls in pretty villages might attract more recruits. His advice was ignored but gruesome scenes of troops going over the top under fire soon proved too awful for the Derry lads, who grabbed their hats and slipped out of the cinema. Another fiasco occured when the father of a private soldier decorated for gallantry was asked to take part in a recruiting drive. By the time he ascended the platform, the father of the hero was 'drunk as an owl' and had completetly forgotten his prepared speech. He clung to his opening line, 'I am the Father of Michael Brennan,' and repeated it ever more belligerently, eventually challenging to '"knock the bloody snout off" any man who dared to say he was *not* the Father of Michael Brennan.'[4]

Lynch-Robinson's extra duties were more interesting than most. The Donegal coast was on the north-Atlantic steamer route and it was feared that German submarines might lurk in the coves and bays. Moreover, the Tory Islanders had a long established trade with German buyers of kelp seaweed (from which iodine was extracted), and they were considered to be not entirely trustworthy or loyal. The RM was therefore given the temporary rank of lieutenant in the RNVR, to give him some status with coastguards and naval units, and he took on responsibility for matters relating to security. He was instrumental in getting the civilian wireless station on Tory Island closed down (at whatever cost to the local population, who may have needed it in emergencies) and he had one islander 'removed', after discovering that the man had recently sold potatoes to a German submarine officer who had gone ashore in search of supplies.[5] Stories of German U boats off the coast and of their crews slipping ashore proliferated in the coastal counties of Ireland during the war but apart from the Tory Island incident Lynch-Robinson never encountered evidence of enemy activity along the Donegal coastline.

The impact of war was more personal for Katherine Tynan and her husband, Henry Hinkson. They felt very cut off from events at Claremorris, so far from Dublin. Their elder son, Toby, was keen to enlist and he soon joined up. The younger boy went on from his public school to Sandhurst and in the last months of the war Toby was fighting in Egypt while Patrick was with the Dublin Fusiliers in France. The unfriendliness of the Mayo gentry was particularly hard for the Tynan-Hinksons at this time, 'when our two boys were fighting on different fronts' but the RM 'met, week after week, at his courts, loyal magistrates who never asked if the boys lived or died'.[6] The work load of the resident magistrates in Mayo was greatly increased after the RMs for both Belmullet and Ballina districts were seconded for military service. This left only Hinkson, stationed at Claremorris, and John Milling, at Westport, to cover the entire county. Despite the pressure of war, the administrative division of Dublin Castle continued to keep a watchful eye on the RMs. Some of the RMs sent in more detailed reports than usual, or additional memos on matters relating to the war effort. William M. Scott Moore reported from Mullingar in April 1915 that there had been some 'cattle driving trouble' near Tyrrellspass but it had been 'a good month for the farmers and the county is prosperous'. Next month he noted that recruiting was 'very slow' in Mullingar, 'practically no farmers or shop assistants have joined, and will not, except by compulsion.' The farmers, he added, had 'no excuse' as cattle grazing was commonplace and they could not claim that their labour was needed for what little tillage was undertaken locally.[7]

The following year was notable for the Easter Rising, an event that changed the course of Irish history but which has been written about so widely that it will not be recounted here. The resident magistrates were not directly involved in the action in Dublin but in the weeks that followed it was the RMs, in consultation with RIC officers, who recommended to Dublin Castle the names of nationalists to be arrested and interned. Many parts of the country were unaffected or apathetic about what was happening in the capital, although it is generally agreed that the executions that followed brought about a rapid change in popular attitudes. In March of 1916 the Tynan-Hinksons were in Dublin for 'a fortnight's breath of life after the winter stagnation'. They enjoyed their visit as usual but heard a lot of talk of Sinn

Féin, which people seemed to be 'puzzled' by but the general opinion was 'that there was nothing to be afraid about'. The only disappointment in Dublin was that they were not able to see their son, Patrick, at the Richmond barracks as he had unexpectedly been sent to the north. A few weeks later Tynan was 'thanking the Mercy' which had sent him north and kept him there during the Easter rising.[8] Lynch-Robinson was at home in Donegal when rumours spread that 'there was something amiss in Dublin'. Nothing definite was known until the evening of Easter Monday, when the RIC District Inspector from Ballyshannon motored over to tell the RM that he had 'private word' that there was an armed rising of Sinn Féin and that fighting was going on in Dublin. (The rising was generally attributed to Sinn Féin and thereafter all strands of nationalism were commonly described as 'Sinn Féinism'.) Lynch-Robinson was concerned for his wife, who was at Foxrock visiting her parents, and for his parents who lived near his in-laws. Early next morning he set off by way of Enniskillen and Cavan, taking his Colt automatic with him and stopping at every police barrack to ask if any news had come through. It was not until he reached Navan in Co. Meath that he learned anything more. There he was told that he would probably not be able to get across Dublin but he by-passed the city to reach Foxrock, some six miles south, and found his wife at his parents' home where all three were sitting out on the steps, 'listening to the distant battle'. The RM stayed for several days on the instructions of officials at Dublin Castle, as 'everything was normal and quiet in Donegal' and the military did not want people to make unnecessary journeys.[9]

In Co. Mayo, people were soon 'back to their buying and selling' and Tynan tried to get on with her writing but 'the Rebellion, for many weeks, was never out of my thoughts'. She had lived many years in England, where her sons had been born and educated, and had 'come to believe that affection for England and love of Ireland could quite well go hand in hand'. 'To me', she wrote, 'any bloodiness between England and Ireland was unthinkable. All that belonged to the bad old days. And here was '98 come again, and the people who were my own people were being shot and deported by the people with whom we had lived in amity and affection for eighteen long years'. Her admiration for the 'good, impractical' men and the 'almost religious' spirit of Easter 1916 was another element in her conflicting feelings about the 'tragedy' of the rising.[10] Lynch-Robinson was also somewhat ambivalent in his response. He felt some sympathy with English people who were 'bewildered' by the rising and the whole separatist movement but he regretted the 'fine lives' lost in the executions that followed. He had no doubt that both sides believed sincerely that what they fought for was right, but 'the whole thing was damnable'.[11]

At the end of 1916, a few days before Christmas, 600 untried Irish internees were released from the camp at Frongoch, in Wales, and from Lewes prison. They had been jeered by Dublin mobs as they were marched to the quays in the spring but they were welcomed as heroes on their return to Ireland. The remaining Irish prisoners were released in June 1917. In October of that year de Valera was elected president of the Irish Volunteers and of Sinn Féin, which adopted a policy of seeking recognition for the Irish Republic. As support for the advanced nationalism of Sinn Féin grew so politics became increasingly confrontational and violent. In February 1918 restrictions on the carrying of arms were introduced, to apply to all Ireland, and the possession of arms was prohibited in counties Clare, Galway and Tipperary. Clare was shortly afterwards proclaimed a military area. In April the anti-conscription crisis added to the general tension. The Military Service Bill to apply conscription to Ireland was passed by the Commons within seven days of being introduced but the Home Rule MPs withdrew from the House in protest. A conference representing all shades of nationalist opinion was held at the Mansion House in Dublin, as a result of which anti-conscription pledges were issued and at the end of April there were nationwide demonstrations and mass signings. An anti-conscription national strike on 23 April was successful, other than in Ulster. The campaign against conscription attracted much publicity and popular support for Sinn Féin, which had shrewdly judged the strength of opposition to compulsory military service. It was rumoured in Galway, in May 1918, that in remote parts of Connemara people were leaving their work and homes to live in the hills, so 'terrified' were they of the threat of conscription. The intelligence officer for the Midland and Connaught district thought the agitation had been largely 'worked up by the leaders' but as an example of how successfully they had frightened people he described an incident in Co. Longford, when a farmer to whom the local RIC sergeant had gone 'to make ordinary inquiries' had suddenly rushed at the policeman and stabbed him with a pitchfork, shouting 'I will die before I am conscripted'.[12]

On the 17 and 18 May 1918 about 100 leading figures in Sinn Féin and the Volunteer movement were seized for internment in the 'German Plot' arrests. There was no such plot but government claimed to have discovered one, in an effort to discredit Sinn Féin and as a pretext for the arrests. Not all the wanted men were taken in the police raids. One who made his escape was Patrick O'Malley of Leenane, Co. Galway, who exchanged shots with the RIC at his home before getting away; he was still on the run at the end of the month.[13] The arrests did nothing to improve the state of the country. In June martial law was imposed throughout most of the south and west, with Limerick and Tipperary being proclaimed as special military areas. In the following month nationalist organisations, including Sinn Féin and the Irish Volunteers, were banned and public meetings were proscribed. Thereafter the armistice of November 1918 restored international peace but it brought no peace to Ireland, where the post-war general election resulted in the virtual annihilation of the old Home Rule party and considerable success for Sinn Féin. The Representation of the People Act (February 1918) had enfranchised all men over twenty-one and most women over thirty, thus creating almost a full democracy. In December 1918 the Irish electorate decisively rejected limited independence and devolved government, in favour of separatist republicanism. Only six Home Rule candiates were returned but Sinn Féin took seventy-three of the 105 Irish constituencies. The next few years were to be among the bloodiest in Ireland's history and the experiences of the Irish RMs during the period 1919-21 were far removed from the comic exploits of Major Yeates.

In January 1919, while the first Dáil was in session in Dublin, a Volunteer or IRA unit ambushed and killed two RIC constables taking dynamite to a quarry at Soloheadbeg, Co. Tipperary. This later came to be regarded as the start of the 'War of Independence' or 'the troubles', as the violent years were more commonly described by contemporaries. The first RM to die in the troubles was John Milling, shot and fatally wounded in March 1919; his life and death are recounted below in one of the biographical studies of Part III. In May two more policemen were killed, during the rescue of three wounded IRA men at Knocklong railway station. Next month, on 23 June, DI Hunt was shot dead on the streets of Thurles. It was reported that some of the crowd jeered the officer as he lay dying and the news of his murder was allegedly greeted with cheers at Kilmallock and Ballylanders.[14] Such killings were widely condemned but to Sinn Féin and the IRA they were acts of war, legitimised by the results of the 1918 election and the setting up of the Dáil. As a Sinn Féin representative put it when commenting on the Knocklong incident, anyone who killed a policeman 'may rest easy in his conscience, for he is only carrying out the sentence already passed on them by the republican government'.[15]

The year culminated with an IRA attempt to assassinate the Lord Lieutenant, Lord French, at Ashtown on the edge of Phoenix Park. French was returning by train from his country house near Boyle, Co. Roscommon, and was to travel by car from Ashtown Gate station to the viceregal lodge in the Park. For various reasons the plans of the eleven IRA men went wrong and, having failed to block the road, they fired rifle shots at the first car in the convoy. Grenades were thrown at the second car, in which it was assumed Lord French was travelling, and shots were exchanged with an armed guard in the third vehicle. French was actually in the first car and unhurt. The only casualty was Martin Savage, an IRA man who was shot and killed in the encounter. His comrades abandoned his body and cycled back to Dublin, where news of the attack was soon heard. The assailants were subsequently referred to in an *Irish Independent* editorial as would-be assassins, a description which offended the IRA. Its protest was registered by the despatch of some twenty to thirty armed men who held up staff at the newspapers' office and smashed up the linotype machines.[16]

The attack on French was investigated by the resident magistrate Alan Bell. He was born in King's County (Offaly), the son of a Church of Ireland minister, and joined the RIC as an officer-cadet in September 1879. During the land war of the 1880s he investigated the funding of the Land League and he acquired brief notoriety in 1882 when, at Athenry, he arrested the American land reformer, Henry George, who was touring the country. Alan Bell joined the resident magistracy in November 1898 and served in counties Mayo, Down and Armagh before being transferred in 1919 to special duties at Dublin Castle. He had many years' experience of dealing with political crime and he was brought to the Castle to serve on the secret committee set up to improve intelligence gathering. Some covert agents worked under Bell's direction and many police or army raids were undertaken in consequence of information supplied by the RM.[17] In the course of his inquiry into the attack on Lord French he interviewed numerous people including an Ashtown publican, Peter Kelly, and his brother Bartholemew or 'Bartle' Kelly. No hard evidence linked the publican to the IRA but Peter Kelly had 'found it convenient' to be away from his licensed premises on 19 December, even though a local fair and market meant that it was one of the busiest trading days of the year. The RM found no useful leads but he did manage to establish the route taken by the assailants as they returned to Dublin, and his findings confirmed 'statements of witnesses and informers'. The recent murder of Mr Redmond (who had been brought down from Belfast to reorganise the detective division of the DMP) had been 'a great set back' to the investigation as through him Bell was 'able to make inquiries which I should not care to entrust to the "G" division'. Bell went on to refer to several Dublin houses used as 'Dance Halls', which he had under surveillance. They were frequented by young men and women but Bell suspected they were 'drilling' centres, where the clatter of feet and loud music were 'kept up to cover the sounds of words of command'. The inquiry was inconclusive but the RM concluded his report by explaining that he had prepared 'a statement for use for Propaganda purposes' by the Chief Secretary's office, 'and for possible use by the Foreign Office at the British Mission in America'.[18]

Propaganda was an important element in the conflict and Sinn Féin often won the war of words. A large section of British public opinion was critical of

government policy in Ireland and on occasion British actions were also subject to the condemnation of international opinion, especially that of America
with its republican tradition and large Irish immigrant population. Reprisals
taken by state forces against the mass of the people were a sensitive issue in
the latter half of 1920 and on into 1921, though initially these were unofficial
acts perpetrated mainly by the 'Black and Tans' and the 'Auxies'. These were
reinforcements for the RIC, which was below its pre-1914 strength and had
taken the brunt of IRA attacks during 1919. The Black and Tans (so called
because of their combination uniforms of khaki and dark bottle green, and in
allusion to a Galway hunt) were recruited chiefly but not entirely from other
parts of Britain from January 1920 and went into service in Ireland at the end
of March. Recruiting for the Auxiliary Division of the RIC was in hand by
May 1920 and the 'Auxies', a body made up of former officers in the British
army, went into service in July. Resident magistrates were involved in the
recruitment of these men and the Auxiliaries were organised by the grandson
of an RM.[19] Both groups were soon notorious for their ruthless brutality,
which may well have been somewhat exaggerated but was undoubtedly characteristic of these supplementary forces. Their behaviour caused some unease
even among the Anglo-Irish gentry, many of whom hoped to see 'the Shinners'
put in their place by firm government.

Life went on much the same for most of the Anglo-Irish during 1919 but
already some families were leaving the country, especially from the western
counties.[20] The atmosphere of the big house during the early 1920s, as tennis
parties and dances competed with raids for arms and ambushes on lonely
roads, has been captured in literary works of some documentary value, such
as J.G. Farrell's *Troubles* and Elizabeth Bowen's *The Last September*,[21] in
which the characters' experience is often similar to that of the RMs during
those years. Indeed, one factual incident that Farrell included in *Troubles*
involved John St George. St George was resident magistrate for a district in
Co. Tipperary but in January 1920 he was at his family home in Co. Kilkenny
and had arranged to hold a ball at Kilrush House, Freshford. On the night of
the ball, two young men travelling in a covered car where held up at Troyswood,
some three miles from Kilkenny. They and the jarvey were kept prisoner
while their captors barricaded the road with the car and a 'wall' of stones.
About an hour later a party of military officers on the way to Kilrush House
with their wives and friends was brought to a halt by the road block. They
were ordered out of their six motor cars by masked and armed men in search
of weapons. The petrol tanks of the cars were riddled with bullets and the
engines smashed with hammers, according to newspaper accounts, before the
attackers left the scene. As they were six miles from the RMs home and the
ball, the party set out to walk back to Kilkenny, which they reached around

eleven o'clock. The few people out late on that stormy night were reported to have been 'astounded on seeing a number of "Society" folk proceeding in evening dress along the streets', one of the women minus a dancing slipper which she had somehow lost in the ambush. The tone of the report was lightly amused at the plight of the gentry, and it concluded 'We understand that "Cinderella" can have her slipper on applying to the nearest police station. A pleasing feature of the affair is that nobody was injured.'[22]

Meanwhile Alan Bell was settling in at 19 Belgrave Square, Monkstown, with his wife and two servants, and travelling daily to Dublin Castle where he was engaged in trying to trace money subscribed to the Dáil National Loan. A raid on Sinn Féin headquarters in January had yielded only £1,000 as the bulk of funds was deposited in banks, in the names of private individuals. By early March Bell was ready to serve summonses on officials of the Hibernian Bank and of the Munster and Leinster Bank, and he took preliminary depositions from those officials in the period 8-11 March. When the manager of the College Green branch of the Hibernian Bank appeared before Bell in an interview room at Dublin Castle he asked, at an early stage in his examination, 'can we be represented by counsel?' 'No', replied the RM, 'nobody is allowed inside here except myself, yourself – the witness, and the shorthand writer'.[23]

Bell was now a marked man. He had been attacked in the nationalist press and in the Dáil publication, the *Irish Bulletin*, as a secret agent long opposed to nationalism. Moreover, he was the key figure in the investigation into the Dáil funding and Michael Collins, as Minister of Finance, acted quickly to protect the loan. On 26 March Alan Bell was shot dead. He had taken the tramcar from Salthill into the city as usual but when the crowded car reached Simmonscourt Road in Ballsbridge a young man alighting with other passengers immobilised the tram, by pulling away the overhead connecting wire. Other men surrounded Bell, who was reading a newsapaper, and hustled him onto the road where they fired several shots at him. An ambulance was called by passers-by, but he was dead on arrival at hospital.[24] Lady Taylor, wife of the Under-Secretary, broke the news to Mrs Bell. Her husband had not been under police protection 'in the ordinary sense of being guarded by officers in immediate attendance', because he had refused such protection. As an 'old and experienced police officer himself' the RM had believed, according to the Chief Secretary, that 'any ostentatious protection would defeat its own object'.[25]

All of the resident magistrates were now regarded as legitimate targets by the IRA. In May, Edward Wynne, resident magistrate for Tralee, Co. Kerry, was ambushed and fired at by seven or eight masked men as he drove on a side car to the Causeway petty sessions. Wynne was an Englishman born in

Essex, who had served in the RIC for over twenty years before joining the resident magistracy in 1903. In an interview with a reporter from the *Cork Examiner*, he said that he had fired five shots from his revolver at the attackers and had seen one man fall. It was further reported that 'The others, seeing their comrade drop, ran back, two of them over the fence, and the others hesitated. [Wynne] shouted "Come on, you cowards", holding his revolver up. He then called on the driver to drive on . . .'.[26] The RM saw his attackers return to pick up the wounded man and he then travelled on to hold the court at Causeway before returning to station in a police motor car. He told the press that he hoped he had inflicted no fatal injury, adding that he did not believe any Kerryman would attack him. This response was not unusual, for most RMs liked to think they were personally popular in their districts and they commonly ascribed attacks to 'outsiders'.

In the most disturbed districts special crimes courts were adding to the work load of the RMs and as the situation deteriorated they were increasingly inconvenienced by petrol shortages, travel restrictions, curfews, train strikes, raids for arms and transport, raids on the mail, blocked roads and ambushes, and burnt out courthouses. By mid-summer 1920 Sinn Féin courts had replaced the petty sessions in many areas. William Orr attended the 'ruins of Lismore courthouse' in June only to find the place deserted,[27] and in Co. Louth Christopher Lynch-Robinson noticed a sudden falling off in civil cases at his courts.[28] Police prosecutions, the transfer of publicans' licences, and other semi-official cases continued for some time but it then became increasingly common for defendants to fail to appear in response to a police summons. County JPs began to desert the courts, for fear of IRA violence, and the RIC abandoned routine patrols, so there were no prosecutions for drunkeness or other minor breaches of the law. Lynch-Robinson's summary of duty for July 1920 revealed that the petty sessions at Louth village had not proceeded ('Courthouse burnt down') and that on the 7 July no justice had been administered at two other courts: 'Litigants failed to appear at Mell – Tormofellin courthouse burnt down this morning'.[29] He sent Jimmy Brogan back to his parents in Donegal, much against the young man's will, but there was no escape from danger for the RM, who endured the 'remarkably unpleasant experience' of driving to his courts expecting to be ambushed on every journey.[30]

As the duties of the RMs became more onerous and dangerous they became increasingly dissatisfied with their salaries. They had been making their feelings known since 1918 and in April 1919 a deputation met the Chief Secretary to discuss pay and allowances.[31] The matter was under consideration for many months thereafter until legislation in 1920 brought in 'somewhat higher rates' than had prevailed since 1874.[32] Some RMs were also concerned about the financial security of their families, if they should be killed in the course of their duties. Joseph Kilbride, RM for the Galway district, decided in the summer of 1920 to insure his life for £1,100 for a five-year period but he was asked for an additional premium of over £20 per annum because of the high risks of his occupation. He wrote to the Castle to ask if the Treasury would pay all or part of the excess but it was some time before he received a final ruling. His correspondence progressed slowly through the system until, in late July, a Treasury official wrote a long missive to Dublin Castle. All the implications of Kilbride's request were considered in detail before the official concluded that if government paid the premium it would amount to 'free insurance' for civil servants in Ireland. Numerous objections to this were raised and it was finally dismissed as being 'impractical in view of the impossibility of distinguishing loyalists from Sinn Féiners. No doubt Resident Magistrates could be treated specially as a class that is bound to be loyal, but if they were given special terms an awkward precedent would necessarily be created'. Moreover, it 'would be cheaper to pay the death claims direct, as they arise', and the officials' superiors believed that provisions under the Criminal Injuries Compensation Act (1919) were sufficient to compensate for the life of a resident magistrate.[33]

A fortunate few RMs retired in 1920, among them Charles Paston Crane. He had been seconded for military service at the outbreak of war but he was seriously ill in 1917 and on the sick list for over a year. When he resumed his duties as a resident magistrate in Kerry he was appalled by the lawless state of the county. He was faced in court by young men who treated him with 'studied insolence' and refused to recognise British authority, declaring themselves 'Soldiers of the Irish Republic'. As he left court after sentencing some IRA men he was 'surrounded by a savage booing mob, some of whom shook their fists in my face, shouting "You will be dead in six months".' Crane blamed many years of 'weak administration' for the unrest and, like many Englishmen, he held to the 'murder gang' theory that a minority of violent nationalists had terrorised the mass of the people into support for a republic. Yet he had little sympathy for those in fear of their lives, people such as 'my man, whom I had taught to drive, [who] came to the conclusion, "for his wife's sake", that he could no longer bear the danger of driving me. He had what the local doctor called an attack of mauseritis.' Morning after morning the doctor met the RM with the cheerful remark 'Well, are you alive still?' Crane was warned by many personal friends that as an Englishman and one of the 'foreign garrison' he was in danger but he 'never suspected or believed in the possibility of any harm' coming to him during his last days in Kerry. He and his wife abandoned plans to stay in Ireland after his retirement because the future seemed so uncertain. When his wife's family offered them a house in London they were glad to take it and leave the country. Crane was a 'free man' by June 1920 and he and his wife sailed for England in July.[34]

For those left in Ireland life was to become ever more dangerous. In August the recently appointed RM for Kilkee district of Co. Clare, Captain Lendrum, was ambushed at Tullerine as he and a District Inspector were on their way to a petty sessions. Both men escaped unhurt but the RMs car was riddled with bullets. In late September there were press reports of attacks on the RIC and the military in the Miltown-Malby area of Co. Clare and of reprisals against the local population. It was also reported that Captain Lendrum was rumoured to have been fired at and wounded while travelling from Kilkee to Miltown-Malby.[35] The RM had disappeared between Doonbeg and Craggaknock on his way to the Enystymon petty sessions. When he failed to arrive, police and military searched the area and found evidence to suggest that he had been wounded and kidnapped. Houses along the coastline were subsequently searched but no trace of Lendrum was found and, on 27 September, notices were posted in Kilkee announcing that if the RM had not returned to his station within forty-eight hours, Kilkee, Kilrush, Carrigaholt, Doonbeg and Kilmihill would be burnt. Visitors to these places were reported to have quickly left.[36] Official steps were taken to prevent the threatened reprisals, according to the London *Times*,[37] but on the night the notice expired troops and police drove into Kilkee intent on destruction. The parish priest pursuaded them that the townspeople knew nothing of the whereabouts of the RM but a local man came forward claiming to be under IRA orders to give information to the authorities. The reprisals were 'temporarily postponed'.[38] According to the informant, the RM was dead and his body would be returned but it was not readily available. It was eventually found on 1 October, abandoned conspicuously on the West Clare railway line between Cragarode and Kilmurry stations. The remains were contained in a crudely-constructed coffin on which was written, 'He died for a foreign Hunnish government, and his body is given up regardless of threatened reprisals.'[39] There were two bullet wounds to the head and the state of the body indicated that it had been recently dug up. More detailed examination suggested that it had been in contact with salt sea water. The manner of Lendrum's death was never fully revealed but Lynch-Robinson wrote in his memoirs of a resident magistrate said to have been 'caught and buried alive in the sands'.[40] It seems that this was widely believed to have been the way that Lendrum met his death; the story was recounted in the anonymous *Tales of the RIC*, published in 1921, in which a resident magistrate was wounded in an IRA attack and then buried up to his neck on the shore. He was left to drown as the tide came in. The same brutality was used against the central character in Farrell's *Troubles*, although he was rescued from his fate.[41]

Four resident magistrates were to die during the troubles, a small number in the total loss of life but the proportion killed was actually greater than the one in twenty members of the RIC killed in just over two years.[42] Few of the Irish RMs came through the conflict without some unpleasant encounter with one side or the other, although not all such encounters were life-threatening. Walter Callan, stationed at Queenstown (Cobh) in Cork, was perhaps little more than embarrased by a military raid in October 1920, when officers and troops from a Highland regiment 'visited' the house of Miss Geraldine Penrose Fitzgerald, an elderly novelist 'known to be a warm supporter of the Irish people in their desire for self-government'. Her papers and correspond ence were 'closely looked over' before the search was checked by the military discovering that 'an occupant of the house, then in his bath, was the Resident Magistrate for the district'.[43] 'Visits' from the IRA were made on several RMs, especially after that organisation began to 'requisition' transport for its war effort. Lynch-Robinson was confident that a gadget he had devised effectively immobilised his car but when the IRA came calling one night, facing the RM with a revolver when he answered a knock at his door, he was mortified to see the men start up the vehicle and drive away. The car was found abandoned next day, with fifty extra miles on the clock.[44] William M. Scott Moore had a more alarming brush with the IRA when he and a county JP were 'captured by Sinn Féiners' on the morning of 14 October 1920, as they drove to the Castlepollard petty sessions. For an hour or more they were driven around, blindfolded, in Scott Moore's car. Then, as he reported to Dublin Castle,

> We were taken to three different filthy cow houses and were wet through walking over the mountain between them, and given wet hay to sit on. We were released about 8pm on the night of 15th, separately, and sent off in the opposite direction to Castlepollard – it being night we could not see or know where we were – after wandering about we arrived at Castlepollard about 1.30am on the morning of 16th, and reached Mullingar about 2pm on that day.[45]

There were, unusually, some quick arrests in this case and the RM indentified some of his 'guards' detained at the Mullingar military barracks. He also located one of the houses where he had been held, and was told by the RIC that they had found his abandoned car in a ditch, 'considerably damaged'. Scott Moore went on sick leave to Londonderry in late October, suffering from rheumatism and other after effects of his ordeal, but in November he was summoned to Dublin to assist the court martial officer dealing with the case. In December twelve men appeared at the Kilmainham court-

house charged in connection with the affair. The magistrates' were said to
have 'left written notes hidden, and also cut notches in the woodwork', in
order to be able to identify the places where they were held. Eight of the
accused refused to recognise the court and declined to plead. The other four
were found not guilty but the decision in regard to the main body of accused
was undecided when the court rose.[46]

For Patrick Sullivan, a former barrister and RM in Co. Kilkenny, the
threat of violence came not from the IRA but from the forces of the Crown.
In December 1920 questions were asked in the Commons about Sullivan,
who had complained publicly that he had been assaulted in the precincts of
his Kilkenny court by a man supposed to be one of his peace officers. It
transpired that the RM had arrived at the courthouse as a police search was
in progress and he had been refused entry by an Auxiliary who did not know
him. The Chief Secretary acknowledged in the House that the officer had
been guilty of a technical assualt, by 'placing his hands' on the RM's shoul-
ders, but he emphasised that 'no violence or threats were used'. A local RIC
man had intervened and vouched for the RM, and both the Auxiliary and the
County Inspector had apologised to Sullivan for the incident. The Chief
Secretary suggested that the RM's statement arose from some 'misunder-
standing' but his questioner in the House doubted if Sullivan would have
spoken out so strongly unless he had been 'brutally assaulted'. The MP went
on to ask 'is not this [Auxiliary] police force getting out of hand in Ireland?'[47]

The Auxiliaries and the Black and Tans were generally unpopular but
they were particularly detested in Cork, which was one of the most disturbed
counties throughout 1920. The experiences of the RM for the Bantry district,
which encompassed the Skebawn (Skibbereen) of Somerville and Ross, were
among the grimmest of any endured by those resident magistrates who were
not actually killed. Patrick Sarsfield Brady, a former Belfast solicitor, was
kept busy with many special courts and extra duties during the first part of
1920. In July two motor cycles were stolen from his home, in what was
assumed to be an IRA raid, and in December he witnessed the murder by
Auxiliary Cadet Harte of Canon Magner and Timothy Crowley. The murder
was only one of many bloody incidents in Co. Cork and elsewhere. At the end
of November the IRA had wiped out an entire Auxiliary patrol, with the loss
to themselves of two men, at Kilmichael on the Macroom–Dunmanway road.
Martial law was declared in counties Cork, Kerry, Limerick and Tipperary on
10 December but next day the IRA made another major attack on the RIC in
Cork city. Auxiliaries and Black and Tans later burned large parts of Cork in
reprisal and the military, which was responsible for the city during the hours
of curfew, did nothing to prevent them. On 15 December, Brady was motoring to the Skibbereen petty sessions when his car broke down. Canon Magner,

the elderly parish priest of Dunmanway, came upon the scene and while he and the RM were in conversation a young labourer, Tadgh or Timothy Crowley, cycled by and was called over by the priest. At this point two Crossley tenders carrying some thirty Auxiliaries passed by, on their way to the funeral in Cork of one of their force who had recently been shot dead. The second lorry stopped some distance from the trio at the roadside and the officer in command, Cadet Harte, jumped out and ran back towards the three, carrying a revolver. He wanted to see some identification and did not believe Brady when he said he was the district RM. He then began to question Crowley aggressively, pushing and jostling him as he did so. When the priest protested at this behaviour, Harte shot the young man dead. Two other Auxiliaries approached at this stage but they did not intervene effectively and, within minutes, Harte had also shot Canon Magner dead.[48]

Harte was disarmed, placed under arrest, and soon reported to be 'out of his mind'. The Prime Minister, Lloyd George, is said to have wanted Harte tried and hanged on the spot but General Sir Nevil Macready, commandant of the ADRIC, insisted on a proper investigation.[49] A court of inquiry into the deaths of Manger and Crowley found the Auxiliary 'guilty of Homicide in both cases'. It emerged that Harte had been 'greatly affected' by the killing of his close friend, Cadet Chapman, but he had not been thought unfit for duty. The general feeling of the Auxiliary company was that the shooting of Crowley 'was not unjustified as they did not know if he used threats or [was] in possession of arms'. One of the Auxiliaries gave evidence that Harte 'had been drinking and as he went down the road his steps were unsteady' but an officer who had seen him shortly before the funeral party set off, and the officer in the first lorry, both swore that Harte was perfectly sober.[50] The brigade commander in Cork commented on the report of the inquiry that 'The action of the two Cadets who walked back to Cadet Harte after he had shot Timothy Crowley and was talking to Canon Magner, also the reason why Cadet Harte was allowed to be in Command of a lorry if he was the worse for drink, requires investigation'.[51] No further investigation seems to have taken place but Harte was charged with murder and tried by courtmartial at Cork on 5 January 1921. Officers again attested to Harte's sobriety at the time but the RM described him as smelling strongly of 'and suffering from' drink. Brady suggested that, if not actually drunk, Harte must have been drinking heavily the day or night before. He also told the court that, after the priest was shot, he had said to the other two Cadets 'He'll surely shoot me too,' to which one of the men replied, 'Yes, you'd better clear.' Harte was said by the defence to be of unblemished character. The court was told that on the outbreak of war in 1914 he had sold up his fruit farm in Tasmania in order to join the army and he had served for the duration, with 'honour and distinction'. One of the escort party described how, on the journey to Cork after his arrest, Harte seemed unaware of the shootings and talked as if he thought they were still on the way to Chapman's funeral. The escort's evidence alone was insignificant but six of 'the greatest mental experts in the United Kingdom' swore that Harte was insane at the time of the murders.[52] The Cabinet in London recognised that this was a 'particularly unfortunate' finding, as the killer in the infamous Sheehy-Skeffington case in 1916 had also been declared insane; the civil servant Mark Sturgis (joint Assistant Under-Secretary at the time) commented in his diary that if Harte was insane, 'those who let him loose on the world in charge of a party armed to the teeth should take his place in the dock'.[53] He was still being held in detention at Cork in late March 1921, 'pending the completion of inquiries into another crime', although the Chief Secretary had already signed the order for his transference to Broadmoor hospital for the criminally insane.[54]

By the end of 1920 the six-county state of Northern Ireland and that of Southern Ireland had been created by the Act for the Better Government of Ireland (December 1920). The 'partition act' was boycotted by Sinn Féin but after elections in May the Northern Ireland Parliament, attended only by unionists, met in June. The Act did nothing to reduce violence, and from January 1921 there was official support for reprisals. Lynch-Robinson had nothing but admiration for the Auxiliaries he met in Co. Louth, some of whom were occasional visitors to his home, but he was highly critical of the Black and Tans he encountered, being nervous of them himself and aware that some of the old RIC were afraid of them. When a local RIC sergeant told the RM of the arrest and wounding of a Drogheda publican by a Black and Tan, who had 'planted' evidence, he was so outraged that he took the train to Dublin with the intention of raising the matter at the Castle. His Sinn Féin friend, the lawyer Albert Wood, and his father, Sir Henry Robinson, persuaded him that no action on his part would do any good. He returned to Louth consoling himself that 'a humble RM' was not in a position to influence events but he was uncomfortably aware that the RIC sergeant thought he had 'funked it'.[55]

Relations with the army were perhaps more straightforward than those between RMs and the police reinforcements but early in 1921 the resident magistrates in Cork came under criticism from the military. Colonel Willis wrote to HQ complaining, 'I am unable to fathom the position of the RMs in my area at the present time, and will ask to have their position explained to me'. The RM at Queenstown (Cobh) seemed to doing the work of the RM for Cork city and the RM for Bantry, 'though present', was leaving most civil cases to the summary court official. The RM for Macroom was apparently on leave, but no temporary replacement had been sent there. In mid February it was explained to the officer that at the period in question the Cork RM was on transfer leave, which was why the Queenstown RM was doing his duties. Patrick Brady, stationed at Bantry, was on extended sick leave and the Bandon RM had recently retired but would be replaced shortly.[56] Brady was given six months' leave from 17 January because of fears for his safety, as there were rumours that the Auxiliaries or Black and Tans meant to kill him because of the evidence he gave against Harte at the inquiry into the murder of Canon Magner and Timothy Crowley.[57]

When Brady resumed duties at Bantry, Co. Cork was still very disturbed and there was a final trying experience ahead for the RM. Lord Bandon was kidnapped in June 1921 and his home was destroyed by fire. Two county JPs were kidnapped at Clonakilty on 22 June, and next day a local magistrate from Bandon was abducted. It was announced that more troops were to be sent to Ireland and that, drawing on experience in the Boer War, cavalry would be used in 'carefully arranged drives, on the South African principle, through the mountainous regions where the rebels are in force'.[58] When Patrick Brady returned to Balilicky House, he found that there had been a break-in and a large quantity of jewellry and other property was missing. There was no indication as to who was responsible. Around midnight on 2 July he and his wife were woken by loud knocking at the door, whereupon Mrs Brady went to the window and asked what was wanted. She was told it was the RM that was wanted. Brady dressed and went down to find some eight armed men around the house, who said they wished to take him to identify his stolen property.[59] He had little choice other than to comply but the men promised Mrs Brady that he would be safely returned by morning. That promise was not kept. As the RM later noted in his summary of duties performed during the month, having been kidnapped in the name of the Irish Republic on Sunday 3 July he remained a prisoner in the hands of the IRA until 21 July.

The RM was at first detained in a house where, after a few days, a man saying he was from 'headquarters' arrived to tell him that he was being held as a hostage. That night Brady heard loud talk and 'tremendous cries'. Next morning the woman of the house told him that but for her appeals he would have been 'executed'. He was then moved to another place where he was lodged for a fortnight in semi-darkness, in a room without windows or fireplace and furnished with only a bed. When he was eventually released he was medically examined and said to be 'suffering from nervous shock'. He resumed duties immediately but had no petty sessions until the Bantry court on 25 July, where fifteen cases of unlicenced dogs were scheduled for hearing. The court was adjourned because the RM felt too unwell to attend. In October Patrick Brady was awarded over £2,000 compensation for his illegal imprisonment and loss of property.[60] His experiences epitomise those of the resident magistrates' as a whole during the years of the troubles, when the threat of death was as ever present as the mundane list at the petty sessions.

The troubles had officially ended while Brady was incarcerated. Between 4-8 July a representative of southern unionists, Lord Midleton, had met with de Valera and Arthur Griffith and acted as an intermediary with Lloyd George in London. Draft terms for a truce were published on 9 July. Several days of serious rioting followed in east Belfast, with loss of life, but the Truce came into effect on 11 July. Thereafter, the Anglo-Irish Conference met in London from 11 October and articles of agreement for a treaty between Great Britain and Ireland were signed in the early hours of 6 December 1921. The Anglo-Irish Treaty was ratified by the United Kingdom Parliament in mid-December and approved by Dáil Éireann on 7 January 1922. These political events were not unaccompanied by controversy and they did not bring immediate stability to the country but a new Ireland had emerged from the conflicts of 1919-21.

7

The RMs and the New Ireland

Events moved swiftly after the signing of the Treaty and its approval by the British Parliament and the Irish Dáil. By the middle of January 1922 a provisional government had been formed and formal control of Dublin Castle, the seat and symbol of British rule in Ireland, passed to the new regime. British troops began to leave the country and the disbandment of the RIC was soon underway. The transfer of full powers to the provisional government took place on 1 April and, after elections in June, the Irish Free State came officially into existence in December 1922. Yet the threat of violence persisted. Nationalist opinion was ominously divided in its attitudes to the Anglo-Irish Treaty and before long the anti-Treaty 'Irregulars' of the IRA were engaged in armed struggle against the Irish government they had fought to bring into being. Fighting in the civil war continued until May 1923. In Northern Ireland internal conflict continued with unabated ferocity throughout much of 1922 and many lives were lost in sectarian clashes in Belfast during June and July of that year.

The resident magistrates north and south of the border found themselves in very different circumstances. Northern Ireland remained a part of the United Kingdom, albeit with certain powers devolved to its own Parliament in Belfast. The resident magistrates' stationed in the six counties that made up the new province created by the 1920 Act for the Better Government of Ireland remained in post largely unaffected by political change. They were appointed and supervised by the Ministry of Home Affairs in Belfast, in place of the Dublin Castle administration, but otherwise their working lives and duties continued much as before. The institution exists to this day in Northern Ireland, with some modifications, but its future development is beyond the scope of this study.

The resident magistrates in the southern part of Ireland were faced with uncertainty at the beginning of 1922. For months past their normal duties had been disrupted by the troubles but between January and April, during the period of transistion between the Treaty and the transfer of full authority to the provisional government, they were frustrated by enforced idleness and the bureaucratic niceties of the Castle. Whereas disbandment of the RIC was

promptly undertaken, the resident magistracy with which it was closely associated was left in a state of limbo in which the RMs were officially regarded
as still fully employed in carrying out their normal duties but had, in reality,
no duties to perform. Monthly summaries returned to Dublin Castle in January to April listed 'no duty' for an increasing number of days each month
from resident magistrates around the country. At this stage the RMs were not
sure what government intended for their future and, as troops were withdrawn and the RIC was stood down, the RMs and other officials were 'left at
the mercy of any thugs that happened to take a dislike to us'.[1] Questions were
asked in the Commons in March 1922 about the 'exceptionally low' rate of
pension on which RMs were retired and it was put to the Chief Secretary that
they should be dealt with more generously than ordinary civil servants because of the personal dangers to which their work exposed them.[2]

Under the terms of the Treaty the Irish Free State had agreed to pay fair
compensation to any resident magistrate discharged by it, or who retired in
consequence of the change of government, but what this amounted to was a
scheme to enhance pensions by taking into account 'additional years' that
might have been served if British rule had continued. The RMs were not
satisfied with this because although the terms were generous in themselves,
they were dependent on current rates of pay. The resident magistrates' argued through their professional Association that the new salary schemes introduced in 1920 had not materially improved their financial circumstances in
regard to pensions, having not been in effect long enough to do so before
what seemed likely to be imminent 'compulsory retirement'. The resident
magistracy was transferred to the authority of the Irish Free State in April, as
part of the judicial system, and it seemed inevitable to the Association that
after the elections were held the first government would quickly dismiss all
thirty-eight of them. Christopher Lynch-Robinson was secretary to the RMA
at this time and he wrote in May to Lord Long to ask his advice about the
position of the RMs. Walter Long (created first Viscount Wraxall in 1921)
was a Conservative-unionist politician who in the course of a long career had
been Chief Secretary for Ireland in 1905, and was widely known to have been
a sympathetic supporter of the RIC and the resident magistracy. There was,
perhaps, some personal sympathy too for Lynch-Robinson from Lord Long,
who knew the RM as a son of the unionist civil servant Sir Henry Robinson.[3]
In response to advice from Long, some amendments were made to a memorial prepared by Lynch-Robinson for submission to the British government.[4]

In the memorial no fault was found in principle with the Treasury terms
for adding years, for pension purposes, to actual years served but it was
argued the RMs would not benefit fully from changes introduced in 1920.
The three classes of RMs had been abolished then and the starting salary had

been raised to £800 per annum, rising by annual increments of £20 to a maximum of £1,100 (later raised to £1,200). The Under-Secretary had confirmed by letter in May 1920 that the new scales were 'permanent and pensionable' but the Treasury, keen as ever on economy, had taken advantage of the continuance of a war bonus to limit its expenditure on the salaries of the RMs. A war bonus for all civil servants was introduced in early 1919 in recognition of the abnormal inflation of prices and because it was still in place in 1920 the resident magistrates' annual incomes closely approximated to the new rates. The Treasury would therefore only grant a salary scale from £500 to £800. Only 75 per cent of the war bonus had counted towards pension rights and, meanwhile, the bonus had been reduced as the first stage of phasing it out. Pensions would be fixed more or less on the rates of pay existing before 1920 (which had remained unchanged since 1874) and it was calculated that without another ten years' annual increments these pensions would be inadequate. A return submitted with the memorial showed that the ages of the RMs ranged from thirty-four to sixty, with eight of the total being over fifty-five. Few would have expected to retire before their mid sixties but they were now 'faced with the prospect of having to start their lives afresh in a new country, and to support their families and educate their children' on pensions insufficient for those purposes. It was pointed out that their dismissal, and the 'ruination of their prospects', arose from their loyal service to the British government in Ireland. The RMA had no wish to give the impression that the new regime in Ireland was 'vindictive or hostile' to its members but it was concerned to emphasise that the resident magistrates' connections with the RIC and the 'Imperial Government' in the past made them a part of 'the old gang' which had no future in public employment in the new Ireland.[5]

A stark reminder of the risks attached to the office came in June 1922 when James Woulfe Flanagan, RM for Newry in Northern Ireland, was shot and killed. In the south, Major Colley was one of the intended targets of three Irregulars who were killed by their own device in early August, while in the act laying a land mine outside the RMs residence near Tipperary town.[6] On the 23 August the resident magistrates were instructed by the new Dublin government to consider themselves on leave, pending the abolition of the office in a reform of the Irish judiciary. The 'RMs Notice to Quit' had been foreseen by them since the signing of the Treaty although it was reported in the *Freeman's Journal* to have 'come as a surprise to the gentlemen concerned'. The newspaper carried an article in which the resident magistracy was described as 'one of the most deservedly unpopular of the English institutions in Ireland'. Readers were reminded of the role of the Irish RMs in relation to the coercion acts and special crimes courts, and of the 'truculent

part' they had played 'in some of the bloodiest episodes . . . when public
assemblages were swooped down upon by the police and bludgeoned with
savage fury. No body of men in any country has been so obedient to the nod
and beck of an Executive.' The 'iniquitous tyranny' of coercion and the
'disgrace to civilised Government' of the courts of summary jurisdiction were
recalled in relation chiefly to the 1880s land war but it was acknowledged that
'in later years' the resident magistrates had been 'recruited from a better
class, and did not excite quite the same opprobrium as formerly.'[7]

   The question of pensions was raised again in August, when Murray
Hornibrook wrote to Lord Long in England to explain that 'a new difficulty'
had arisen. Hornibrook was a Cambridge graduate who had been private
secretary to the Attorney General for Ireland and afterwards to the Chief
Secretary, before joining the resident magistracy in 1905. He explained to
Long that he was writing as senior member of the RMA because recent
letters to the secretary, Lynch-Robinson, had gone unanswered. Hornibrook
assumed this was because of the 'uncertain' state of the postal service but he
now felt obliged to act as it was a matter of some urgency, and he hoped Lord
Long would take it up with the British government. Earlier efforts to raise
the salaries on which the pension would be calculated had come to nothing, as
the British authorities disclaimed responsibility for the RMs after April 1922
and advised them to approach the Irish government. The RMA, Hornibrook
wrote, accepted that the new regime would 'naturally get rid of us as quickly
as possible' and there had been 'no opportunity' to take up the issue of
salaries with the Irish government, which 'had told us quite frankly that it
was unthinkable that [it] could continue a service so connected with coercion
legislation and the only thing that surprised them was that the Imperial
Government had ever "handed us over" to them in the first place'. The RMs,
Hornibrook added, were not so surprised as they had long experience of the
'peculiarity of Departmental methods'. No criticisms of their treatment by
the Irish government were made but Long was reminded that in many cases
the 'very small' pension would be the sole income of a former resident magistrate. It was 'next to impossible' for men over fifty to find other employment and it would be 'hopeless' for the majority 'to remain in this country
with any hope of other work or happiness in retirement'. Many members of
the Association were said to 'have already left and others are hoping to leave,
to go to England, but if they do so there at once arises the question of Income
Tax.' If tax was deducted in Ireland and a pension was then taxed again in
Britain, 'the result would be that no retired Resident Magistrate will be able
to live in the British isles'. Hornibrook expressed the hope that Long would
take up the matter because a direct approach to government from the RMA
was thought likely to be met with only vague assurances of changes in due

course, probably along the lines of an existing arrangement between Australia and the United Kingdom, which entailed a modified double income tax on similar pensions. It was Hornibrook's personal opinion that what the British government 'ought to do' was guarantee tax-free pensions for the former resident magistrates. He was realistic about the chances of such a concession being made and was not over optimistic about any satisfactory solution being offered. With a touch of bitterness he suggested, 'It would possibly be a fitting epitaph to the service that, in consequence of its loyalty to the British Empire, its members were compelled by the British Government to remain forever exiles from their native lands.'[8]

By the end of September the Irish government was resolved to restore civil administration as soon as the military situation made this possible. It was announced that all commissions of the peace granted by the British administration or by the Dáil were to be withdrawn and that, as a temporary measure to meet an emergency situation, some twenty-six salaried magistrates would be appointed to sit each in his own area as a 'court of summary jurisdiction', with the same jurisdiction as ordinary JPs had in the past. The magistrates were to be drawn from both branches of the legal profession and would be expected to administer the law strictly but impartially, and no man would be appointed to a district where he had 'ties or associations'.[9] In the Dáil debate on these measures one speaker called for 'new blood, men with some national record as well as legal training'[10] and most of those whose appointments were announced in late October had some claim to have been 'Helpers in the Struggle for Freedom', as they were described in the *Freeman's Journal*.[11] James Crotty was one of those nominated by the Minister of Home Affairs to take office as a 'District Justice'. He had been educated at St Kieran's College, Co. Kilkenny, before reading law at the National University and qualifying as a solicitor in January 1918, since when he had practised in Wexford and New Ross. He had some 'knowledge of Irish' and had served a term of imprisonment as a result of his activities in the Sinn Féin courts. The post of District Magistrate was a temporay, non-pensionable appointment at a salary of £1,000 per annum plus a commuted allowance of £200 for travelling expenses. The new magistrates' held office at the 'pleasure' of the Minister.[12] The irony of the first elected government of Ireland replicating the old resident magistracy and doing away with local magistrates was not lost on Christopher Lynch-Robinson, who observed in his memoirs that he and others had individually and through the RMA frequently urged that the county judiciary should be abolished and replaced by resident magistrates' adjudicating alone. Lynch-Robinson was not uncritical of the system under the British but he also thought it 'typical of English government' that the state should pay resident magistrates yet 'withold from them the powers which would make them really effective'. He claimed that every chief secretary interviewed about this by the RMA agreed that impartial administration of justice would be more likely without unpaid JPs on the bench, but that 'nothing would convince any of them that such a change would not provoke an immediate and bloody revolution'.[13] Circumstances were, of course, significantly different in the Irish Free State of 1922, under an elected Irish government, and the district magistrates all had legal training and experience. Nonetheless, to some cynics it seemed that it was a coup rather than a revolution that had taken place. New institutions were often little more than modifications of the old British ones, rather than radically different bodies perhaps better suited to circumstances in an independent Ireland, and place and pay in the service of the state seemed still to depend on influence with those in power rather than upon merit alone.

The new Ireland had the support of southern unionists and the old ascendancy in general, although there were some who raged against the British 'betrayal' of them and of the Union. Christopher Lynch-Robinson regretted that Home Rule had not been established long before the 1914-18 war and he 'recognised the justice of what had happened' in Ireland but this, he noted wryly, 'only made things worse by depriving me of the satisfaction of feeling a martyr'.[14] He had qualified as a barrister in expectation of the resident magistracy becoming a professional body of lawyers but by early 1920 he was thinking of what his future might be if he survived the conflict. He began to look around for another job before the truce of July 1921 and seems to have considered himself a free agent from about the time of the Treaty. He saw 'no use in staying on in Collon', Co. Louth, and he went with his wife and young son to live with his parents at Foxrock in Dublin. By the time Murray Hornibrook was trying to contact him in August 1922 it seems likely that Lynch-Robinson had left the country. He had heard that Lord Dunraven was looking for a private secretary and though he did not know Dunraven personally he knew many people who did; 'taking a great gamble', he went over to London and managed not only to see Dunraven but to fix a date on which to start working for him. Before he left Ireland he had one last memorable experience at Foxrock in the comfortable home of his parents. As the family sat in the hall after dinner one evening they heard a scuffle near the side door into the servants' quarters and then two men burst in, firing revolvers. The men of the family were armed, as was not uncommon, and fired back at the intruders who dived out through the windows onto the lawn. The house was under seige for some time, with shots exchanged between the parties. Lynch-Robinson's Mother, 'with the courage of a lion', boarded the hall windows with leaves from the dining table. The telephone wires were discovered to have been cut but, in any case, there was no authority that could be called upon for help with any degree of confidence. It was agreed during a lull in the attack that an attempt should be made to get across the fields to Horace Plunkett's house and from there try to contact Walter Edgeworth-Johnstone, former RM and ex chief commissioner of the DMP. Lynch-Robinson was confident that Edgeworth Johnstone would somehow raise help and 'take the attackers in the rear' but the plan was abandoned after the RM was fired on when he tried to make a break from the house. After some parley with the 'soldiers of the Irish Republic', the gunmen were let in. The women of the house were put in another room and an armed man guarded Sir Henry Robinson and his son, while others searched the premises. The guard, according to Lynch-Robinson, observed that 'These is terrible times we're livin' in', and tucked his revolver under his arm while accepting a cigarette from his captives. Eventually the men left with their pockets 'full of loot', after telling the family that they would be 'court martialled' next day for resisting Republican soldiers in the execution of their duty.[15] It was later discovered that the intruders were not the IRA but 'local hooligans' taking advantage of the lawless times by carrying out robberies in the name of the IRA.

Next morning Michael Collins arrived to see Sir Henry Robinson, having travelled by way of the Stillorgan road where there was an attempt to ambush his armoured car. Collins advised them that they 'had much better clear out, and come back later on when things had settled down a bit'. Most of the night after the raid had been spent packing and although Sir Henry and his wife would not consider leaving before storing their furniture, the former RM decided that he and his wife, with their young son and his nurse, would cross to Holyhead that evening and wait there for his parents to join them. Leaving for England on the boat from Kingstown (Dun Laoghaire) was a part of Lynch-Robinson's way of life. From childhood onward it had been the starting point of setting off for the school term, or when going to Sandhurst or to rejoin his regiment, and when going to visit his relatives or to take holidays in England or on the continent. On this occasion, Lynch-Robinson left with no regrets or anticipation of homecoming but only a feeling of 'enormous relief' as the boat pulled away. 'I was sick to death of the country and of everything in it, of clever talk, of intellectual posturings, and of philosophical radicalism', he later recalled, 'I longed for a little security and peace, and to get out of the atmosphere of killing.'[16]

The attitudes of his colleagues as a whole to the new Ireland cannot be ascertained but C.P. Crane, like Lynch-Robinson, wished the country well although he too abhorred the violence of the times. Crane was strongly committed to the Union and his devotion to the Empire made it inevitable that he should fear the wider implications of the British conceding to nationalist aspirations in Ireland. After retiring in 1920, Crane and his wife moved to London where they lived at Sloane Gardens. Events in Ireland were still of interest to the former resident magistrate, who in March 1922 wrote to *The Times* from the Wellington Club, on the plight of 'the ruined, homeless loyalists' of southern Ireland. He urged that compensation claims for damage to their property should be 'regarded as a debt of honour – to be discharged in full without any further haggling'.[17] In retirement Crane took up charitable voluntary work and local politics. He became a trustee and sometime chairman of Gardiners' Trust for the Blind, and represented central Wandsworth on the London County Council from 1922 to 1925 before serving on Chelsea Borough Council, from 1925 to 1930.[18] He also wrote his memoirs (published in 1938), in which he concluded, 'when I think of the past, "before the war", I still remember the "grace" of life in those days, and from my heart I wish the best of good wishes for the future of Ireland'.[19]

Crane had spent the best part of his life, some forty years, in Ireland and he undoubtedly loved the country in his own way but, as an Englishman, he did not have the same sort of emotional ties with it as those of the RMs with an Anglo-Irish background, nor did he feel the dual loyalty that was shared by so many Irish servants of the Crown. Even the Catholic Home Rule sympathisers, appointed to the resident magistracy from mainly middle class origins, had been loyalists – 'Castle Catholics' who felt as Katherine Tynan did that affection for both countries and their peoples was not only acceptable but the fundamental core of the relationship between Ireland and England. Their dual loyalty was tested to its limits during the troubles but for most of the resident magistrates Ireland was their home, the place where their future lay whatever political changes came about. It was generally felt by many people with similar backgrounds and outlooks that getting the British out, restoring law and order, and giving the new regime a fair chance was the best option available by the time of the Treaty. The resident magistrates, in all likliehood, adapted in the same way as many of their class by giving their support to the democratically elected government of their country but playing little part in public life, while retaining their links with England and an affection for some of its institutions. The destinations of the resident magistrates who retired during the period 1919-21 and of those of the thirty eight RMs transferred to the Irish Free State in 1922 cannot be traced in every case but it is evident that some of them stayed in Ireland.

Among the resident magistrates who retired in 1919 was P.J. Kelly, the Catholic barrister and former Belfast journalist who had taken up residence at the Junior Club in Limerick on his appointment as RM for the district. He was still a permanent resident at the Club some three years later and probably found the new Ireland south of the border more attractive than Northern

Ireland, as the loyal north developed into a Protestant stronghold where the rights of the Catholic minority looked increasingly insecure. Captain the Hon. Harry de Vere Pery had settled in Blackrock, Co. Dublin, after his retirement but he continued to administer the law as a JP until this office was abolished in 1922. George Butler, who retired in 1921 and was knighted in that year, was living at Rathgar in Dublin during 1922-3. At the same time, Julie Newton, Lady Brady (the second wife and widow of Sir Andrew Newton Brady, who died in 1918) was living at Greystones, Co. Wicklow. Personal and practical reasons would, of course, have influenced the choices made by individual resident magistrates but the early retirement of Patrick D. Sullivan in 1921 followed on from his encounter, described above, with an Auxiliary and his public complaint that he had been assaulted by the man. Sullivan (a Catholic, whose Father had been President of Queen's College, Cork) was educated in England at Prior Park, Bath, before studying at Queen's in Cork and then at Balliol College, Oxford. He was called to the English Bar in 1888 and joined the resident magistracy in 1895. There were obvious attractions to early retirement at the height of the troubles but it is possible that Sullivan's unease about British policy in Ireland was one factor that contributed to his decision to give up the job at the age of fifty-seven. In 1922-3 his address was Castle Bamford, Co. Kilkenny. Patrick Sarsfield Brady, after his harrowing experiences in west Cork, was then living at Kilkee, Co. Clare.[21]

Of the thirty-eight resident magistrates still in office when the post was abolished two, Edmund Dease and William O'Reilly, are the subjects of biographical studies in Part III, below. Three of the others went to Northern Ireland. Robert Webster Glass was a fifty-two year old solicitor, who had served in the Great War and been appointed RM for Ballina, Co. Mayo, in April 1919. Major Thomas Wallace Dickie was a younger man, aged thirty-four, who had been appointed RM for Carrick-on Shannon, Co. Leitrim, in June 1919. The third was Henry Toppin, a former RIC officer aged fifty-three in 1922.[21] Toppin had been stationed at Ballina, Co. Mayo, when war broke out but early in 1915 he was seconded for military service with the temporary rank of Lieutenant Colonel. He applied for demobilization in 1919 but this was refused [22] and he was still serving with the army, in Co. Cork, in the autumn of 1921. It was reported to the Under-Secretary in October of that year that Toppin had applied to be demobilized 'as soon as possible'.[23] General Sir C.N. Nevil Macready (GOC British forces in Ireland) forwarded the application to the Castle and placed on record his appreciation of Toppin's service. 'His experience of the country and knowledge of legal regulations have been of the utmost value', Macready wrote, 'and he has never spared himself in any way'. The GOC regretted that Toppin felt unable to continue in his work but hoped that 'when released of the strain that has been put upon him, he may long be spared to give his talents and experience to the service of the country'.[24] For resident magistrates' with backgrounds similar to that of Henry Toppin moving to Northern Ireland was a sensible option. As a Protestant former police officer and retired RM his future in the Irish Free State would have been at best uncertain and perhaps dangerous, especially as he had not merely served in the British army during the 1914-18 war but also with British forces in Ireland during 1919-21. For younger men, such as Major Dickie, there was time enough to build a new career but whether or not to stay in either part of Ireland, or to go to England or even overseas, must have presented hard choices to some of the last of the Irish RMs.

For Captain W.A. Woods it was a matter of going home, for he was an Englishman born in Yorkshire. He had joined the RIC in 1905 and had family connections in Ireland, in counties Meath, Westmeath, Antrim and in Belfast. He served in the Royal Irish Fusiliers from October 1914 until taking up the post of private secretary to the Inspector General of the RIC in March 1918. He was appointed RM for Tuam district, Co. Galway, in July 1920. One of the Irish-born RMs who chose to leave the country was William Stewart Balfour Leatham, who was born in Co. Down but had relatives in the south, in Co. Tipperary, as well as in Tyrone and Londonderry. He was a Protestant who joined the RIC as an officer cadet in 1898, and was appointed instructor of musketry at the Phoenix Park depot in 1912. In February 1916 he went into the Royal Irish Rifles with the rank of Major and served in the army until February 1919. He was appointed to the resident magistracy in March 1920. Both Woods and Leatham made some claim on the British government for disturbance allowance and a subsistence allowance following their dismissal by the Irish government. Their cases were taken up by Lord Long but to no avail, as all resident magistrates had to be content with drawing their salaries until August 1922 and thereafter relying on pensions paid by the Irish Free State. In January 1923 Long was informed by letter from the Irish Branch of the Colonial Office that Major Leatham's claim for damage to and loss of effects on removal from Ireland had been referred to the RIC tribunal for consideration. Lord Long believed that 'the service that has been rendered by the RMs of Ireland, ever since their creation, constitutes an unanswerable claim upon any British government'[25] but such recognition was of little comfort or practical help to men whose lives were so completely disrupted by the changes in Ireland.

Christopher Lynch-Robinson thought it 'pretty hard on us all', to have to 'clear out to a strange land and a new life', leaving both home and country. He felt especially sad for his Father, who had 'loved Ireland devotedly and worked for her exclusively and unselfishly all his life' in his capacity as a civil servant.[26] Sir Henry's personal feelings were summarised in the dedication of the second volume of his memoirs, 'To the lovers of Ireland who have been driven from their country by stress of circumstances, but whose affection for Ireland nothing can wholly obliterate, and who still find a pleasure in recalling the early years spent in their old homes among the Irish people.'[27] His son also retained a deep affection for Ireland. He claimed that he felt more at home when visiting France than while living in England, where he looked upon his Second World War service in the Home Guard as the least he could do as a 'guest' in the country, but there was perhaps some special pleading in this assertion. England was hardly a 'strange land' to Lynch-Robinson and it seems that the former RM rather relished the role of the outsider. His memoirs suggest that he shared the Anglo-Irish tendency to become exaggeratedly 'Irish of the Irish' in the face of English people who all too often knew very little of his country of birth, and even less about the troubled history of relations between the two islands. Like many another of these exiles of Erin, he lived the life of middle England and perhaps was wistful for the status and certainties of his earlier years in Ireland. The sons and daughters of the old ascendancy were to be found in England in the later 1920s and 1930s earning their bread in occupations hardly known of by their parents' generation. Lynch-Robinson himself eventually worked in a managerial capacity for the Cross and Blackwell food processing company, a far cry from his experiences as an Irish RM.

He went back to Ireland in 1946 and he wrote of his feelings and impressions in a chapter of his memoirs entitled 'The Return of the Exile'. His grandparents' home, Athavallie, in Co. Mayo, had become a convent day-school for girls. The Mother Superior showed him around and he found the place almost unrecognisable and looking 'awful'. He was particularly shocked to find the drawing room converted into a chapel, with a stained-glass window let into one end wall of the room. Despite his inner certainty that he was no bigot, Lynch-Robinson felt as if this represented some 'terrible outrage' perpetrated on the memory of his grandfather, the 'rugged old heretic' whose grave lay only a few hundred yards away. The time he spent in Mayo was bitter-sweet, visiting places much changed yet full of childhood memories. In Donegal he was delighted to renew acquaintance with Atty Dunlevy, who had been a Sinn Féin clerk at one of his petty sessions courts. Dunlevy was still holding the equivalent office, some quarter of a century later. A group of people gathered outside Dunlevy's house while the former resident magistrate recalled old times within, and among the throng was Jimmy Brogan. This was the Donegal lad that the RM had taken with him to Co. Louth, where he taught him new skills before sending him home to his parents for fear that his life was endangered by working for a resident magistrate. Lynch-Robinson did not immediately recognise Jimmy, to his embarrassment, but afterwards consoled himself that 'thirty years can change a man a lot'.[28]

Ireland itself had changed in many ways since a largely Catholic democracy had replaced British rule in 1922. Safeguards for southern unionists in the new state fell somewhat short of what had been promised and the upper house of the Irish Free State government, the Senate, was not as powerful a body as unionists had hoped for. They were most strongly represented in the Senate. The civil war, and especially the burning of many big houses belonging to senators and to 'imperialists' who had served the British government in Ireland, drove many Anglo-Irish families out of the country although there were also numerous stalwarts who refused to leave what they regarded as their homeland, even if the ancestral pile was reduced to a heap of smouldering rubble. It became rather a lonely life in Ireland for those Anglo-Irish who clung on to their much-reduced estates while friends and neighbours fled to the comforts of Bath or the mild contentment of a bungalow in Bournemouth. Rents from land had long gone as a means of subsistence and few of the class had marketable skills or the entrepenurial drive to make money in the new Ireland.[29] Mark Bence-Jones suggests that the most usual reason for leaving Ireland was 'because the money ran out . . . the real reason in the case of many who left ostensibly because of the unrest or the loneliness or their dislike of the new Ireland.'[30]

During the later 1920s and the 1930s 'house parties, hospitality and hunting' continued in the upper social circles.[31] Servants were still plentiful and standards were maintained in many a big house but living in genteel poverty was an increasingly common experience for the old ascendancy. Yet some of the sons of the last of the Irish RMs had much the same schooling and careers as the previous generation had and, in many cases, they continued to serve British interests. This was so in the family of the resident magistrate John Edward St George. He lived on at Kilrush House in Freshford, Co. Kilkenny, until his death in 1940, when his elder son, Howard E.G. St George, inherited the property. Lieutenant Colonel Howard St George (born in 1900) was educated in England at Cheltenham College and the Royal Military Academy, Woolwich. He served in the Royal Engineers, 1919–45. His younger brother, Arthur John (born in 1914) was an officer in the Durham Light Infantry. He died in action during the Second World War, killed in the Normandy landings of June 1944.[32]

When the RMs were swept away in the formation of the Irish Free State their passing from the scene was not entirely unmourned. Katherine Tynan paid tribute to them in an article in *The Times*, whose readership was predominantly a Conservative-unionist one in sympathy with loyalist officials out of place in the new Ireland. The RMs were, Tynan wrote, 'very typical, very racy of Ireland . . . I have never known a resident magistrate who was not kindly Irish of the Irish'. They had, she added, 'a heart for the people, and they stood for justice where there else would have been miscarriage of justice'. She concluded her tribute to the Irish RMs with the plea, 'let them not go unwept, unhonoured, and unsung.'[33]

Within a decade or so of the demise of the resident magistracy, the *Cork Examiner* published a piece by Louis McQuilland on the Somerville and Ross stories, in which *Some Experiences of an Irish RM* was described as the jolly tales of Major Yeates and his neighbours, in 'the bygone period of a happy-go-lucky Ireland'. The years of 'the garrison' may have been years of 'political slavery', McQuilland observed, 'but they continued to embrace a lot of fun in a country leisured and, to some extent, carefree'.[34] Fiction was already proving more influential than fact, and if the resident magistrates are remembered today they owe it largely to Somerville and Ross. Their immortal Major Yeates and the enduring popularity of their stories have shaped public perception of the Irish RMs for many generations but, as we have seen, the image of the resident magistrate portrayed in the comic universe of Skebawn has obscured some of the complexities of historical reality.

8

John Charles Milling, 1873-1919

John Milling was born on 27 March 1873 at Glasson, near Athlone, Co. Westmeath, the second son in a family with a tradition of service in the constabulary. His grandfather, Oliver Milling, was appointed parish constable in Ardee, Co. Louth, in 1828 and ended his career as RIC County Inspector for Tyrone from 1873 to 1877. During the abortive Fenian rising of 1867, while stationed at Kilfinane in Co. Limerick, he led the force of constabulary that lifted the seige of Kilmallock police barracks.[1] John Milling's father, also named Oliver Milling, served in the police force in various parts of the country until, in 1887, he was appointed County Inspector for west Mayo. He and his wife, Lissie, with their four sons and three daughters, took up residence in Co. Mayo at Barley Hill, a large gentry house at Attyreece about three miles from Westport, on the Newport road.

The Millings were Plymouth Brethren. This Protestant sect was founded in Ireland during the 1830s by the curate, John Darby, and attracted many of the gentry and the aristocracy, including Sir Richard O'Donnell of Newport House in Co. Mayo.[2] The presence of other Brethren in the area may have pursuaded the Millings to take Barley Hill (instead of living at Castlebar as the county inspector was officially expected to do) because members of the sect relied upon each other in the practice of religion and were generally very exclusive in their friendships and personal relations.[3] Around the turn of the century the Millings employed a young Plymouth Brethren widow (who had been born in New Zealand) as governess to their daughters, although their cook and a male domestic servant were both Catholic.[4]

John Milling attended the Ranelagh Endowed School at Athlone, which was founded by the earl of Ranelagh in 1708 for the education of Protestant children but developed over the years into an establishment offering a broad education to fee-paying day and boarding pupils, and a few scholarship boys. In the late 1880s there were 117 pupils on the roll, mainly Episcopalians but with some nonconformist Wesleyans and Presbyterians among the boarders and seven local Catholic day-boys.[5] Little is known of Milling's school days but he was awarded a good conduct medal in 1890, when he was seventeen or so and probably about to leave Ranelagh. Holidays had been spent in Mayo with the family and it is likely that over the next three or four years he was living at Westport, enjoying the social and sporting life appropriate to a young gentleman of his class. As he approached his majority he may also have put in some effort at one of the numerous 'crammers' in Dublin, where many private tutors specialised in preparing the sons of the middle classes for the entrance examinations for the civil service and the RIC.[6] Milling was accepted into the RIC in August 1894 at the minimum age of twenty-one and after undergoing basic training at the Phoenix Park depot[7] he was stationed at Derrygoanelly, Co. Fermanagh. He later served at Ballyshannon, Co. Donegal, and in Ballymena, Co. Antrim. He was presented with an illuminated address on leaving Derrygoanelly, where he was said to have been a popular young officer, and in Ballyshannon the resident magistrate, C.P. Crane, knew Milling as a diligent and efficient district inspector.[8]

In 1897 John Milling married Elizabeth 'Lilla' Malcolmson, the third daughter of the late Robert Malcolmson of Bennekerry Lodge, Carlow, who was a solicitor and an author of some note who had written on the lives of the MPs of Co. Carlow. The engagement was announced in January but the forthcoming marriage was overshadowed by family tragedy when in February John's twenty-year old sister, Emma, died from what may have been a brain tumour. John and Lilla were married the following month by special licence and according to the rites of the Plymouth Brethren, at 54 Wellington Place, Dublin, where Lilla and her sisters were living with their widowed Mother. In May 1898 one of Lilla's sisters married another RIC officer, Charles Arthur Walsh,[9] a Tipperary-born Catholic who had worked for some eighteen months in the Ecclesiastical Commissions Office before joining the police. John and Lilla's first son, Robert, was born in 1899 but the Millings were again touched by tragedy in 1903 when John's brother, Henry Desmond, was killed in a railway accident.[10] There were further family changes in the next year, when Oliver Milling retired from the RIC and moved from Co. Mayo to Armagh. He was in failing health and soon decided to settle in the English seaside resort of Margate in Kent, where he died in 1906,[11] the year in which John and Lilla's daughter, Marjorie, was born. Meanwhile John Milling progressed in his career with several grants of good service pay and commendations for his zeal and ability in detective work. He was a keen sportsman and played both rugby and soccer for the RIC first teams. His enthusiasm for his job and an interest in the law led him to write a 'handbook' which was published in 1908 as *The RIC ABC or Police Duties in Relation to Acts of Parliament in Ireland*.[12] In that year he was posted to Belfast, where the family first lived at Newton Terrace, 147 Clifton Park Avenue. There a third child, another son, was born but he died in infancy.

Milling was stationed at Brown Square barracks and while there he gained three favourable records for his conduct during the riots of July 1909. The *Belfast Telegraph* carried a lively account of 'rowdyism' on 12 July, in McDonnell Street and other thoroughfares between Grovesnor Road and Albert Street, where there had been many previous encounters between the people and the police. Reinforcements were sent into the district but there was no trouble until nightfall, when 'occasional stones began to come over the roofs of Grosvenor Road from the disaffected area. Shortly before ten o'clock, volleys of stones were fired down McDonnell Street, and the police had eventually to clear the street with a baton charge.' Rioting continued, with further baton charges, until a crowd of stone-throwers was 'neatly caught by the police. By a series of whistle signals, simultaneous charges were made up McDonnell Street and Albert Street, and the mob flying before District Inspector Milling's detachment ran into the arms of the force which Detective Inspector Clayton had brought up from the Cullingtree barracks.' Several policemen were injured in this encounter, including DI Milling who was hit by three or four flying stones and suffered what was described in press reports as a serious leg wound.[13]

In August of 1910 Milling was transferred to the Glenravel Street barracks and he was again highly commended in 1912, in the aftermath of another disturbed summer in Belfast. Tension and conflict over the Home Rule Bill were such that for several months troops stationed at Mullingar were on standby to go up to Belfast at short notice.[14] During June and July some 2,000 to 2,500 men were driven out of the shipyards by the violence and intimidation of Protestant workers associated with Unionist Clubs. Most of those expelled were Catholics and nationalists but the total included some 500 Protestant trade unionists and others regarded as sympathetic to Home Rule. The victims of an attack made in early June made a complaint to police at Henry Street barracks, where they named some of those they held responsible. Weeks went by without any police investigation of the allegations. The case was only taken up by the RIC when it was reported to Glenravel Street barracks where it was dealt with by John Milling, who made it clear to higher authorities that his colleagues at Henry Street were not helpful to him in bringing the cases to court, and that he was appalled by their conduct.[15] All those who had been injured were Catholics while all those accused of causing their injuries were Protestants. When the men in the shipyard cases first appeared in court the RM, Andrew Newton Brady, was careful to use neutral language in asking if the defendants were 'all of the one way, or is it give-and-take?', to which a police officer replied that all the prosecutions were 'against men of one party'. At this point the defending solicitor intervened to say that it was 'quite evident all the summonses are against persons who are Protestants', to which the RM responded: 'I did not ask you that, and I did not want to know.' Newton Brady, a Protestant-unionist himself, was perhaps not wholly unsympathetic to those in the dock. He certainly played down the seriousness of the charges, commenting that 'the height of the damage' to one of the beaten Catholic workers seemed to be a 'discoloured eye' which, 'when he came to think of it, that might have arisen among a lot of boys, and it seemed a very ordinary thing'.[16]

These cases were adjourned but in late October and early November they came to court with others arising from charges brought after a riot at Celtic Park football ground, which involved both Catholic and Protestant defendants. The Crown wanted all these cases sent for trial at the Derry Assizes, fearing that a fair trial in Belfast was unlikely in the circumstances, but the Belfast Recorder insisted on the shipyard cases being tried in the city.[17] At the County Courthouse in Crumlin Road a jury found a number of Protestants not guilty of the alleged attacks on William Parkes and six or seven other Catholics who had been expelled from the shipyards.[18] When the Recorder's Court reassembled next morning the Crown entered a *nolle prosequi* in respect of the seventeen remaining cases, which led to a 'tiff' between the judge and the Crown Solicitor.[19] Some of the accused were rearrested (the legality of which action was later questioned) to appear at the police court next day before Garrett Nagle, the Catholic RM. Nagle and a borough magistrate, Mr Davison, heard a number of routine cases before seven magistrates, all of them stated to be unionists and one said to be the secretary of a Grand Orange Lodge, arrived unexpectedly and packed the bench. When the contentious cases came up, the Crown asked the RM (as the magistrate before whom the informations had been sworn) to return the defendants for trial at a higher court. Nagle declined to do so on the grounds that he had no power, under the Petty Sessions Act, to exclude the other magistrates. The proceedings then degenerated into farce. The Crown Solicitor withdrew from the court and, after some consultation with magistrates and solicitors, so too did Garret Nagle and Mr Davison JP. Then the unionist magistrates' elected a chairman and called the prisoners one by one, but the police would not produce them. Meanwhile Mr Davison took new depositions elsewhere and eventually an improvised court was held at the 'police office', where Mr Emerson JP sent the cases for trial, while irate Unionist JPs were kept out by DI Milling and a constable.

James Craig MP (later the first Prime Minister of Northern Ireland) complained that all this was done 'by the Government to once more blacken the fair name of Belfast, which hitherto on all sides had been admitted to be the one spot in Ireland where a fair trial could be had without fear or favour',[20] which was not a view that the bulk of the Catholic population of the city would have shared. As the editor of an English newspaper commented, the affair 'threw a curious and not pleasing light on the administration of justice in Orange Belfast'.[21] Mr Davison stated publicly that he had been subjected to a series of threats of personal violence and damage to his business because of his part in events. John Milling, who had acted as liason between the RM and the Crown Solicitor and was involved in all stages of the proceedings, was praised at a hearing in the King's Bench Division at the Four Courts in Dublin, where the ensuing legal wrangle between the Belfast Unionist magistrates and the Crown was eventually resolved. The Attorney General spoke in the Dublin court of 'the integrity of Detective Inspector Milling, who, in trying circumstances, discharged his duties loyally and well'.[22]

John Milling was an ideal candidate for the Inspector General to recommend for the resident magistracy and his RIC career ended in December 1914 when he was appointed RM for Westport, Co. Mayo. He had been generally well thought of in Belfast, where the Corporation marked his departure from the city with a presentation of a canteen of cutlery. He was actually appointed for Castlebar (which Henry Hinkson had just relinquished for Claremorris because he could not find a suitable house in Castlebar) but he was given permission to make Westport his headquarters as he too claimed that there were no suitable houses in the county town. He spent several months in a Castlebar hotel while house hunting but in April 1915, with Lilla and the children, he moved into a house at Rosmalley on the southern shore of Clew Bay, some two miles from Westport.

He was given a cordial welcome at his first petty sessions court in the town. Mr Staunton JP commented that 'the people of Westport knew his family for a long time and they were glad that he had been sent back to them as their resident magistrate', and Mr Berry, on behalf of the legal profession, observed that he had known the RM for many years before he left the district. Berry went on to speak of John Milling as 'not coming amongst them as a stranger', and wished him 'many long years to enjoy the well-merited post he occupied.' Similar sentiments were expressed by the clerk and, in reply, the RM spoke of his pleasure at being stationed in Mayo where he had been 'brought up a boy in Westport'. He declared himself 'very glad to be back', and added, 'I hope the friendliest relations will exist between all'.[23] Much of this was mere conventional politeness but there were people in Westport who remembered Milling as 'Master Jack', a popular and likeable boy and young man.[24]

The RM was soon into the routine of petty sessions, hearing charges of drunkeness, unlighted carts, and innumerable cases arising out of family disputes or quarrels between neighbours. At the Newport sessions in January 1915, Mary Masterton of Murreagh summoned Thomas and James Masterton and James Mulgrew, of the same place, for alleged malicious injury, involving damage to a galvanised shed or outhouse. The case was dismissed, which greatly pleased James Mulgrew who complained that it had only been brought 'to stain our characters'.[25] Some of the Mastertons of Murreagh were back in court next month, when Michael Masterton summoned Catherine Masterton for assault and there was a cross-case. This was adjourned but the next case up was one in which Catherine Masterton, senior, summoned Catherine Masterton, junior (her daughter-in-law, and the defendant in the first case), for using abusive language and throwing a bucket of water over her.[26] At Castlebar sessions there was recurring 'Tucker Street Trouble' between quarreling women and at the October sessions in Kiltimagh there were various cross-cases arising out of 'the disputed ownership of a cabbage garden', when Dan Connell, 'an emaciated old fellow, bent with age', and his daughter, Bridget Kelly, summoned Patrick Connell (son of Dan and brother of Bridget) and his wife, Mary Connell, for alleged assault.[27]

There were usually ordinary magistrates sitting with Milling but it was the RM who guided the bench and many cases arising from family or neighbourly disputes were dismissed, often with a paternal lecture from Milling about all parties needing to make an effort to live on friendly terms. Six men who appeared at Kiltimagh after an affray were told by the RM that they could talk among themselves for five minutes and that, if they agreed to be friends, he would dismiss the charges. The alternative was to be bound over to keep the peace, so there were handshakes all round, and John Milling sent them off saying 'It is a shame for neighbours to be fighting . . . in fine weather like this you should be looking after your crops.'[28] He also showed sensitivity in dealing with marital disputes, as in a case where a wife summoned her husband for assault. The RM adjourned the hearing for a fortnight, directing the couple to 'go to Fr O'Hara and have the case settled' but warning the husband that if he attacked his wife again he would certainly go to jail.[29] When a defendant was found guilty the sentence passed often recognised individual circumstances, as in the case of Michael Dolan. Dolan appeared at Westport sessions on a police charge of drunkenness and when it came to passing sentence the RM asked him was he 'able to pay 2s. 6d.?' [12½p]. Dolan, causing much laughter in court, replied 'Oh, make it less', whereupon Milling imposed a fine of 1s. [5p].[30]

Promotion to the resident magistracy did not greatly improve the material position of the family. John Milling was one of those RMs with no private income and it was not easy to maintain an appropriate life style on a salary of little more than £400 a year. A resident magistrate was expected to keep up appearances and it became increasingly difficult to do so during the war years as inflation pushed up the cost of living. The Millings had no resident do-

mestic staff and it seems likely that it was John Milling who Katherine Tynan
had in mind when she wrote of a resident magistrate, whose circumstances
she knew intimately, who was 'driven to taking in paying guests and could not
afford a meat lunch on his long journeys'.[32] Family expenses grew in 1915
when another son was born (named Henry Desmond, after John's dead brother)
but Robert Milling was independent from early 1918, when he joined the
army.

The Tynan-Hinksons and the Millings became good friends despite their
differences over religion and politics. Tynan remembered Jack Milling as 'the
kindest of the kind' and commented on how unexpected it was that he should
be one of the Plymouth Brethren; she and her husband, rather tactlessly,
'roared with laughter the day he solemnly said that he lived by the Bible',
because that 'excellent sentiment seemed so strange in his mouth'. He was
certainly not the dour puritan that one of the Brethren might have been for,
as Tynan describes him, he was 'an eminently sociable man . . . who might go
without himself' but was ' always willing and eager to entertain his friends'.
At Brookhill he would stride in through the open hall door and, if he found
the drawing room empty, would 'go through the house "bawling" for his
friends'. Katherine and Henry Hinkson found him irresistible to tease by
singing Jacobite songs after dinner or professing 'disloyal' sentiments. When
Jack Milling had 'worked himself up into a fine rage', they would 'give in
handsomely, remarking that the English were the superior race and rightly
the dominant one', whereupon Jack would 'roar like a bull at us for degener-
ate Irish'. Love of Ireland and loyalty to the Crown were inextricably linked
for the RM, but he always declared that he had never seen an Englishman
that he would compare to a good Irishman.[33]

In early 1915 the resident magistrates for the Ballina and Belmullet districts were seconded for military service. Hinkson's duties remained confined
largely to his Claremorris district (perhaps because his health was not good)
whereas John Milling was responsible for all the rest of the large county. He
was 'always on the road' and he told Katherine Tynan that 'They are working
me like a galley slave'. 'Ye Gods', he added, 'who would be an RM?'[34] He
sent many memos and unsolicited reports to Dublin Castle on matters that he
considered of importance. In June 1915 he reported that numbers of young
men 'chiefly of the farming class' had recently emigrated to America, apparently because they feared the introduction of compulsory conscription. Recruiting was 'bad' in Westport, where some of the people were 'disloyal' and
many had 'pro-German tendancies'. At the end of the year he reported to
Dublin Castle that 'Boy Scouts (Sinn Féin section)' and about sixty Irish
Volunteers had caused some disturbances during and after a recruiting meeting at the Town Hall. They had followed the Connaught Rangers' band

around the town, 'cheering for the Sinn Féin party and the Irish Volunteers' and chanting 'Will we fight for the Saxon? No! Up with the Kaiser.' The police could identify twenty or so of the young demonstrators and the RIC had made a full report to the competent military authority but Milling evidently had little confidence that the incident would be regarded as serious or that the full rigour of the law would be applied. Such anti-recruiting demonstrations were having 'a most prejudicial effect', he claimed, and he urged that if there were no proceedings under DORA then those indentified should be brought before him and bound over.[35] No action was taken against the demonstrators.

The Volunteer movement had lost support in Mayo, as elsewhere, after war broke out and Redmond urged his followers to enlist. Membership declined by about 2,000 over the twelve months of 1915, to some 4,500 in December, of whom 350 were reported by the intelligence service to be 'Sinn Féiners' or Irish Volunteers. Sinn Féin was not numerically strong in the county, where it was outnumbered by both the GAA and UIL, but it had four branches with an estimated total membership of 121. The 1916 Rising made little immediate impact in Mayo, where there was 'general satisfaction' at its quick suppression but then a wave of sympathy generated by the executions. By late 1916 Sinn Féin had 'a strong following at Westport', where the movement was said to be 'carefully nursed' by Joseph MacBride (brother of John MacBride, one of the executed leaders of the Rising). At the end of 1917, the authorities knew of forty-three Sinn Féin clubs in Co. Mayo, with an estimated membership of over 3,000, while the Irish Volunteers remained a small but significant group of 353, much the same as two years previously. Westport was now reported to be 'the stronghold of Sinn Féinism' and the only exception among the generally loyal county press was the *Mayo News*, published in Westport.[36]

The *Mayo News* was of some importance in the local nationalist movement. It was founded in the early 1890s by the Westport brothers, William and P.J. Doris, who owned a printing works in James Street. William Doris, the elder of the two, was one of the organisers of the 1879 meeting in Westport at which the Land League of Mayo was set up, and later he acted as legal secretary to the National Land League. He was a founding member and first secretary of the UIL, established in Westport by William O'Brien in January 1898. After the Local Government Act of 1898 introduced elected councils, William Doris was variously vice-chairman and chairman of Mayo County Council until 1910, when he was elected to Westminster as MP for the Mayo West constituency. Thereafter he spent most of his time in London, leaving the running of the *Mayo News* to his brother. He retained his parliamentary seat at the 1915 election. The *Mayo News* continued to support Home Rule

and cultural nationalism but it was not sympathetic to Sinn Féin, which the
editor sharply criticised for a 'confidence trick' attempted on St Patrick's Day
1916. For several years past the Gaelic League had organised a procession
through the town on 17 March, which other nationalist groups were invited
to join although there were no political speeches made at any stage of the
event. The 1916 procession marked Irish Language Week, as well as the
Saint's day, and it was expected that members of the Gaelic League would
address the crowds on the language issue but when the processionists reached
the Octagon they found a brake drawn up and occupied by Joseph MacBride,
The O'Rahilly, Darrell Figgis and 'Other well-known Sinn Féiners'. Seeing
who was to address them, three-quarters of those in the parade 'wheeled off
and marched away, followed by the majority of the people' who had gathered
at the Octagon. 'They saw [the event] was to be used as a Sinn Féin meeting',
the *Mayo News* reported, 'and they wisely resolved to have no part in it. The
whole trick was a transparent fraud and was treated as such.'[37] The Easter
Rising and its aftermath radically altered the attititudes of P.J. Doris and soon
the *Mayo News* was a Sinn Féin paper. The paper supported the Sinn Féin
candidate, Joseph MacBride, at the 1918 election when William Doris lost his
seat. This led to the Doris brothers' becoming permanently estranged by
their different political views.[38]

Against this background, the RM carried out his routine and exceptional
duties. Political protest was already being expressed in violence by the autumn of 1915, when there was an attempt to blow up Lord Sligo's motor
yacht cruiser as it lay at anchor near the steamer sheds at Westport quay.[39]
Following the Easter Risng of 1916, the RM was busy with the RIC identifying those involved as leaders in nationalist movements. Early in May, there
were dawn raids by armed RIC men on houses in Westport and ten young
Irish Volunteers were arrested. The show of force seems to have been no
more than that, for the police did not take Joseph Gill of the Quay when he
simply refused to give himself up to three policemen carrying guns. Gill was
'persuaded by friends' to surrender at the police barracks later and, with the
others, he was taken in handcuffs to the station *en route* to Castlebar jail. The
Volunteers had been among 200 or so who had been on a route march and
exercise on Easter Sunday.[40]

News soon reached Westport of the execution on 5 May 1916 of John
MacBride. John Milling went to see Mrs MacBride at the family home as a
show of sympathy for her, and dismissed suggestions that this was a brave
thing to do, saying 'Didn't I know her since I was *that* high? And wouldn't
anyone feel sorry for the poor woman?'[41] This was a warmly human response
but a more thoughtful man than John Milling might well have decided against
the visit because of his official position. He was, after all, the RM and as such

was the physical embodiment of the state that had put to death a beloved son and, what is more, he was the man on whose recommendation to Dublin another son was about to be taken and incarcerated. Joseph MacBride was taken by the authorities shortly afterwards, when a troop of 150 cavalry blocked the main roads out of the town while the RIC made eighteen arrests including the editor of the *Mayo News*, P.J. Doris.[42] Some of those arrested were released at the end of May but others were interned in Wales or held in English prisons.[43] Joseph MacBride was let out of Reading jail in the general release of the Irish prisoners just before Christmas 1916.

Milling used to joke with Henry Hinkson that they should swop districts, as Westport was the stronghold of Sinn Féin nationalism and Hinkson was 'on their side', which was a slight exaggeration of Hinkson's constitutional nationalism although the *Mayo News* did once publish an open letter praising him as an impartial magistrate without 'political humours'. This took Milling to Brookhill, where he dashed in '"bawling": "How did you get around the *Mayo News*, Hinkson, and what did you give them for *that*"?' Hinkson was not merely more sympathetic to nationalism than Milling but almost certainly also more tactful either by instinct or as a result of his training as a barrister, which would have made him cautious in his speech and careful in his language. Milling, in contrast, was a blunt policeman who said what he thought and apparently cared little if people were offended by his opinions. He was often 'scolded' by Henry Hinkson for the 'careless and imprudent things he was in the habit of saying publicly'[44] and his forthright remarks in court gave the *Mayo News* plenty of copy that could be used to whip up hostility to Milling. He was a passionate advocate of the British cause in the Great War. In 1917 he applied for permission to join the army himself and was recommended for a commission but nothing came of this. He did his best for the recruiting drive by frequently telling young men brought before him that they should be in the army but the youth of the Westport was, it seems, more interested in the nationalist cause. The RM heard growing numbers of cases of unlawful assembly and illegal drilling under the Crimes Act, and many charges of sedition in proceedings under DORA.

In February 1917 a 'sensation' was created in Westport when Miss Kathleen McLoughlin was arrested and brought before a special court presided over by John Milling. The young woman was charged with having sung songs likely to cause disaffection, at a recent concert in Cushlough, where she had given performances of 'Who Dares to Speak of Easter Week' and 'Who is Ireland's Enemy'. Some 200 to 300 people had attended the concert where they heard the words of the songs which the RM believed to be 'very seditious'. He ordered the defendant to find £20 bail and two sureties of £10 each to keep the peace and be of good behaviour or, in default, to go to prison for two months. The fines were paid but Kathleen McLoughlin's father stated that 'Only for her health is not good I would advise her to go to jail.'[45] At Kiltimagh and other places similar cases were heard, arising from the shouting of such 'slogans' as 'Up with the Kaiser' and 'To hell with the King'. A sixteen-year old youth appeared in court at Kiltimagh after having been heard shouting, while drunk, 'Up the Sinn Féiners' and 'To hell with England'. A gang of younger boys had been within earshot and one of them was asked in court, by the defending solicitor, if he 'had felt in anyway disaffected towards His Majesty'. This caused some laughter but Milling commented, 'Perhaps he is already so'. The bench found the youth guilty and a small fine was imposed. One of the JPs remarked, rather obscurely, that he 'did not mind so much the shouting about Sinn Féiners, as that was politics, but it was certainly treasonable to say anything in favour of the enemies of England.'[46]

As the editor of the *Mayo News* pointed out, the application of DORA was 'a powerful weapon for the creation and stimulation of disaffection and dissatisfaction'. Its 'victims' were mainly young men and women who were 'absolutely indifferent to its terrors',[47] and who relished the chance to go to prison and earn the status of nationalist hero. Young men and women who were fined a nominal sum for making an unauthorised collection for the Gaelic League were denied this chance when the League organiser stepped in and payed the fines[48] but the Volunteer Edward or Ned Moane became a Westport celebrity when he served six weeks in Sligo jail in the late spring of 1917. He was imprisoned after refusing to pay a £1 fine, 'holding he had committed no crime' in singing 'The Soldier's Song' and 'God Save Ireland' at a concert, where he had also been heard to shout 'Up Sinn Féin'. On his release the *Mayo News* published his photograph and commented, 'It is a unique distinction to do six weeks in jail for singing a song, so that in this Mr Moane has made a record'.[49]

The situation deteriorated as 1918 approached and not even the RIC was immune to the spreading disaffection. A young constable in Claremorris, Timothy O'Leary, resigned in December 1917 giving as his reason that his sympathies were 'with Sinn Féin, with the men who fell in Easter week, and with those who are trying to free Ireland'.[50] In January 1918 there was an attempt to blow up 'George's monument' (which commemorated George Glendinning, a local banker and philanthropist who had been for many years land agent to Lord Sligo and 'wielded despotic sway' in the Westport district) at the Octagon in Westport.[51] In March 1918, Ned Moane was again arrested, on a charge of unlawful assembly and illegal drilling. When Moane was brought before the special court a group of Volunteers, led by Joseph Ring, paraded outside the courthouse in Castlebar Street until they were dispersed by a police baton charge. Moane refused to recognise the court and he was remanded to Sligo jail. The town remained 'in a state of excitement' until a late hour, with crowds out on the streets and the RIC on patrol.[52] Arising out of the day's events, more Volunteers were arrested and subsequently Joe Ring, William O'Malley, William Malone, Charles Garvin and Tom Kitterick were taken before Milling at a special court held in the RIC barracks. The first man charged answered with the standard reply, 'I am a soldier of the Irish Republic and do not recognise this court.' The clerk asked the RM if he should write all that down but Milling, according to the *Mayo News*, told him there was no need to record any of 'that nonsense'. Joe Ring was wearing his Volunteer cap and refused to remove it; Tom Kitterick lit a cigarette; all the prisoners, turning their backs on the RM, 'industriously devoted themselves to studying documents on the wall'. Milling ordered DI Shore to bring up a couple of policemen, to make the accused show more respect for the court, and a 'rather lively scene' ensued before the young men were forcibly turned around. Joe Ring then claimed that Milling had come to court with the verdict and sentence decided upon. 'You said already at the hotel below', he alleged, 'that you were going to "give Ring eighteen months".' The RM did not respond to this allegation but offered to admit the prisoners to bail. Ring told him not to 'insult' the prisoners, who were all remanded in custody with the exception of William Malone; it was discovered that he was not actually named in the deposition and, cheated of a hero's role, he was rather ignomini- ously 'sent home'.[53]

There were riots in Westport that night. Policemen and civilians were hurt in the clashes, and the RM sent a wire to Dublin Castle urging that a military curfew should be imposed if more trouble broke out. The next night was quieter but on the Saturday there were further disturbances and more baton charges by the RIC. John Milling went into Westport at eight o'clock on the Sunday evening, anticipating another night of disturbances. He called on the Catholic parish priest to accompany him around the town and use his influence with people on the streets, which effectively lowered the tension, and no disorder occurred. When the Westport prisoners appeared before the 'coercion court' at Castlebar during the following week, there were unprec- edented scenes in and around the court house. Large crowds sang patriotic songs and shouted the usual slogans, 'Up the Irish Republic' and 'Up De Valera'. The prisoners' refused to recognise the court and gave a rendition of 'The Soldier's Song', followed by a chorus of 'Whak fol the Diddle'. They were encouraged by a defendant in an earlier cattle-driving case, who called to them 'Well done, boys', and who was rebuked by John Milling for convers- ing with the accused. Milling did not sit alone but with a more senior RM, Joseph Kilbride from Galway. Nine months hard labour was imposed on each defendant with a further nine months in default of paying sureties for good behaviour. As none of the 'Soldiers of the Republic' were likely to pay, they were in effect sentenced to eighteen months for offences that Milling described as 'nothing but Hooliganism', which would 'serve no cause under the sun'. When the RMs left the court Kilbride was allowed to pass through the crowd unhindered but when John Milling appeared the throng surged forward, jeering and shouting at him. The police drew their batons and cleared a way for him but he was 'hooted' and verbally abused as he went.[54] It was later alleged that there were many strangers to the district among the crowd outside the courthouse and it was suggested that the demonstration was a carefully planned and orchestrated protest directed specifically at John Milling.

The sentences imposed at Castlebar were criticised in the *Mayo News* as 'excessive' and the RM was vilified in editorial comment and in some letters to the newspaper. The press censor was keeping an eye on the *Mayo News* and he decided that there was now 'a case calling for action under DORA'. In a memo for the attention of the Chief Secretary, the Attorney General and others, the censor wrote that 'the tone of the *Mayo News* has been bad for a long time'. He explained that the paper had a large circulation and that its articles and editorials were considered likely to cause disaffection, or perhaps even attacks on the police. On 29 March, HQ Irish Command issued a warrant to the county inspector in Mayo to seize the plant at the James Street printing works and search the premises. The warrant was executed on 1 April and some 'not very important' documents were found. The editor protested that he had always acted openly and asked if he could continue to fulfil his printing contracts with the Board of Guardians and other bodies. The military authorities did not approve 'of any such concessions'[55] but P.J. Doris was nonetheless allowed to meet his printing contracts and the *Mayo News*, although still 'closely watched', resumed publication within a month or so. The press censor had made no mention of the possibility of the RM being endangered by press attacks on him but from March 1918 John Milling was the recipient of annonymous treatening letters and warnings. His motor boat was burned in an arson attack on Lord Sligo's boat house, an attack which was believed to have been aimed at Milling. He continued to antagonise nationalists and it was the language issue that caused conflict in August, when the RM was involved in heated exchanges with Castlebar JPs. He initially refused to sign the licence certificate for the Castlebar Town Club because the parish priest, a trustee of the Town Hall, had signed the application in the Irish form of his name. Milling declared that as he was unacquainted with that language he could not be certain that the signature was that of the priest.[56] Incidents such as this contributed to the increasingly hostile atmosphere, which created such concern for the safety of the RM and his family that their house at Rosmalley was guarded from dusk to dawn by constables from the Quay barracks. Milling asked the Castle for a transfer to a station in the north of Ireland and, in October 1918, moved into Westport where he believed the family would be less vulnerable to attack. They took a villa near the town centre, on the Newport Road. DI Captain Scott had lodgings next door and police patrols from Westport barracks were instructed to pay particular attention to the resident magistrate's house. In January 1919 he learned that his friend and colleague, Henry Hinkson, had died at Claremorris. Hinkson's death left John Milling very isolated and when he wrote to Katherine Tynan in sympathy for her loss he told her, 'I feel so lonely and I cannot bear this country now.'[57]

He adjudicated in many special courts but when three Louisburg Volunteers where charged in early January 1919 it was Joseph Kilbride, the Galway RM, who actually presided over the court at Westport. Milling appears to have said very little and the sentences imposed were moderate terms of six weeks to two months. There is no evidence to suggest that the executive had any hand in this, but if Milling had been advised by the Castle to keep a low profile he would probably have resented the advice. His determination to uphold the law was made explicit in an exchange of correspondence arising out of disturbances at the Lowpark (Charlestown) petty sessions on 10 January. Four JPs withdrew when a case came up that was 'a local one and of a party nature', having decided (as local magistrates did so often in similar instances) that it would be 'wiser' to leave the RM to adjudicate alone in these circumstances. A young man named O'Donnell, described by Milling as 'evidently a Dillonite', had organised a dance in the Town Hall one night in December, with the permission of the parish priest. When the dance was in progress some forty to fifty young men, 'wearing bandoliers and Sinn Féin caps, and headed by a man carrying a Sinn Féin flag', entered the hall and 'took possession' of it, while O'Donnell pleaded that he was responsible for keeping order. He told the intruders they could stay if they would pay the 1s. (5p) entrance fee, whereupon a man named Walsh, 'evidently a ring leader of the crowd', struck him in the face. The RM found Walsh guilty of assault and imposed a fine with costs and sureties of £20 for good behaviour. When the judgement was delivered, Walsh said 'I'll do the gaol', and an outburst of cheering followed. The few policemen in court found it difficult to restore order and the hundred or so people carried on cheering for some time. They continued to do so outside after the court was eventually cleared. Milling then directed the RIC sergeant to swear an information as to what had happened, and he wrote to the Castle to report that twenty-two men had been identified. He proposed to issue warrants for them to be brought before him on charges of contempt of court, stating that 'If conduct of this kind is allowed to pass unchallenged the administration of summary jurisdiction in this country will become impossible and as far as I am personally concerned I shall uphold the dignity of the Court and suppress lawlessness of this kind by every means in my power.'[58]

The Solicitor General agreed with the RM but thought it 'would be better' to make the charge one of unlawful assembly. However, before warrants were issued, the Bishop of Achrony intervened. The Solicitor General was told that His Lordship urged that 'in the interests of the peace of the neighbourhood' no action should be taken over 'a mere passing outburst not intended in any way to display contempt of court, and he thinks proceedings would only embitter feelings of resentment and animosity to the authorities'. Unless the Solicitor General felt that his earlier advice should be acted on 'as a matter of principle', Milling would be told 'to let matters rest'. This instruction was duly forwarded to the RM, who was given no information about the intervention of the Bishop but was merely notified that the decision had been reached 'Having regard to the view of the local police' that this was 'in the interests of the peace of the locality'. This was an example of what Christopher Lynch-Robinson called 'the curse of the country . . . the usurping by the executive of the functions of the courts' not, as nationalists believed, by directing their findings or instructing them as to the sentences they imposed but by not allowing the resident magistrates to prosecute clear breaches of the law because of sensitivity to public opinion, or in response to pressure from such people as the Bishop. Milling was not pleased by the decision and wrote to this effect to the Under-Secretary's office, saying that he would like to know on what grounds the RIC based their view and asking if he could see the police report on the matter. He added that 'Personally I am of the opinion that magistrates should be supported when a case of this sort arises, but of course I submit to the ruling of the Executive.' The Under-Secretary ruled that no useful purpose would be served by sending the police reports to the RM, adding that 'The matter is closed and I think the correspondence had better close also.'[59]

The RM continued to adjudicate at special courts around the county, including several held in Castlebar in February and early March. By then the Castle was considering a transfer for him, to Ballymena, Co. Antrim, but the administrative division moved too slowly to save him from his fate. On the night of Saturday 29 March 1919, John Milling was shot and fatally wounded at his home in Westport. About eleven o'clock, he left the dining room and crossed the hall to the drawing room, where he was going to wind the clock and move it on to British Summer Time. The curtains were drawn back and the blind was up, the room illuminated only by the lamp he carried. Shots rang out, fired through the window, hitting the RM in the shoulder and the abdomen. He staggered back across the hall to the door of the dining room but then more shots were fired through that window, one of them missing Lilla by a hairsbreadth. James Sheridan, who lived next door, heard what he thought were gun shots and looked out his front door but, seeing no one about, went and knocked at the Millings' door. The RM opened it, bleeding profusely, and told Sheridan that he had been shot. Lilla had fainted briefly but soon revived and she and Sheridan helped the RM upstairs to his bed, where they tried to make him comfortable. DI Captain Scott, who lodged with the Sheridans, was soon on the scene and he checked the rooms for evidence. A doctor also hurried round, from his nearby club, and he was later joined by the family's regular doctor. The Castle was informed, and sent specialist medical help from Dublin overnight. A telegram brought the Galway county inspector, Lilla's brother-in-law, from Ballinasloe to the bedside of the wounded RM. John Milling was a robust man in good health and he lingered on in great pain until ten o'clock the following night. As he lay dying he commented, 'they've got me at last', and he asked particularly that his wife should be looked after. He told Dr Jordan that he had repeatedly requested a transfer, 'but they would not grant it and this is the result'.[60]

In the aftermath of the murder Westport was declared a military area. Police searched various premises, troops were called in, an aircraft flew low over the surrounding countryside, markets and fairs were suspended, and all movements in and out of the town were controlled. At the inquest the jury initially failed to agree on the wording of their verdict. The foreman told the Coroner that five jurors objected to the wording agreed by nine others, that John Milling had been 'murdered by bullets fired at him by some person or persons unknown'. The dissenters wanted to 'put pious verbiage into this', the foreman said, adding 'I protest against any lesser word than murder, and I would say foul murder'. He was sent back to tell the others that the Coroner would have a unanimous verdict, even if the jury was there a week. 'Foully murdered' was the term used in the final verdict, to which riders were added expressing sympathy for the family and condemning 'the murder of an upright, honest and just public servant'.[61] The RM was buried in the Protestant cemetery with his brother and sister,[62] his coffin borne to the grave by four RIC sergeants followed by the Wesport and Newport district inspectors and a body of constabulary. The chief mourners were his brother and sister, Richard and Hilda Milling, and his brother-in-law Charles Walsh. The Marchioness of Sligo and Lord Altamont attended, as did the Catholic priest, Father Canavan. Lilla was too distressed to go to the funeral, and shortly afterwards she and her children left Westport to settle in Armagh.

The crime was widely condemmned and many tributes were paid to John Milling. In the *Belfast Telegraph* he was remembered as 'an extremely popu-

lar' RIC officer, and described as 'A man of splendid physique, affable characteristics, and sporting instincts – no one was better known on Ulster golf
links than he.' He was 'a great favourite in the North of Ireland', and the
writer believed that he was 'also held in the highest esteem by the better class
of the population in the West.'[63] Katherine Tynan's appreciation of her friend
Jack Milling was warm in praise of his 'good will to everyone. . . . He was a
great, jolly, hospitable Irishman, with always an open hand and an open
house.'[64] In the House of Commons an MP for one of the northern Ireland
constituencies, T.W. Brown, spoke of 'a great personal friend of mine, a man
to whom I had to look up physically and in every other way'. He went on to
describe John Milling as 'a most charming fellow, one of the most charming
personalities in Ireland'.[65] Down in Mayo, Father Canavan denounced the
shooting at last Mass on the Sunday morning after it happened, as the RM
lay dying, and the Catholic Archbishop of Tuam was later vehement in his
condemnation of the killing. He stated that the perpetrator was, if not insane,
a criminal of the first order and urged it as the 'duty of all good citizens to do
all in their power to bring to justice one who is an enemy of God, an enemy
of society, and an enemy of Ireland'.[66] The editor of the *Connaught Telegraph*
regretted that the people of Westport had not followed the example of Castlebar,
where a public meeting was held to condemn the incident. It was acknowledged in the editorial that the 'overwhelming majority' of Westport people
were shocked at the 'awful occurrence' but the editor added that 'it was only
one among many lesser ones, and unless they do their duty and stamp out the
spirit of anarchy that has been rampant so long in their midst there may be a
repetition of [the] tragedy'.[67]

The *Mayo News* was quick to adopt a conciliatory editorial tone and to
argue that no blame could be attached to Westport. As RM for the district
Milling had held an office 'not always popular' but the discharge of his duties
could 'scarcely have created for him an enemy so bereft of Christian feeling as
to take his life', the editor declared. Nonetheless, he went on, 'an attempt will
be made, and is already being made by a section of the Unionist press, to give
the crime a political tinge and fasten it, if possible, on the popular organisation . . . what the motive was cannot even be guessed.' Mention was made of
John Milling's long association with the district and its people, and it was put
to the readership that he would have been the last man to suggest that the
inhabitants of Westport were 'the wild, murderous race that the Unionist
Chronicles would now paint them'. The hope was expressed that the truth
might come to light and justice be meeted out to whoever had committed the
murder, and sympathy was offered to the widow. If the crime was proved to
be attributable to the discharge of his duties, 'we think it is slanderous fallacy
to fix on the small area of Westport as responsible for it in any way', the

Mayo News insisted, because the RM had adjudicated all over the county, and any 'murderous criminal determined to assassinate him' would have done so wherever he lived.[68]

Lilla Milling was not entitled to any pension as a dependant of a resident magistrate but she was paid £425 by the state, one year's salary for a third class RM. She could not make a claim for compensation under the existing Criminal Injuries (Ireland) Act but that Act was quickly amended, in April 1919. Thereafter a claim could be made where a magistrate, a policeman, a member of the forces or of the civil service was murdered or maliciously injured in the execution of his duties, or on account of the office he held.[69] She lodged a claim for £5,000 compensation but raised that to £6,000 before the case came before the Westport Quarter Sessions in June, coinciding with the lifting of military restrictions in the area. Mr Featherstonehaugh appeared for the claimant, and he drew the court's particular attention to the cases in March 1918 and to the criticism of the RMs sentences in the *Mayo News*. Such criticisms, the Judge observed, did not amount to incitement to murder. Mr Kenny, for Westport Rural District County, argued that there was nothing to prove that it was a political motive that had instigated the crime. He also pointed out that 'they did not know what offence Mr Milling might have committed in his private life', but he was warned by the Judge not to 'suggest anything'. Kenny and Mr Bewley, for the UDC, insisted that the kind of demonstrations the court had heard about took place in every county in Ireland, and that Westport should not be forced to pay for the crime. Featherstonehaugh made the case that 'There was no earthly reason why Mr Milling should be shot, no more than any other member of the community, if it were not because of his position and of his having done what his duty required him to do.'[70] Lilla Milling and her children were awarded £6,000 with full costs, with two-fifths of the sum assessed on the rates of Westport UDC and another two-fifths on the rest of Co. Mayo. The County Council appealed against this and a later ruling put the whole burden on Westport where, by August, the *Mayo News* was complaining about the 'The Milling Tax'.[71]

Who killed John Milling is likely to remain a mystery but all the evidence points to it being a murder for political motives, despite the reiterated denials of nationalists in Westport and of some Irish MPs in the House. On the night of the murder a regular RIC patrol left the Shop Street barracks just before the shooting but the party was diverted by sounds of a disturbance in Peter Street. Nothing was found there but the delay was enough to ensure that the patrol was still some distance from Newport Road when the shots were fired. The attackers perhaps expected Milling to present an easy target just then, because they knew at what time the household usually retired and also that

Milling wound the clock last thing at night. The fact that the murder took place almost a year to the day after the events of March 1918 may have been coincidence but it might be of some significance that only a fortnight before the shooting the Volunteer Ned Moane was released from prison and arrived back in Westport. So too did Joseph MacBride (arrested in May 1918, in the 'German Plot' affair), the older man who had so carefully nursed the Sinn Féin movement in Westport, whose brother had been executed by the state, and who was almost certainly a member of the IRB. Moane and MacBride had been held in the same British prison. Their names do not occur in the tales told in Westport about the incident, tales in which the shooting is often attributed to 'the three Joe's'. This may have some truth in it but although Joe Ring and Joe Duffy were local Volunteers, Joe Baker was an Omagh-born IRA man who did not move to Westport until 1920. In his memoirs Baker wrote of his experiences with the West Mayo flying column during the War of Independence and of fighting with the anti-Treaty Irregulars duing the civil war.[72] He claimed to have served with two of three men involved in the Milling affair and to have been told by one of them that DI Shore was their target. According to this account the three men, armed with only one rifle, passed Shore on the street but did not recognise him and simply seized the opportunity when Milling appeared in the dimly lit room as they reached his house in the Newport Road, yet the spent cartridges found by DI Scott at the scene were of two different calibres, which indicates that more than one weapon was used.

No one was charged with any offence in connection with the death of John Milling but James McLoughlin was questioned and held by the police for some time. McLoughlin, aged about twenty but described as 'a boy', was arrested at his place of work on 3 April and taken to Westport RIC barracks. Police also searched the premises of the boy's father, an unemployed agricultural labourer, when the man was not there to give his permission. McLoughlin senior saw his son at the barracks next day but could get no information about why he had been arrested. The DI told him the lad would be 'all right' there until next morning but James McLoughlin was later moved to Castlebar. Questions were asked in the Commons about his detention and in the middle of May his father applied for an order directing the RIC to release his son. Sergeant Matheson subsequently produced McLoughlin, explaining that 'We want to return the boy . . . we wish to return him to his Father. But our case is that the boy was retained by the police for his own protection'. The sergeant claimed that the RIC had not considered it safe to 'let the boy home' after he had been helping them with enquiries into the murder of the RM.[73] The RIC officer responsible for the arrest and illegal detention of John McLoughlin was DI Scott, the neighbour and friend of John Milling, who it seems had promised McLoughlin a sum of money if he would give satisfactory evidence leading to an arrest. Scott was rapidly transferred to the North of Ireland, which provoked some questions in the Commons, and McLoughlin was later awarded £25 compensation for his illegal detention.[74]

The *Mayo News* reported that what DI Scott wanted from McLoughlin was a statement that he had seen two particular members of the local branch of the Irish Transport and General Workers' union (ITGWU) coming from the direction of Milling's house immediately after the murder. There was a strike going on in Westport at the time and the foreman at O'Malley's shop had been assaulted as a 'black leg' about a week before the killing. Cases arising out of this incident were not heard until after Milling's death but rumours of some ITGWU involvement lingered on. In October the *Mayo News* reported that a cutting from the *New York Herald* had been sent to the editor by an American friend. It contained what purported to be an account of the 'true story' of how Westport became a military area and it implicated the ITGWU but all this was dismissed by the editor as a tale that could only be read with amusement and amazement by anyone who knew the district.[75]

John Milling was a man of principle, doing his duty in ever more difficult and dangerous circumstances. Other resident magistrates also used the strategy of binding over Volunteers to keep the peace or, in default of finding sureties, to go to prison for a term. Christopher Lynch-Robinson was not alone in considering this 'effective preventative justice', if it resulted in young men being locked up for a year or more,[76] but inevitably those on the other side of the conflict took a different view. John Milling's unpopularity with nationalists in the Westport area was understandable in the circumstances but it was encouraged by the criticism of the *Mayo News*, and he was somewhat unfortunate in becoming a focus for local anti-British feeling. Wider opinion in Co. Mayo judged the RM more kindly. A *Connaught Telegraph* reporter wrote of John Milling that he gave offence to only a few and was 'highly popular' as far as the journalist knew. 'Why he should be made a victim to some vile fanaticism, or at the behest of some secret society, can hardly be explained', he added, 'a fairer-minded man could not sit on a bench'.[77]

9

James George Woulfe Flanagan, 1864-1922

James Woulfe Flanagan was born on 27 January 1864, the fourth son of the Rt. Hon. Stephen Woulfe Flanagan and his wife, Mary Deborah (*d.* 1886), a daughter of J.R. Corballis QC. The family name derived from a marriage in 1813 between Terence Flanagan of St Catherine's Park and Johanna Woulfe from Co. Clare. The Woulfe Flanagans were a Catholic professional family from the wealthier strata of the upper-middle classes which, through the ownership of landed estates, merged with the upper classes. In the late 1870s Stephen Woulfe Flanagan owned over 2,000 acres in Sligo, more than 1,500 acres in Roscommon and 869 in Clare, with an annual valuation of £2,049.[1] He also owned a property at Ballybrack, Co. Dublin, and at sometime acquired a town house in a fashionable part of Dublin, at 20 Fitzwilliam Place. His career began when he was called to the Irish Bar in 1838. Some twenty years later he was appointed QC and was a Bencher of the King's Inns, and Judge of the Landed Estates Court 1869-85. He was also a Privy Counsellor for Ireland and Great Britain. This was the sort of family from which many of the JPs, grand jurors, high sheriffs, deputy lieutenants of the counties and resident magistrates were drawn for much of the nineteenth century.

At his death in December 1891 Stephen Woulfe Flanagan left, 'with other issue', six sons and five daughters. They were Johnny (John, 1852-1929), Stee (Stephen, 1854-1940), Terry (Terence, 1859-1914), Jim or Jimmy (James, the RM, 1864-1922), Dick (Richard, 1868-1955), Eddie or Eddy (Edward Martyn, 1871-1954), and Sis, Sissie or Sissy (Johanna, *d.*1924), Jenny (Jane, *d.*1953), Mary (who joined the order of the Sisters of Charity and took the name Sr Scholastica, *d.*1924), Fan (Frances, *d.*1898) and Molly (Elizabeth, *d.*1939).[2] Private correspondence suggests that they were a close and affectionate family but inequality of opportunity made the lives of the brothers' and sisters' very different. With the exception of Richard, all the sons had the advantages of an Oxford education. Johnny was called to the English Bar in 1877 but later took up a career in journalism and was for many years a member of the editorial staff of *The Times*. Stee and Jimmy were also barristers. Terry became a doctor and Dick and Eddie were British army officers. Their sisters, other than Mary, who took the religious option, seem to have been restricted to the often rather empty existence of so many women of their class. Marriage partners for the daughters of the Irish gentry were in short supply, and none of the Woulfe Flanagan daughters married.

Sissie and Jenny did the Castle season, which began in early February with a levee and continued with 'drawing rooms' (at which the debutantes were presented to the Viceroy), dances and dinners until its culmination in the St Patrick's Ball on 17 March.[2] Jenny came out in 1882 and she described some of the fun with girlish enthusiasm, in a letter to Johnny dated 4 February:

> I've been out six times this week, two balls and the drawing room, which was awful, much worse than I expected even but won't be so bad next time as I know what it is like now and I won't have to be presented any more, though indeed I did not mind that much, Sissy said you got a sort of 'nun's kiss' on the top of your forehead, but he gave me a regular smack on the cheek, I heard it. . . .[3]

Sissy would not go to the drawing room, declaring that 'Castle Balls were awfully stupid', but Jenny had enjoyed herself at one the night before she wrote, although she 'did not get very many dances'. One of her few partners was an impressive naval officer 'in full uniform, blue and gold'. This was clearly not a triumphant debut such as that made by Daisy Burke the following year, when she carried off the prize catch, Lord Fingall, after a whirlwind courtship.[4] Few were as fortunate as Daisy, and Sissy's dismissive attitude to social events may have reflected her unwillingness to become one of the ageing girls who competed in the marriage market for many seasons before finding a husband or giving up the search.

While all the sisters remained single, only the three eldest sons married. This was not unusual in such famililies because financial circumstances often precluded marriage for younger sons. John married the second daughter of Major General Sir Justin Shiel, Maria Emily, in 1880 and they had two children, John Henry (Jack, *b*.1881) and Jane Mary (Baby or Pussy, *b*.1883). Maria died in 1886 and thereafter Jenny seems to have played the familiar Victorian role of maiden aunt in her widowed brother's household. Stephen married Eleanor McTernan, in 1898, the youngest daughter of the former RM Captain Hugh McTernan. These marriages were with Catholics from similar social backgrounds but Terry married, in 1892, the daughter of a Protestant clergyman. The family's reaction to this is not known but, although Catholics and Protestants generally mixed easily enough at this social level, so-called mixed marriages were not widely approved.[5]

For James Woulfe Flanagan 'family' meant his sisters and brothers and nieces and nephews. As the eldest son, John took over the role of head of the extended family after his Father's death but it was James, in Dublin, who oversaw the winding up of the estate and dealt with immediate financial matters. Many of his letters written from 20 Fitzwilliam Place to John, in London, were concerned with money matters, with the annuities paid to 'Old Feyther' (a priest, in Adare, Co. Limerick) and to Barbara or 'Babs' in Leesson Street, Dublin, or with the familiy investments in railways, corporation stock and other shares. In February 1892 James wrote to Johnny that, 'unless we very quickly get rid of this house I shall infallibly be swamped. I feel bound to stay – indeed I have no doubt I am better off here and living cheaper than in lodgings – but it is impossible to live on here.'[6] He had already had the library valued for probate and was hoping to sell a brass harness to Stee, 'for £4, if I can screw that much out of him'. He was keen that Dick should pay his late father's estate, back-dated to December 1891, for the upkeep of any horses he chose to keep from the Rathtermon stable in Co. Roscommon. By the end of February he was confident that 'we have (at least) £2,000 to invest'.[7]

The sisters' had little or no say in these matters it seems, with their brothers' taking major financial decisions. The family lawyer, 'Old Lynch', was not in full agreement with James over some details and Johnny was appealed to for advice in March:

> I am anxious at the earliest possible moment to be able to say to the girls, 'Your money is all invested and your income will be so much'. . . . Are we entitled to pay off (at their request) the girls' debts to the date of our distributing the estate, out of their capital, and so start them fair and clear of debt? I say Yes, Lynch says No![8]

James' career at the Bar was not making much progress. He added a postscript to the letter above, telling Johnny, 'I got a brief yesterday – one miserable guinea', but he later wrote that he was at least solvent, with enough money to clear his debts and provide for his funeral expenses, 'if Terry disposes of my remains as requested.' All this and more was written in a lighthearted tone but James was clearly seriously worried about the situation at Fitzwilliam Place. It cost over £660 a year to run the household and, unless major changes were made, 'the girls will have only £18 to dress, wash and amuse themselves with.' The house was probably sold shortly afterwards, as over the next few years letters to Johnny were sent from Baggot Street, from the University Club or the St Stephen's Green Club and from an address in Simmonscourt Road. The sisters presumably took lodgings or made extended visits to the wider family while James struggled on with increasing despondency about his prospects. Early in 1894, as his thirtieth birthday approached, he wrote from the University Club:

> I am quite sick of stopping here earning a kitchen maid's wages and loafing in a room all day, so badly ventilated that it would never pass the tests required by the factory Acts. . . . I am quite seriously thinking of going to 'seek my fortune' abroad. . . . I see absolutely no opening at the Bar here and I fear there is no one eager to do a job for me and I confess I don't like the idea of licking people's boots to encourage them – the blacking over here is so very bad![9]

He had hoped that the lawyer, Lynch, might put some legal work his way but, as he recognised, law was an overcrowded profession and there were numerous young men in Dublin with more experience than he possessed. There were many men in similar situations who, unable to earn a living in Ireland, went abroad in search of opportunities but James stayed on in Dublin, perhaps partly because of a sense of responsibility towards his unmarried sisters. By 1898 he was living with them again, at 16 Upper Fitzwilliam Street.

This was to be a year of change in the Woulfe Flanagan family. Fan died early in July and the event affected Sissy's health. She was to visit the family in London shortly afterwards but she delayed her journey, which seems to have irritated Johnny. James wrote a conciliatory letter on 18 August, saying that he did not think Sissy should be blamed for changing her plans and that it was in no one's interest to hurry her as she 'would almost certainly get ill again'. He suggested that Johnny did not understand 'how much her health depends on freedom from bustle and anxiety'. Worry had 'already laid her up for days in the past week or so and if she must be shuttlecock I'll not do battledore', he added, but he assured Johnny that, 'unless her health breaks down in the meantime', she would travel in a few days. In the event, James accompanied Sissy across to Holyhead from where he wrote on 22 August: 'With the aid of Caffrins and Sal Volatile Sis effected a start today and is now *en route* for London where I think it probable she will break down, but she may not'. Whether Sissy's threatened breakdowns were anything more than a retreat into illness is impossible to say with certainty. Invalidism of hysterical origin can be seen as a form of protest and there were many women of the nineteenth century who took to their couch as a kind of passive resistance to their state of powerlesness. There was, perhaps, some family tendency to 'suffer from nerves', in the parlance of the times, as both Terry and Dick experienced episodes of illness attributed to mental rather than physical causes. Whatever the cause, Sissy became a permanent invalid and she was later confined to a wheel chair.

Back in Dublin, James was commissioned to buy a bicycle for his nephew Jack. His particular outdoor pursuits were walking, sailing and mountaineering but he was also a keen cyclist and he was regarded as the family expert on the best type of machine to buy. He had to ask Johnny for £18 on account, as he could not afford 'to fork out so much', but for people like James Woulfe Flanagan shortage of money was essentially a problem of liquidity or cash flow rather than actual want of necessities. Genteel poverty did not preclude continental holidays, which could actually be taken as an economy measure because it was possible to live quite cheaply abroad. James, Sissy, and Molly were in Switzerland by late September, staying at Lucerne, and in early October James was at a hotel on Lac Majeur in Italy. Family responsibilites followed him even on holiday. He wrote to Johnny from Italy that he had left his cheque book behind when he crossed the border, and asked him to 'send old Barbara her usual quarterly', with a reminder that Jenny and Molly's 'quarterlies' would also be due soon. It was to be a short holiday for James but his sisters' plans were uncertain. They might keep moving, he told Johnny, although it was possible that they would settle 'in a big city – say Frankfort [*sic*]. Molly (not unnaturally) gets bored after a short time in a small place as she has no occupation whatever (except praying). Sis is willing enough to halt anywhere but I don't think objects to "moving on" until she gets home'.[10]

It was a less than happy homecoming for James. He had a very rough crossing from Holyhead to Kingstown (Dun Laoghaire) and was 'SICK, SICK, SICK' on the boat. He arrived at 16 Upper Fitzwilliam Street 'calculating on grand hot bath – "there's not a bit of coal in the house, Sir!" No bath.' He found a pile of post accumulated but nothing of much interest, and the worry of 'bill, for Sissy's pills, bill for Molly's blouses'.[11] What was in the post was of more than usual importance, for by now James Woulfe Flanagan was hoping to be appointed to the resident magistracy. This would provide a solution not only to his problems but also to those of Sissy and Molly, and also Jenny in the long term. They could all live together more comfortably in greater security if James had a regular income of over £400 a year. He had received a 'very diplomatic' reply from the Castle when he applied on his own behalf but he was not at all hopeful of his prospects until a mutual friend intervened and asked John Woulfe Flanagan to use his influence. James would 'not have asked' his brother for help but he was delighted with the outcome of this friendly interference. A letter to Harrell, the Under-Secretary, brought an invitation to attend an interview with the Chief Secretary on 1 November. After meeting Balfour, James reported that although no distinct promise had been made he was given the impression that he would be appointed in the future, and added that Balfour had said his name would go on his 'select list':

I was not ten minutes with him. He is evidently quite satisfied with my
qualifications and asked no awkward questions as to my experience of
adjudicating the criminal law and said as well as I recollect 'I have sent
for you to tell you – to be quite candid – that I do not think I can
appoint you now.' He asked me my age and then told me I could afford
to wait a bit![12]

At almost age thirty-five James Woulfe Flanagan was still five years' under
the age limit of forty but he was spared a long wait on Balfour's select list.
Only eleven days after his interview at the Castle he sent a telegram to Sissy
and Molly in Florence, with news that he was appointed to a district in Co.
Kerry.

James Woulfe Flanagan's letters to his brother offer an intimate glimpse
of his family life and the circumstances that encouraged him to apply for the
appointment. They also give unique insight into the interview procedure
under Arthur Balfour, and other letters are equally valuable because of the
light they cast on the experiences of an Irish RM as he settled into his new
role. Some six weeks after taking up his post in Listowel, the RM wrote that
the hotel was 'quite good for a country town' but he feared that he would
have to 'eat my plum pudding in solitary grandeur'. The former RM, John
French (a brother of Lord de Freyne) had moved on to his new station in
Limerick and two bachelor acquaintances were going away for Christmas.
'We don't rise (as far as I know) to a stationers in Listowel,' he explained, by
way of excuse for not having sent a Christmas card to Jenny. He had found a
house that 'would suit us nicely' but 'unfortunately there is a widow in
possession and though I dare say I could get the house and widow together,
I fear it will be hard to split the lots'.[13]

UIL activity and 'moonlighting' were disturbing the peace of Co. Kerry
at the time and it was something of a baptism of fire for the RM to take up
his duties during the land agitation. While familiarising himself with the new
job and the routine of petty sessions he had also to accustom himself to the
particular difficulties of a resident magistrate in a disturbed district. Shortly
after arriving in Listowel he drove out to a meeting to be addressed by
William O'Brien, which was expected to be a gathering of the people in their
thousands. It was a 'frightful' day and the RM found 'the thousands were
represented by about 150 to 200 very damp and unenthusiastic patriots',
while the law was represented by himself, a police sergeant and two constables. He commented that press reporting of the event gave a very different
picture to what he had seen that day. There had been some moonlighting
cases of intimidation and he thought there might be an 'epidemic' of them,
although the priests were 'tired of agitation' and some had made themselves

unpopular by denouncing outrages. There had been an attempt to boycott a fourteen year old boy who had given evidence in court that led to the conviction of a moonlighter and a sentence of three years. The boy's schoolfellows had walked out in protest at the presence of an 'informer' but the master, with the co-operation of the parents, soon had them all back in school under threat of expulsion. The boy and his father were being 'watched' by the RIC, and the RM hoped he would 'not be shot' although he later decided that his life was in real danger and asked Johnny if he knew of any English firm that might employ the lad.[14] Woulfe Flanagan quickly became well known in the district, because of his adjudication in cases arising out of the UIL campaign.

The RM was 'by no means comfortable in the saddle yet'. He felt that to do the work 'really right' would require more extensive legal knowledge than he possessed and he was of the opinion that most decisions in the petty sessions courts were 'illegal', if straightforward cases of drunkenness were discounted. He claimed that it had been the custom for years for the local magistrates' to 'sign the orders in blank for the clerk to fill in at his leisure'. Although none of the orders made out by the clerk (who took the 'keenest professional pride' in his work) had ever been quashed, the RM suspected they 'were everyone bad, nevertheless'. He had another 'phase of Kerry justice' to recount after a JP called upon him, not to welcome the new RM but to try to plead for his son, who was to appear in court at the next petty sessions. The JP was sent on his way, 'not altogether pleased with his reception'. After hearing a few cases of drunkenness and unmuzzled dogs at one of his more remote sessions, some distance from Castleisland, the RM was asked by the district inspector to take depositions from a Crown witness who had been badly beaten and had his arm broken by a man now in custody. This was 'not pleasant work', as Woulfe Flanagan described the encounter:

> now you will see the fixes a poor Kerry RM gets landed into. The injured man's hovel was the most miserable human habitation I ever was in – very picturesque and very 'niffy' – but still it was his Castle. 'Get out of this, I don't want you, I won't be sworn' – was our welcome. There we were 'trespassers *ab intro*'! Then we proceeded to clear the house of neighbours and invited guests (I wonder is it 'forcible entry', or what?). Then I tried to coax my man to take the oath – but no he wouldn't.[15]

The RM ordered a warrant to be drawn up, to commit 'the poor broken-armed wretch' to gaol, and cross-examined him 'sweating there and all but fainting twice with fear of Tralee gaol on one hand and the Moonlighters on the other.' The man 'gave way', or so it seemed, but when he had taken the oath he swore that the statement he had made the day before was all false.

There were lighter moments in the RMs life, as in January when he visited Ballybunion for the first time and wrote to Johnny: 'You are to tell Baby that I expect her and her Nanny there about the 1 of June for a long stay'. He had an anecdote to tell about the Listowel council, 'all elected on the "labour ticket" ', whose chairman was a publican but refused 'tick' to his fellow councillors. He was thinking of selling his books, now that he was 'a nomad' and money was still scarce. All he had left of a £500 legacy from his sister, Frances, was £300 and there were temptations to extravagance in Kerry. 'I don't know what I am to buy that lovely little thoroughbred chestnut with, that I saw a couple of days ago', he told Johnny in February, 'I am trying to persuade myself that it would be a reasonably prudent thing to do, to have a horse and trap of my own, but I can't!'[16] He lived at Cahirdown, Listowel, during his stay in Co. Kerry, where his nephew Jack visited him in April 1900. It was perhaps not the most enjoyable of visits. The RM was unavoidably absent for part of each day and Jack, sick with a bad earache, was left much to himself. James was concerned about his nephew's future and worried that the boy seemed to have no opinion as to what he might like to make his career. Another family visit was being planned in the summer, when James went to Kenmare on transfer leave before moving to his new station in King's County (Offaly). He stayed at the Great Southern Hotel but recommended Johnny to the Caragh, a 'much less grand' but more 'genuinely comfortable' place which had a good cook and 'would "do" you and your son and daughter at 10s. (50p) each a day.' There were also, he noted, 'two "villas" to be let a few miles off, specially constructed for the Saxon',[17] which was perhaps a brotherly jibe at Johnny's having become a true West Briton after long residence in England.

James' own culture and values were derived largely from English models, as his observations about his new district illustrate. Writing from Hayes Hotel in Tullamore, the day after he took up his duties, he told Johnny: 'It is a very different station to my last. I drove to Clara yesterday in a rubber-tyred car over splendid cycling roads through very English scenery.' At the petty sessions he had 'nothing but drunks and a "cattle wandering" – not a single sore head or application to bind to keep the peace – Disgusting!' He was impressed by the 'Quaker settlement' at Clara, where there were lots of fine villas all belonging to 'Alpha beta "Good Bods"' and a 'great factory' employing many hundreds of workers. With its English scenery, its good roads, its villas and industrial workers, and 'Good Bods' in place of Moonlighters it was 'a d—d civilized prosperous hole of a place.'[18] First impressions were confirmed as the weeks went by and the RM found that he had 'nothing to do here except carp at Dublin Castle and its ways – I am a perfect sinecurist!'[19] In September he wrote of a day when two courts were scheduled but one was cancelled as there were no cases, 'tho' it is a monthly court', and at the other there was only 'one drunk and a civil case which was settled beforehand'. 'I have over 3,600 people in my district, according to Them', he told Johnny, 'but they really have not committed anything that could be called a "crime" since I came.'[20]

Family affairs and money matters also featured in the RMs letters to his brother, with affectionate greetings being sent to Jenny and the children and references to 'Old Feyther' and Babs. He was pleased to hear that Johnny had 'taken to Friday cycling', as a means of exercise. The plinth and cross on Fan's grave at Glasnevin were in need of repair, and there was some confusion over £600 'due by Eddy' which perhaps ought to be divided in equal thirds between Fan's estate and Jenny and Molly. Sis and Molly were apparently to join the RM when a suitable house was found. In reply to a query from Johnny as to where the two would go in the interim, James sent him a letter he had received from his younger sister, 'the hapless spendthrift'. He was quite sharply critical of her and wrote of the letter he had enclosed:

> Observe she begins 'Sis has no more money of mine'. Sis writes by same post 'Molly owes me £12', but it is all one to her!! I have referred her to you and sent her £20 to go on with as a loan. I think you ought to make her confess her financial sins to you. I really do not think she ought to be in debt this year. I incline to think it would really be better for her in the long run if we told her to instruct Jas. McCann to sell out some stock she owns absolutely and which she got under Fan's will. She has had some hundreds of pounds capital in dribblets of twenties and thirties – how much I know not and am sure she does not either. Sis will I know be applying for capital too but of course it is a wholly different case with her.[21]

Sis, it seems, always had the greater share of her brothers' sympathy because of her ill health but Molly deserves some understanding. As the youngest sister she was perhaps particularly patronised and as she was apparently treated like a child where money was concerned she cannot be entirely blamed if she behaved like one. Her role in life, like Jenny's, was shaped by her unmarried status and the needs of other members of the family. No doubt there were emotional satisfactions for Jenny, in taking on some responsibility for the children of her widowed brother, and for Molly in acting as companion-nurse to her invalid sister, but few women would have chosen such lives for themselves.

The RMs quiet life in Tullamore was sometimes enlivened by extra duties at courts in Queen's County (Laois), where he would on occasion look up old friends. He may also have been marginally involved in one of the criminal sensations of Ireland around the turn of the century, for according to later newspaper accounts of his career he once signed a warrant for the arrest of the notorious James Lynchehaun, who was convicted of the brutal assault of an English landowner, Agnes MacDonnell, on Achill Island, Co. Mayo, in October 1894. It has been suggested that his exploits while on the run were the model for J.M. Synge's *Playboy of the Western World*. Lynchehaun was eventually arrested and tried at Castlebar where he was found guilty and sentenced to a term of imprisonment, but in September 1902 he escaped from Maryborough (Portlaois) jail and eventually fled to America.[22] As for the RM, Woulfe Flanagan had few exceptional duties in this calm period of his career but his pleasant routine in Tullamore ended shortly afterwards, when he was transferred back to Listowel, Co. Kerry, in May 1903.

He again lived at Cahirdown, Listowel. Few of his letters from this period survive but it is evident that family life went on much as before. There were concerns over the health of 'poor Terry' in 1907 but better news of nephew Jack, who seemed to be making something of himself at last. He had taken a City and Guilds diploma at the Central Technical College in London and after gaining this qualification he had gone out to Canada to work on a land survey of British Columbia. In April 1908 he wrote from McGill University in Montreal, where he was visiting a friend, and he was enthusiastic about his first attempt at skiing and about his prospects. He would earn £24 a month with all his expenses paid and, if he studied for a further qualification, might earn more than double his starting salary. He enquired after Sis and Molly, asked if there was any news of Terry, and concluded: 'How goes the great garden? How are the eyes?'[23] In later years the RM was off sick on several occasions with 'optic neuritis' and it seems that this recurring eye problem had set in by 1907.

This second posting to Listowel lasted nine years, time enough to make a 'great garden', but in March 1912 James Woulfe Flanagan was transferred to Co. Down where he and Sis and Molly settled at Savalmore, Ardarragh, some three miles from Newry. They were later joined by Jenny, whose services as substitute mother were no longer needed in brother Johnny's household. The Newry district encompassed all of south Down, south Armagh, and north Co. Louth. Woulfe Flanagan replaced the resident magistrate Robert Bull, a Protestant former RIC officer who had a reputation for being 'fearless but rugged and austere, a terror to evildoers'. In contrast, Woulfe Flanagan was later described by a journalist and personal friend as noted for his 'kindliness', a man often 'pained' by the sordid stories that he heard in court but always cheered by any 'signs of reformation'. His meticulous care could sometimes be irritating in court as, even in the most trivial cases, he would 'probe into the smallest detail' to get at the truth and ensure that no injustice was done. His respect for the law was, however, to the benefit of defendants who could not afford to be legally represented. They found in the RM, according to his friend, 'an advocate as well as a judge'. Still an active man in his fifties, the RM remained a keen mountaineer and he was a member of the Tyrolese Mountain Club. From day to day he put his energies into gardening but also spent many hours in his workshop-garage, dismantling and rebuilding his several cars. He kept two in running order, to meet the needs of all the household, but for preference he drove his sporty little two-seater De Dion. He was widely known as a devout Catholic and as a man with a great affection for his family, and he was often to be seen pushing his invalid sister along in her wheel chair.[24]

The appointment of a Catholic RM to Newry in 1912, when feelings were running high over the Home Rule issue, was perhaps intended as a gesture towards the Catholic population of the district. If so, it was futile, for as the political situation deteriorated attitudes hardened and a Catholic serv-ant of the Crown was increasingly likely to be regarded with suspicion by Protestant-unionists because of his religion and to be unpopular with nation-alists because of his loyalty. For most of the time James Woulfe Flanagan's experiences in Newry were much the same as those of the resident magis-trates in general, although like all those serving in northern districts he dealt with numerous cases arising out of sectarian conflict. It is not the intention here to chronicle his routine duties from 1912 onward but to focus on the period after the Government of Ireland Bill, offering a six-county state to unionists, was put before the Commons in February 1920.

A vicious summer followed in the north of Ireland. Sectarian violence broke out in Derry and, on 21 July, Protestant and unionist workers yet again expelled Catholics, nationalists and socialists from the Belfast shipyard of the Workman and Clark company. Three days of disturbances in the city left seven Catholics and six Protestants dead. Woulfe Flanagan, who held an additional warrant for Belfast, was ordered there on 22 July and remained on special duty until 27 July. More violence followed the murder in Lisburn on 22 August of DI Swanzy, the RIC officer believed by nationalists to have been implicated in the murder of the Sinn Féin mayor of Cork, in March 1920. Reprisals for Swanzy's murder were taken against nationalists in Lisburn and Belfast and, on 24 August, a church in a Catholic area of north Belfast was attacked by Protestants. By the end of the month over twenty people had been killed, hundreds of Catholic families had been driven out of their homes, and the damage to property ran into many thousands of pounds. The Newry RM was sent to Belfast when these disturbances began and he was involved in hearings at several courts, although it was James Roche (a former solicitor and one of the two Belfast resident magistrates) who first heard the charges against the taxi driver and two other men charged with the murder of DI Swanzey.[25] In response to the mounting violence, the military authorities imposed a curfew on the city at the end of August and this remained in force until 1924.

1921 opened with a spell of bad weather and James Woulfe Flanagan was delayed by snow and ice in getting around his district. Some six months later he found that he had more ominous forces than the weather to cope with, when on his way to the Warrenpoint petty sessions in July he was 'held up by strange "specials" in Newry.' This was his first encounter (other than in court) with any of the special constables enrolled from the previous November, in three categories: A, full-time temporary constables; B, part-time constables serving in their local area; C, an emergency reserve force. Like the Black and Tans and Auxiliaries in the south, they were reinforcements for a hard-pressed constabulary but they were to remain in being for many years longer and they became (especially the B Specials) as detested by northern Catholics and nationalists as their southern counterparts had been. There were other similarities between north and south, such as the disruption to courts in areas where Sinn Féin was particularly active, and the coexistence of routine lists with special courts. When the Newry RM attended Ravensdale petty sessions on 19 May 1921 he found 'nobody there but Clerk and myself'. At the Newry petty sessions in June the bench, presided over by the RM, was confronted by cases and cross-cases arising out of 'More Womens' Disagreements' and 'A Drover's Troubles', as the local paper informed its readers, but on the same day and in the same court house James Woulfe Flanagan and W. Gore Moriarty RM heard twenty-two prosecutions for breaches of the curfew. Some of the cases were dismissed and most of those found guilty were fined 5*s*. [25p] but there were complicating factors in the case of Patrick Tate. He had been issuing threats and challenges to some troops and was arrested by Constable Jones on the order of a military officer, Captain Crawford. Tate had also threatened the constable. He was charged only with breaking the curfew and had nothing to say except that he had been drunk. 'I think you must have been drunk', Woulfe Flanagan commented, 'when you were prepared to fight the whole lorry full'. This brought laughter from the court but the RM told Tate, 'If you had kept a bit quiet you would have got off a bit cheap - you will have to pay 10*s*. instead of 5*s*.'[26]

The state opening of the Parliament of Northern Ireland took place in June 1921 and in early July negotiations were underway to bring about a truce in the south. A few days before the Truce came into effect (on 11 July), Patrick Murphy was up before the RM at the Newry petty sessions. A constable had found Murphy drunk and staggering on the streets, shouting 'Up De Valera', 'Up Dublin' and 'To Hell with the King'. The policeman had decided to arrest the man for his own good and had kept him in custody overnight. It was certainly unsafe to express such sentiments in parts of Newry, and Volunteers in the south had been charged with serious offences for shouting similar slogans, but Murphy was treated as nothing more than a case of drunkenness.[27] His treatment suggests some ambivalence on the part of the local RUC and the RM himself towards nationalists in their district but as the tension mounted in the border area Woulfe Flanagan felt himself increasingly at risk. In the autumn he wrote to one of his old Oxford tutors and sent him a list of ten murders or attempted murders that had taken place during one week in July in Newry. He added, 'If I get a sentence of death by tomorrow's post, I should not know whether I was sentenced for being a Catholic or a loyal subject of HM'.[28] Yet the job still attracted a few applicants and among those who wrote to Dublin Castle about appointment as RM in 1921 was Major Jack Woulfe Flanagan,[29] the nephew of the Newry RM. Jack had returned from Canada at the end of 1908 but continued his engineering career until joining the army for service during the 1914-18 war.

Meanwhile, at about the time of the peace negotiations in the south, James's bother Stee came under threat on the borders of counties Sligo and Roscommon. As Stee was about to set off from home for the Sligo petty sessions he was 'visited' by two men who threatened him with 'arrest' if he tried to attend the court. He shut the door in their faces, and decided to travel by road rather than taking the train as usual:

> But I was overtaken at Hollybrook and, on my refusing to go home, was forcibly taken a short way up the mountain, and detained there for nearly seven hours, when I was released with emphatic warnings not to attempt the English Court on [the] following day, as I should be well watched. I was not ill treated, and most of the men were civil enough.[30]

The threats 'proved groundless'. He was not interfered with in any way when he went to the Boyle petty sessions in Co. Roscommon on the following Friday, but he took the precaution of asking for a police escort to accompany him there and back. It was generally believed in the locality, he wrote, that 'the job was the private work' of a tenant against whom he was taking legal proceedings but, he added, 'If it was an "official" command to abstain from "English Courts", my position may prove difficult, and even intolerable'. Pending the results of the peace conference, he did not think he was in any immediate danger.

His brother, the RM, was by now finding that there was a sectarian tinge even to seemingly commonplace cases of neighbourly disputes that came before him at the petty sessions. In Devonshire Court, off Lower Water Street, a woman in a 'mixed marriage' was harassed and verbally abused by neighbours who hoped to drive her out to join her husband, who was working in Belfast. The woman claimed she was often told that 'there should not be an Orangeman left in Newry.'[31] As in many of the border towns, the community in Newry was polarised and there was a large section of the local population which wanted no part of the unionist state of Northern Ireland. The Port and Harbour Trust reflected the mood of many people when, in December 1921, it unanimously resolved to co-operate with other bodies trying to secure the inclusion of the southern parts of counties Down and Armagh in the Irish Free State.[32] Many nationalists were still hopeful that the boundary would be redrawn and so place them within the Irish Free State and, meanwhile, some northern nationalists held the view that the terms of the Truce should be observed in the state of Northern Ireland. The perceived injustice of the situation sustained violent republicanism and the courts were kept busy in consequence. The RM adjudicated in only comparatively minor cases involving the carrying of weapons, as more serious charges were sent up to the assize courts, but in February 1922 a young man was brought before him at a court in Rathfriland, Co. Down, charged with possession of a revolver and ammunition. It was stated by the police that James Keenan had a revolver and eleven rounds of ammunition in his possession when he was arrested in January 1922. He declared himself a soldier of the Irish Republic and refused to recognise the authority of the court to try him. His solicitor contended that, under the terms of the Truce, Keenan had as much right to carry arms as the Ulster Special Constabulary or any member of the British forces in Ireland. The RM said in response to this that he could not take any notice of the Truce in the south because he had 'no official intimation' that he could do so. Keenan was given a moderate sentence of three months' imprisonment, without hard labour.[33] The *Freeman's Journal* used the heading 'Where the Truce is Unknown' in March 1922, when it reported on the 'heavy sentences' imposed on three IRA men at the Downpatrick Assizes. The men had been arrested by B Specials in the early hours of 14 February, near Kilkeel. Patrick Murray was armed and carrying a 'passbook' detailing the issue of firearms, ammunition and explosives to local IRA battalions and James Monaghan, from Newry, had in his possession four ordnance survey maps of Belfast, Newry, Monaghan and Drogheda. Michael Murney had on him a coded police message sent out to district inspectors, and a document addressed to a Father McKee. The men refused to recognise the court but Murney stated that he was 'not ashamed to say that I am an Irish Republican' and he admitted responsibility for the documents found on him, 'especially the one relating to the Irish Republican Brotherhood'. He denied that Father McKee had anything to do with the matter, even though, as the Judge remarked, the priest's name had not been mentioned in connection with the charges. 'I don't think this is fair', Murney complained later in the hearing:

> The Northern Government can't have it both ways. They are living in comparative peace as a result of the Truce, but at the same time they are acting on their own initiative, holding up the like of me along the road and bringing such flimsy charges against me . . . the sentence does not matter much to me, but it is a matter, I would say, that is not for me and this tribunal at all, but for the Northern Government, which you recognise as yours, and for Dáil Éireann, which I recognise as mine.[34]

Murney was found guilty of illegal assembly and sentenced to twelve months with hard labour. The others, and a third man found guilty at the same court of possession of firearms and explosives, were given terms of three to six years penal servitude.

Fighting along the border was continuing meanwhile in such episodes as that reported from Co. Tyrone at the beginning of April, when police on the northern side came under fire for nearly an hour from snipers in the south. There were also many indiscriminate sectarian killings, like that of a young man whose body was found lying on the roadside near a bridge just outside Newry, with two bullet wounds to the head. His bycycle lay beside him and it seemed that he had been shot while returning from a Saturday night out in Newry.[35] The RM heard a growing number of cases involving the possession of ammunition, most of them instigated by B Specials and many of them involving possession of only one cartridge. Virtually every defendant was a Catholic. All these coincidences clearly worried Woulfe Flanagan, who was committed to the principle of impartial justice and was a man of probity in his professional and personal life. When such cases came before him, he usually made some pertinent observation during the course of giving his judgement but, with apparently solid police evidence before the court, there was little more that he could do short of taking up the matter with higher authorities. There is no evidence to suggest that he did so but perhaps, like Christopher Lynch-Robinson with the Black and Tans in the south,[36] he wrestled with his conscience and came to the conclusion that there was not much a resident magistrate could do about the behaviour of police reinforcements who had the backing of governments. Nonetheless, even in cases where there were no grounds for suspecting that the police had planted the evidence, the RM drew attention to what seemed to be going on in general. He did so in May 1922 at a special court in Newry, where Michael James McAvoy appeared on a possession charge. McAvoy had been out after curfew when he was stopped and searched by B Specials who found a cartridge in his waistcoat pocket. He did not deny possession but explained that a cousin of his, now a clerk in the Provincial bank, had served through the 1914-18 war and had at some time past given him the bullet as a souvenir. He had put it into his pocket and forgotten that it was there. The RM said that in all arms cases, 'unless there was something extraordinary about them', he had 'made up his mind not to give bail on the first hearing.' He therefore remanded McAvoy in custody for eight days. He also took the opportunity to observe once again 'that it was an extraordinary thing that in a number of cases that had been before him the men charged had only a single cartridge' in their posession. The worst of it was, he added, that 'people who are otherwise of the highest respectability were mixed up in offences of this kind at the present moment.'[37]

Towards the end of the month, on 27 May, the Newry RM was in Belfast hearing charges of illegal assembly brought by the police against twenty-five young men from the Rathfriland district. Secondary charges of possessing or having in their control arms and ammunition, with intent to endanger life, were withdrawn. The dock, greatly congested by the large number of prisoners, was guarded by the 'Special Constabulary' as was the entire court house. The accused were admitted to bail for trial at the next Downpatrick Assizes.[38] This was the last of James Woulfe Flanagan's duties performed in Belfast and among the last of his duties as an Irish RM. On Pentecost Sunday, 4 June, he was fired at and mortally wounded as he was leaving the eleven o'clock Mass at Newry Cathedral.

Newspaper reports of the incident are agreed that as he left the cathedral, accompanied by Molly, three men approached him and their leader said 'Come along with us'. The RM refused, whereupon about five shots were immediately fired at him. Molly was reported to have 'made a plucky effort to capture one of the murderers, but he flung her off, and the rest of the congregation was too stupefied to interfere.'[39] There was 'a wild stampede' after the shots were fired and many people on their way to attend mid-day Mass turned home in fright. The RM, shot twice in the chest and wounded in the left hand, was carried to the nearby shop or house of Peter Fox where several doctors attended him, together with a young newsboy who had been wounded in the leg by a glancing bullet. James Woulfe Flanagan survived for some fifteen minutes, his dying moments attended by Molly, who 'gave him water and tried to make him comfortable'.[40] Two priests administered the last rites to the RM, whose final words were variously reported as 'I expected this' or 'I forgive them'. The three attackers, said to be 'respectably dressed' young men in their twenties, made their escape in a car driven off at speed by an accomplice who had waited nearby with the engine running. The *Freeman's Journal* reported that the car headed in the direction of Warrenpoint but that it was 'not actually known which road' it then took, whereas several other newspapers' stated that the vehicle made off 'towards the Free State'.[41]

The remains were not taken home to Savelmore because 'Miss Flanagan considered this would have been too great a shock for her invalid sister, as she was devotedly attached to her brother.' The body was removed to the mortuary at Newry Hospital in a Red Cross ambulance escorted by armed Specials in lorries. The murder was widely condemned, particularly by the Catholic and Protestant clergy of Newry, and the family received many condolences. One sympathiser wrote to John Woulfe Flanagan after discovering that the murdered RM was his brother, not merely 'a distant cousin . . . a member of the same clan'. 'The great tragedy of Ireland', this correspondent remarked, 'involves numberless individual tragedies about which it is difficult to write without exasperation . . . it will, I fear, be little consolation to have given in your own intimate circle a martyr to the cause of civilization in Ireland.' From all accounts he had read it seemed, he added, that the RM had been 'a fine fellow' who did his duty 'regardless of lurking danger, knowing himself to be suspected by Loyalists for his Catholicism, and hated by Sinn Féiners for his Loyalty'.[42] The letter, sent from the Athenaeum Club, expressed the feelings likely to have been shared by many of John Woulfe Flanagan's Conservative-unionist friends in England but sympathy came also from other quarters. In Dublin, the secretary of the Ancient Order of Hibernians wrote from Mountjoy Square to Sister Scholastica in the nearby Gardiner Street convent of the Sisters of Charity, to offer condolences from himself and on behalf of the members of the AOH.[43] In Newry Father McGee, preaching in the Old Chapel on 11 June, said 'that he never thought he would live to see a gentleman leaving God's sacred building murdered by a band of assassins, who lay in wait for him and cruelly shot him'. It would 'go down as Newry's Black Sunday on account of the foul crime committed at the Cathedral door', the priest said, and he later paid tribute to the RM as a man who had 'died the death of a martyr.'[44]

There was generous praise of Woulfe Flanagan in the local and national press, in which he was widely reported to have been greatly respected for his passion for the law and the care with which he administered it in the Newry district. It was suggested in the *Belfast Telegraph* that it was his very 'fearless' adherence to the law that had made him a man 'marked for destruction'[45] To his former Oxford tutor it seemed there was little doubt now as to which side in the conflict had been most likely to assassinate the RM, and the general assumption was that this was an IRA killing. It was referred to in a *Times* leader, in which it was stated that the Irish question was trembling in the balance between peace and war with the Treaty under threat from 'active aggression'. Britain, it was claimed, had done all that lay within its power to establish peace in Ireland. 'We bear no malice. We have no ulterior aim to serve', wrote the editor of this influential newspaper, but he went on to declare that a murder like that of Mr Woulfe Flanagan:

> tells trumpet-tounged against the wicked conspiracy that has too long been sufferred to present itself as a political opposition. Sunday's foul deed may have been perpetrated by irresponsible desperadoes, but the stain of it lies on a people that has consistently acquiesced in the employment of murder as a political weapon.[46]

The assassination achieved no purpose but to further antagonise unionist and liberal opinion and to add weight to arguments for more stringent measures to be taken with regard to closing the border.[47] The Downpatrick RM, Walter Garden Duff (a Scottish-born Presbyterian and former RIC officer), took over the Newry district for some weeks until Major J.D. McCallum was appointed in Woulfe Flanagan's place. A 'night of terror' followed the killing of the RM in Newry, when the main street through the town was 'the scene of a huge conflagration'. Later in June six Protestants were murdered and their homes burnt to the ground near Newry in an outrage which prompted rumours in the Dundalk area that eleven B Specials had been killed by the IRA, although none of the male victims were members of the special constabulary. There was said to be 'great uneasiness' in Newry after this incident and many persons were 'fleeing to the Free State'.[48]

Meanwhile in Dublin, following the general election and a split in the subsequent IRA convention over whether to resume the offensive against British troops, anti-Treaty Irregulars had taken over the Four Courts. Troops of the provisional government bombarded the building from the early hours of 28 June until the garrison surrendered on 30 June but street fighting continued until 5 July, marking the start of the civil war. Sister Scholastica wrote to Johnny from Gardiner Street on the first day of the action, telling him that the Republicans had taken over two hotels near the convent and that the sound of firing could be heard all around. 'If I could only face death with the courage dear old Jim did I would not mind getting a bullet,' she wrote, 'but I must confess I am a real coward and everything combined is making me a bit "jiggy" at present.' A few weeks later she wrote again, in a calmer atmosphere, to explain 'a little difficulty about money poor Jim used to send me'. He had customarily forwarded the sum of £3 to her in June and December each year, 'towards a weekly allowance for Teresa', but since his death another source of charity would have to be found.[49] It seems that the RM had been a kindly man, 'the personification of good nature in all his social and other relations in life', as his journalist friend remembered him. He recalled the resident magistrate's consistently helpful attitude to the press and his habit of offering lifts to reporters to his remote petty sessions, although the journey was often tedious as Woulfe Flanagan would never exceed fifteen miles an hour because of his 'horror of running things down'. Such was his personal probity that when the RM was forced to take to his bycycle after using up his petrol allowance during the Great War he refused the offer of a couple of cans from the local RIC stock, saying that he must obey the law and put up with the inconvenience like any good citizen.[50]

The compensation claim relating to his murder was dealt with by a Belfast solicitor but Johnny kept in close touch with the legal advisor, and he argued that 'The state of Johanna's (Sissy's) health seems to entitle her to claim more than she could have done, if in normal health for her age'. Her condition did not 'materially affect her expected life', he thought, although her doctor's opinion should be taken about that, but he explained that because of the wheelchair she needed to live in a house with large rooms and her requirements for medicines, personal service and special foods all added 'seriously to her necessary expense'. Johnny had been through the housekeeping receipts and tradesmens' order books for the last few months of life at Savalmore but earlier accounts were not readily available as they had been packed up when the sisters' left the place prior to its auction. He did not think it advisable that Jane (Jenny) should be called as she 'has a horror of swearing to anything and is very nervous'. She had made a statement of household expenses ('without telling me') and he was sure it was scrupulously fair but was certain that 'she would not swear to it, or hardly swear that she thinks it is even approximately correct'. Stephen had been checking out 'payments before 1919' but, 'for much the same sort of reasons' as Jenny's, would be 'a bad witness, but I am afraid he will have to appear'. Johnny understood that Elizabeth (Molly) was herself willing to attend but 'both Miss Flanagan (Sis) and Colonel Flanagan (Eddy) are strongly opposed to her attendance, on the ground that it would expose her to danger.' He did not think the danger would 'be appreciable, unless those concerned in the murder thought that she might be asked to identify any suspected person', in which case the danger to Molly would be 'serious'. She would, he acknowledged, be the right witness 'as to the mode of life at Savalmore' and it was his opinion that she would give her evidence clearly and well but he could himself speak about the family's lifestyle, as he had often stayed there for his summer holiday extending over several weeks. If a second witness was desirable, Eddy could attend, as he had lived there as a member of the family 'for a great part of each year'. Another objection to Molly having to appear was that 'Miss Flanagan can hardly do without her, even for a couple of days. Everybody in Newry knows that Molly very rarely left home and at Savalmore Jim and their own servants were not able to supply her place.' He was adamant that if Molly was to appear the family wanted an official assurance that she would be reasonably safe and adequately protected.[51]

The case was scheduled for hearing on 16 September 1922 but then adjourned. In mid November the Newry district inspector wrote to John Woulfe Flanagan about the hearing and suggested that it would be best if the whole family stayed in Belfast for the duration of the case, as Molly had 'such an aversion to staying in Newry'. Solicitors could talk to her there. The district inspector would arrange to have the place they stayed in 'supervised' and she would 'have only to travel to Newry once', with the party being accompanied on the journey by a police escort.[52] No press report of the much adjourned hearing has been located but on 1 May 1923 the solicitor acting for the family wrote to John Woulfe Flanagan that he was 'only sorry I could do no more in the case'. 'I promised the deceased', he added, 'if the worst happened I would look after the claim of his relatives and I was very pleased that my resignation of solicitorship to District Councils, shortly before the tragedy, enabled me to take charge of the application'. He again regretted that he had not been 'more successful' and referred to a question of domicile raised by the Northern government but confessed himself uncertain of how this 'affects your family'. 'I suppose they are trying to grab more revenue', he concluded, which perhaps suggests that higher compensation would have been paid if the entire family had been living in Northern Ireland.[53] The memory of the RM did not fade quickly for his family or for those closely involved in events. On the first anniversary of his death, his brother Johnny had a Mass said in Newry for the repose of his soul. The parish priest needed no reminder of the dead RM, whom he 'did not forget' on Pentecost Sunday, when 'the memory was very vivid with me of the awful scene on last Pentecost, when I knelt by his side and heard him pray forgiveness for his murderers.'[54]

In May of 1925 an unidentified friend or member of the extended family wrote from Dublin, where he or she was living and working for the new administration, to tell Johnny in London that there was 'a good deal of Flanagan news from Clyde Road.' The correspondent was 'fairly well informed' about recent events despite not having written to any of the family for some time. Johnny's brother, Dick ('looking very fit, but far too fat'), was 'home with me by order of Denis Shiel . . . supposed to have had a breakdown from overwork and worry.' The writer was 'glad to have him' and went on to say, 'I shall be anxious to know where Molly will come to anchor, and whether there is any chance of her and Eddie joining forces'. Stephen had been up at Warrenpoint for Easter where he was told:

> that a man who was shot dead by a RUC constable in Newry, who tried to arrest him, was known to the police as one of Jim's murderers. Did you hear that? The shooting was reported in the newspapers but there was no reference to the other matter. Stephen also told me that the anger of the police and others at Jim's murder had not died down, and that they are as eager as ever to get the culprits. It was all new to me as I thought the matter had been longed dropped.[55]

James Woulfe Flanagan's death was but one among many in the bloody years that witnessed the emergence of a new Ireland. In the annals of the struggle for freedom the resident magistrates who died, like the men of the RIC who lost their lives, have no place except as the enemy, part of the 'foreign garrison' and legitimate targets in a just War of Independence. Yet not the least part of the tragedy of the troubles was that the conflict so often involved Irishman against Irishman, divided by political allegiance but united in love of their country.

10

Edmund James Charles Dease, 1861–1945

Edmund J.C. Dease was born on 1 October 1861, the eldest son of Edmund Gerald Dease of Rath House, Ballybrittas, Queen's County (Laois) and his wife, Mary Grattan, who was the fourth daughter of Henry Grattan MP, of Temlock, Co. Wicklow, and grandaughter of the Irish Parliamentarian Henry Grattan (1746-1829). The Deases were a Catholic family, probably of Old English origin, whose estates were forfeited after the great rebellion of 1641 but later recovered. Their lands in Westmeath were bought back from the Pakenhams with the proceeds of property in Co. Cavan, which had been held in trust by the Pollards of Castle Pollard. By advantageous marriages the Dease's established themselves as members of the Catholic upper class that became increasingly integrated with the old Protestant Ascendancy during the nineteenth century.

Garret Dease of Turbotstown married in 1740 the daughter of Oliver Plunkett, of Rathmore Castle in Co. Meath. Their eldest son, Gerald (1790-1854), married in 1820 Elizabeth O'Callaghan of Kilgory, Co. Clare, who was co-heiress to her father. Three sons of this marriage were James Arthur (1826-74), Edmund Gerald (1829-1904), and Gerald Richard (1831-1903). James Dease strengthened the connection with the O'Reilly family of Co. Louth and established a tie of kinship with the English aristocracy by his marriage, in 1853, to Charlotte Jerningham.[1] Edmund Dease (father of the future RM) contributed to public life as a DL and JP for Queen's County (Laois) and as high sheriff during 1859. He was MP for the county from 1870 to 1880, a Commissioner of National Education and a member of the Senate of the Royal University of Dublin. Gerald Dease, of Celbridge Abbey, Co. Kildare, was JP for counties Kildare and Meath, honorary colonel of the 4th battalion of the Royal Irish Fusiliers, chamberlain to the vice-regal court at Dublin Castle, a director of several companies and also of the Bank of Ireland, of which he was Governor from 1890 to 1892. He was educated at Stoneyhurst, one of the leading Catholic public schools in England, and in 1863 he married Emily Throckmorton, the daughter of an English baronet. He was knighted in 1897, the year in which his eldest son married a daughter of Colonel Lascelles, from Cheshire. This marriage linked the Dease family to the earl of Harewood and so connected them distantly to the royal family of Britain.[2] The Deases were also well-connected with the Irish aristocracy, this generation being cousins to the earl of Fingall and to Lord Kenmare, who were two of the leading Irish Catholic peers.

These aristocratic cousins played some part in the lives of the Dease brothers. The land agent, Sam Hussey, recalled that Lord Kenmare selected one of his Catholic-unionist Dease cousins to stand for election in the late 1880s, in Co. Kerry, against a young Protestant landowner with Home Rule principles. This Mr Dease lost the election and while campaigning 'got a blow on his ribs at Castleisland, which told on his health, and he died soon after'.[3] Relations between one of the surviving brothers, Gerald Dease, and Lord Fingall were particularly close. Countess Fingall remembered Gerald Dease as 'Fingall's cousin and mentor'.[4] He was a frequent visitor at Killeen Castle in Co. Meath and the Fingalls in turn were often guests at Celbridge Abbey, which had been the home of Esther Vanhomrigh, Dean Swift's 'Vanessa'. (After her death in 1723 it passed into the possession of Thomas Marley, Lord Chief Justice and grandfather of the eminent Henry Grattan, and came to the Deases' by way of the marriage of Gerald's parents. Daisy Fingall made a romantic claim to have seen and heard Vanessa's ghost at Celbridge, 'crying in the garden by the waters of the Liffy'.)[5] Dease acted as agent for Fingall in looking after his Dublin property and the two worked together at Dublin Castle when Dease was Chamberlain and Fingall held office as State Steward. These were powerful figures on the social scene, who controlled the issuing of invitations for which competition was intense during the Castle season. The countess recalled her debut during the season of 1883 and remembered 'those tear-stained faces behind some lace curtain in Fitzwilliam or Merrion Square', as the mounted orderly from the Castle rode past the houses of those not graced with a summons to the levee or ball. There were no tears from the seventeen-year old Daisy Burke because 'Fingall saw to it' that she was always invited, but debutantes who hoped to get around Colonel Dease were less likely to find him easily persuaded. The most eagerly coveted invitations were for the small, intimate dances in the Throne Room but Dease 'had the hard heart of the perfect official' and did his duty 'admirably' by following protocol and resisting appeals for favouritism.[6] The chamberlain was just as unhelpful to the writer, George Moore, when he wrote to Dease in the winter of 1884-5 in the hope of an invitation to one of the dinner parties at the Castle. Moore had stayed at the Shelbourne Hotel the previous winter and attended various functions during the season but he was in search of more naturalistic detail for his novel dealing 'with the social and political power of the Castle in Modern Ireland', as he described *A Drama in Muslin*. Moore followed up his letter with notes delivered by messenger but no invitation was forthcoming, and eventually he was told that the lists were 'at present closed'. The writer then capitalised on his position by publishing the correspondence in the *Freeman's Journal*, and asking who were the people entitled to enjoy the costly entertainments given at the Castle if he, as a Mayo landowner and an author of serious purpose, was not to be admitted.[7] It was easy enough for Moore to poke fun at the Castle and scoff at the pretentious show of it all but the young Edmund Dease could hardly have wished for a more influential relative than his Uncle Gerald, whose role in Irish life went beyond playing the part of chamberlain to the viceregal court. Gerald Dease was one of the comparatively few Catholic members of the Kildare Street Club, and he was vice president of the Irish Loyal and Patriotic Union. Family connection and friendship linked him to Fingall's cousin, Horace Plunkett, and Gerald Dease became a member of the first committee of Plunkett's Irish Agricultural Organisation Society.[8] At the time of the second Home Rule Bill, he was one of the thirty-six 'men of rank and station' who joined six Catholic peers, including Fingall and Kenmare, in sponsoring a petition calling on the Commons to reject the Bill.[9]

Edmund Dease almost certainly owed his post as RM to the influence of his uncle. Edmund was educated in England at Oscott College and made his early career in the army, in the regiment of which Gerald Dease was an honorary colonel. Edmund Dease rose to the rank of major in the 4th battalion of the Royal Irish Fusiliers but he left the army when he was in his mid-thirties and it was probably the prospect of marriage (as it was for the fictional Major Yeates) that was the incentive to seek appointment as a resident magistrate. He resigned his commission on becoming RM for the Tralee district of Co. Kerry, in February 1896, and two months later he married Mabel More O'Ferral, the daughter of a Catholic gentry family from Co. Kildare.[10] The couple's first child, Richard Edmund Anthony, was born in Kerry in February 1897.

First appointments were generally made to vacant stations or, if there was a reshuffle of personnel, to one that was deemed appropriate in the light of a man's experience in his previous career but the timing of transfers and the location of postings thereafter were, as we have seen above in chapter four, areas in which resident magistrates' had some control of their working conditions, although their wishes were not always deferred to by the administrative division. It is highly likely that not all such requests were made formally through official channels and it seems that landowning resident magistrates (who tended to come from higher social class backgrounds and to have more extensive networks of influence than, for example, former police officers) often served for many years in districts conveniently located in counties adjoining that in which the family estate was located. So it was with

Edmund Dease, who was transferred to Co. Tipperary in 1900, the year in which his daughter, Marion, was born. He stayed in the same county for over twenty years, until the resident magistracy was abolished in 1922. He was stationed in the Nenagh district of the north riding of Co. Tipperary, which was some distance from his family home at Rath House, Ballybrittas, in the northeastern part of Queen's County (Laois), but considerably closer to it than he had been when serving in Co. Kerry. His father was by now an elderly man in his early eighties and the RM may have wanted to oversee his inheritance while continuing his work as a resident magistrate. Edmund Dease senior died in 1904 but his wife lived on at Rath House until her death in 1918. The RM and his family remained in Co. Tipperary, but while living at Yewston, Nenagh, Edmund Dease combined his duties as RM in Co. Tipperary with the roles of DL and JP for Queen's County.

The Major was an unremarkable RM judged by his infrequent appearances in official records. He seems to have been one of those RMs who lived the life of a country gentleman, kept his paperwork up to date, and was largely left alone by the Castle to do his work in his own way. In Tralee during the period of UIL activity his experiences were similar to those of James Woulfe Flanagan in Listowel, although Kerry was not among the most disturbed counties during 1898-1900.[11] Dease progressed to second and then first class RM by the early twentieth century and he was recognised by the Lord Lieutenant as qualified to adjudicate in special courts under the Criminal Law and Procedure Act (1887). He held an additional warrant for Limerick city, empowering him to carry out duties there at short notice in case of emergency. The people of his Nenagh district were 'well disposed towards the law', Dease reported in early 1914, 'and better disposed towards one another than they used to be.' He considered the Volunteers to be a potential threat to public order as it was his opinion that they were not under proper control or discipline and, if armed, 'would be a menace owing to the number of irresponsible individuals in their ranks.'[12]

Dease was responsible for only seven petty sessions or fourteen court sittings each month, and this light workload was reduced over time. One of his courts, at Borris-in-Ossory, was across the border in Queen's County but only this and one other were more than a twenty-mile journey from Nenagh. He did not attend any petty sessions at Rathdowney during January 1915 and seems to have cited the length of the journey as his excuse for non-attendance, with a suggestion that this court should be the responsibility of the RM in Templemore district. It was the opinion of officials in Dublin that Murray Hornibrook had 'already heavy duties' in Templemore, with eleven petty sessions or seventeen courts every month. Four of these were more than twenty miles from the designated headquarters of the district, but Hornibrook lived at Abbeyleix and from his home address he travelled over twenty miles to seven of his courts. There was little difference in mileage or inconvenience in getting to Rathdowney from either Nenagh or Abbeyleix. For Dease it entailed a journey of over twenty-nine miles, taking a train just after nine o' clock, while for Hornibrook it meant travelling twenty-five miles and getting a train a few minutes before nine o'clock. It was pointed out in a minute to the Assistant Under-Secretary that if Rathdowney was transferred to the Templemore district, Hornibrook would have 239 courts in the year whereas Dease had by this time only 152 courts annually.[13] Dease perhaps had more influence at the Castle than his colleague — he emerged the winner in this bureaucratic battle and Rathdowney was later included in the Templemore district.[14]

When the Great War began, the resident magistrate's only son was seventeen and not of an age for military service but he volunteered at the earliest opportunity. In 1915, Richard Dease joined the Southern Irish Horse and he served with that body in both France and Ireland. He later transferred to his Father's old regiment, the Royal Irish Fusiliers, with which he served until the end of the war. The Major himself offered his services to the war effort in June 1918, shortly after the anti-conscription crisis, when he wrote to the Conservative-unionist politician, Walter Long, who had been Chief Secretary for a short term in 1905. 'I don't know whether you remember me,' Dease began, 'but I had the pleasure of meeting you . . . some years ago, and also you were very kind to me when you were Chief Secretary over here.' He went on to apologise to Long for troubling him but asked to be considered 'for a post where my knowledge of this country would be of service. . . . I have been Resident Magistrate for twenty-two years, and feel I could do better work for the country, if I was required.'[15] Long replied promptly with assurances that he did indeed remember the RM and was very pleased to hear from him, adding that he would gladly do what he could to bring Dease's name 'before the Irish Government'. He wrote on the same day to the Lord Lieutenant and to the Chief Secretary, telling them that Dease was 'anxious, if possible, to help in the recruiting movement' and that he believed the RM to be 'a reliable man' who 'would be very useful'.[16] Nothing seems to have come of this, but resident magistrates' were active in organising recruiting drives in some counties and Dease was probably directed to local efforts in the Nenagh district.

He wrote again to Walter Long in November 1918, shortly after he and other members of the RMA had formed a deputation to the Castle about the resident magistrates' pay scales. The RMs were quite prepared to do additional work if required, Dease wrote, but the rising cost of living made it an urgent necessity that salaries were increased by £150 a year, 'as the very minimum . . . a Resident Magistrate at present, especially if he is married, cannot live on his pay, and unless he has private means, must get into debt'.[17] This was much the same argument as that put forward by resident magistrates' in the 1870s, but there had been no increase in salary for nearly fifty years and they certainly had a genuine grievance in 1918. Long acknowledged the strength of their case and assured Dease that the resident magistrates would have his full support, if he was 'consulted by the Irish Government' on the matter.[18]

Edmund Dease's experiences of the troubles were not in any way exceptional, or so it seems from official records although the local newspapers might well reveal his involvement in some particular incidents. The Volunteers in the area were arming themselves with weapons and explosives by 1917[19] and there was considerable IRA activity in Co. Tipperary during 1919-21.[20] He missed courts because of illness at times, as in the spring of 1920 when he was unwell and did no duty for three days at the beginning of March. He was then on sick leave from 19 March to 5 April. Most of his petty sessions courts were still being held, with the difficulty experienced elsewhere, and at Borriskane on 5 May 1920 he noted that 'local justices attended' but only two cases were scheduled for hearing. The munitions embargo was now underway, lasting from May to December 1920, and as it spread from Kingstown (Dun Laoghaire) throughout the country it came to include a refusal to carry armed troops. The strike was one of the contributions made by organised labour to the struggle for freedom and it caused considerable disruption to rail traffic. The Major missed his petty sessions court at Roscrea on 21 June 'because of train strike' but does not seem to have been otherwise greatly inconvenienced.[21]

In the new Ireland that emerged from the troubles the RMs main concern was for his son and heir. In May 1922 Edmund Dease wrote to Walter Long (now Lord Long of Wraxall) in the belief that Long was 'taking charge of the RIC Bill in the House of Lords'. The RM explained that when his son, Richard, was demobilised after the war he had expressed an interest in joining the RIC. Dease had 'sent him to a crammer' but no examinations were held for officer cadets in the exceptional circumstances of 1920. Cadetships were awarded by a selection board which placed young Dease second 'out of 700 candidates, all of whom had served in the war'.[22] (It is worth noting that Edmund Dease's cousin, W.J. O'Reilly RM, was a member of the selection board that interviewed prospective cadets in Dublin on 26 May 1920.)[23] Richard Dease was appointed on 15 June and after two months training he was posted to Co. Sligo, where he served until the RIC was disbanded. Police records do not identify Richard Dease as a member of the Auxiliary Division RIC but as a standard district inspector, third class, and it seems that he joined the RIC in hope of a conventional career in the constabulary. The process of disbanding the RIC began in January 1922 but it was not until the 25 April that Richard Dease was formally discharged. He then went home to Rath House, where 'he received warnings, that could not be disregarded, that if he remained in the Queen's County his life would be taken, and this house burnt, and that he was to leave Ireland at once, and not return'. Other members of the RIC were similarly intimidated out the country, and as an officer who joined the constabulary in 1920 Richard Dease would have been a particular target of hostility. To his Father it seemed outrageous that any member of 'that gallant and loyal force' should be driven from home, 'to save their lives being taken by their own countrymen.' The RM wrote to Long after his son had gone to England seeking work, with only a small pension for income and no gratuity to 'help him on', but it was Richard's long term prospects that most concerned the Major:

> He, unlike many others, has a stake in this country, as he will have this place on my death, and through no fault of his own, but merely because he did his duty, he has to leave Ireland to save his own life and prevent his home from being burnt. He could not offer to join the North of Ireland police, because if he did, he would never be able to set foot in the Southern Provinces again.[24]

It was Edmund Dease's hope that the particulars of his son's case might be of use to Long and in some way 'help to get better terms' for the officers and men of the RIC.

Richard Dease did not live to inherit Rath House.[25] He continued to serve British interests, by joining the Indian police force. In 1923 he married the daughter of a colonel in the Worcestershire regiment and a daughter was born to the couple in 1925, but the marriage later ended in divorce. During the Second World War, he served as a pilot officer in the RAF Volunteer Reserve and was killed in action on 24 November 1940. Edmund Dease lived on to a great age at Rath House, Ballybrittas, in what was now Co. Laois. He died on his eighty-fourth birthday, 1 October 1945.

William Joseph O'Reilly, 1864-1937

This final biographical study focuses on the historical background and life of W.J. O'Reilly, whose family were of Gaelic origin. The O'Reilly's claim descent from Aodh Finn ('Hugh the Fair'), king of Connacht in the early seventh century. They were chieftains of the eastern part of the ancient territory of Breffney, 'Breffney O'Reilly', which was formed into the county of Cavan in the 1560s. The branch of the O'Reillys with which we are concerned here can trace their lineage to Maolmordha (Myles) O'Reilly, who was elected chief of East Breffney in 1536, and who married a daughter of Hugh Duff O'Donnell, the chief of Tyrconnell. His eldest son was elected chief in 1565 and knighted in 1579. His third son, Edmund, was elected Tanist or heir apparent in 1586 and became chief of East Breffney in 1598.

The first of Edmund O'Reilly's three marriages was to a daughter of the Plunkett family and the second to a daughter of the thirteenth Baron Devlin, which connected the O'Reillys to the earl of Westmeath. Edmund's grandson, Brian O'Reilly, married the Hon. Mary Plunkett, daughter of the eighth baron of Dunsany. The eldest son of this marriage, 'Myles the Slasher' O'Reilly, was high sheriff of Co. Cavan but took part in the rebellion of 1641 and proved himself an able military officer during the civil war that followed. He is said to have commanded a company of horse that successfully defended the bridge at Finea, Westmeath, against an attack in August 1646 by a numerically superior English force. Accounts of his fate differ, in one version he is said to have been the last of the defenders to fall at Finea, just as reinforcements arrived from Granard, but another version states that he fled to Spain and later went to France, where he died in 1660 and was buried in the Irish monastery at Chalons-sur-Marne.[1]

Myles's son, John O'Reilly, was a landowner in Co. Cavan and MP for the county in 1689. He later raised a regiment of Dragoons at his own expense for the service of King James II and two of his sons were captains in this regiment, which fought at the Battle of the Boyne in 1690. Following the defeat of James II, Catholics were excluded from all public life under the penal laws and the ownership of land was subject to complex restrictions and conditions under a branch of the penal code. Property had to be divided rather than passed by primogeniture to the eldest son, but a son who turned Protestant could dispossess his brothers and take over the estate undivided. It seems that the O'Reilly family were predominantly Protestant during the eighteenth and early nineteenth centuries, although in two generations there were 'wild geese' serving in Spanish regiments.[2]

Matthew O'Reilly (c.1756-c.1782) of Knock Abbey, Tallinstown, Co. Louth was remembered in the family and in local folklore of the early twentieth century as 'Matt O'Rua', a red-haired 'Black Protestant' who had 'turned' to save his lands. By his first marriage he had two sons and a daughter, Anna Maria, who married into the Dease family discussed above, in chapter ten. Matthew O'Reilly's second marriage produced five more sons and another daughter. The sixth son, Dowell (1795-1855) became Attorney General of Jamaica and his younger brother, Richard (1814-60), was a judge in Jamaica. The eldest son, another Matthew (1779-1841), married in 1830 the younger daughter of Revd Hon. George de la Poer Beresford, who was the second son of the first Baron Decie and Protestant Archbishop of Tuam. Another of the de la Poer Beresford daughters had married Matthew's cousin, Myles O'Reilly of Queen's County, in 1829.

When Matthew O'Reilly died in 1841 he was succeeded by his half-brother, William, who had married his cousin, Margaret Dowell O'Reilly, in 1820. This William O'Reilly (1792-1844) was a JP for Co. Louth and MP for Dundalk, 1832-5. According to the family tradition it was he who reverted to the Catholic faith. He is said to have been influenced by the Oxford Move-ment for the revival of Catholic doctrine and observance in the Church of England, which began in the early 1830s and led to the 'conversion to Rome' of such prominent people as J.H. Newman (later Cardinal Newman) in 1845 and the Archdeacon of Chichester, H.H. Manning, who joined the Roman Catholic church in 1850.[3] In the O'Reilly family the reversion to the old faith of William O'Reilly was long remembered as a cause of considerable upset and ill-feeling, particularly because of the family's close connections to the Protestant Archbishop of Tuam.

William and Margaret O'Reilly had a daughter and one son, Myles William Patrick O'Reilly, who was born in March 1825. He was educated in England at St Cuthbert's College, Ushaw, Co. Durham, and at London University before taking a degree in law at the University of Louvain in Rome. When he came into his estate at Knock Abbey he also inherited property at Knockengin, Balbriggan, Co. Dublin, and his land comprised over 4,000 acres in Co. Galway as well as more than 400 in Co. Louth. The annual valuation of his 4,561 acres was £1,964 in the 1870s.[4] Myles O'Reilly was a DL and JP for Co. Louth and high sheriff in 1848. He was also a captain in the Louth militia, a JP for Co. Dublin and later an Assistant Commissioner for Intermediate Education. In August 1859 he married Ida Jerningham, the second daughter of Edmund Jerningham of Rutland Gate, Hyde Park, London, and so formed a link with the English aristocracy.[5] (Ida's older sister, Charlotte, had married James Dease, an uncle of Edmund Dease RM, in 1853.) Within months of her marriage, when pregnant with her first child, Ida O'Reilly was at her husband's side as he commanded the Irish Battalion of St Patrick in the Papal army.

Italian nationalists, led by Garibaldi, demanded in 1859 that Pope Pius IX should surrender the northern papal provinces of Romagna, Umbria and the Marches. This the Pope refused to do, and when excommunication failed to bring the nationalists into line he sent emissaries to several western European countries to request arms and men for a Catholic campaign. Some 1,400 men left Ireland for Vienna in the spring of 1860, despite efforts by the British to limit recruiting and a proclamation reminding the people that under the Foreign Enlistment Act those joining the Papal army were liable to punishment. In September 1860, before the largely untrained Irish force was ready for action, the Papal States were invaded. O'Reilly eventually took command of the Irish Battalion, with the rank of Major, and he has been credited with turning an 'undisciplined rabble' into a splendid body of fighting men. He was given the specific task of defending the old fort of Rocca, atop a hill beside the walled town of Spoleto about sixty miles south of Florence. Although heavily outnumbered in terms of manpower and weapons, the Irish suffered small losses and inflicted considerable casualties on the Italian forces before O'Reilly, with virtually no ammunition left and the walls of Spoleto breached, decided to surrender. Ida O'Reilly and the wives of other soldiers had been allowed by the Italian general to leave the fort for safe custody the day before the bombardment began. This gentlemanly way of conducting battle continued after the surrender, when the garrison was permitted to march out as prisoners of war with the officers still wearing their swords.[6] The Irish prisoners were returned to Cork in the following November but, according to the family tradition, Myles O'Reilly was not held in captivity. He brought home from the campaign what became known to succeeeding generations as 'the Pope's table', a personal gift from Pius IX to Myles O'Reilly in recognition of his service at Spoleto.

Myles and Ida O'Reilly's first child, Mary Pia Walburga, was born in December 1860 and within a few months Ida was again pregnant. A second daughter, Edith Mary, was born in January 1862. Newspaper reports show that Myles O'Reilly was in Brussels at about the time of Edith's birth when, back in Ireland, the Catholic clergy of Longford began to organise opposition to the Liberal MP, Colonel Luke White. White had recently accepted the post of Lord of the Treasury for Ireland, despite having been elected as a

Home Rule candidate who had pledged himself to 'keep aloof' from government office. It was reported in *The Times* of 20 February 1862 that at a 'public meeting' attended by 'not a single layman' the clergy of Co. Longford had decided to support 'any honest independent gentleman' who was willing to stand for election.[7] A few days later it was reported that the Longford clergy had resolved to adopt Major Myles O'Reilly as the independent candidate, and to bear all his election expenses. *The Times* correspondent reminded readers that O'Reilly was well known as the commander of the Irish volunteers who had fought for the Pope. Arguing that the priests' seemed to believe it was their 'exclusive right and privilege' to decide who represented Longford, the journalist suggested that if O'Reilly was 'returned to the Imperial Parliament he will be as truly in the service of the Pope as when he was at the head of his volunteers in Italy'.[8] O'Reilly arrived from Brussels in time for the nominations and issued an electoral address in which he promised to oppose the 'sacrilegious invasion and robbery pursued by Piedmont', and to work for reform of the education system to provide 'free Catholic education', for reform of the Poor Law and the grand jury system, and for an extension of the franchise and the secret ballot. 'Seeking no favour of any', he concluded, 'I shall hold myself independent of every Government. My votes shall be influenced solely by the interests of my constituents, of our country, and of our religion'.[9] The nominations went off quietly enough although it was reported that 'a rabble of miserable looking peasants of the Connaught type, who had come in from the country armed with sticks' gathered in front of the court house, shouting for 'the O'Reilly'.[10] The election itself, however, was allegedly such a violent affair that the degree of intimidation 'rendered the polling a farce', although O'Reilly and his supporters denied these charges. He was elected with a majority of over 500 and took his seat in Parliament but within weeks the House of Commons was petitioned to declare the election null and void.[11] The Longford election was discussed in the House in May but it became apparent that his opponents had much exaggerated the violence and intimidation and O'Reilly retained his seat.[12] He was MP for Longford from 1862 to 1879. He spoke most frequently on education in Ireland, on distress in the country, on land tenure and the need for labourers cottages, and the appointment of Catholic chaplains to the Indian army.

Meanwhile the family grew over the years, with the birth of William Joseph (the future RM) on 16 February 1864 being followed by that of Edmund Joseph in 1866, Charles Myles in 1869, and Francis Joseph in 1872. The children were left motherless in April 1878 when Ida O'Reilly died, and in Febrary 1880 the death of Myles O'Reilly made orphans of them at ages ranging from eight to twenty. They were shared about among the extended family in a way not uncommon in the nineteenth century, when death all too often broke up a family unit before the children had reached full adulthood. Ida's sister Charlotte, Aunt 'Chas' Dease, had been widowed in 1874 but she took in Mary and Edith and also provided a home for William when he was on holiday from his school in England. Charles Myles, aged eleven, was despatched to the French branch of the family, to be cared for by descendants of his great-aunt Margaret who had married the Baron de Bellgarde, Siegneur de Laran of Toulouse, in 1765. Edmund and Francis are believed to have been brought up by relations in England. Aunt Chas had a large family of her own but her sons were by now in their thirties. One of her nine daughters had died in infancy, in 1872, and in 1880 the eldest of the girls married (as his second wife) the third earl of Gainsborough. Four of the Dease daughters became nuns and another two married but one remained single until her death in the 1920s. Mary and Edith O'Reilly had company of their own age among their numerous cousins but, no doubt, considerable competition in the marriage market and both were unwed.

William, aged sixteen in 1880, continued his education at his Father's old school, St Cuthbert's College, and followed his example by going on to the University of London; he then studied at the Temple Inns and qualified as a barrister. At the age of twenty-one he inherited Knock Abbey and the rest of the O'Reilly estates. His niece, when in her nineties, summarised what she had heard of her Uncle William's way of life during the period 1885-1900 as follows:

> He inherited a large estate . . . of 2,000 acres, and went to live at Knock Abbey . . . his friends were Lord Louth of Louth Hall and Sir Vere Foster of Glyde Court, these friends also inherited their estates at an early age . . . he kept a string of polo ponies, travelled the world, and spent all his money! He spent his time hunting, fishing, shooting, and travelling.[13]

Knock Abbey (known earlier as Thomastown Castle), at Tallinstown near the village of Louth, was a tower house typical of those found throughout Co. Louth, being four stories high with a barrel-vaulted, stone-flagged ground floor from which stone steps led up to what had originally been a large hall.[14] This had been converted into a private chapel at Knock Abbey. Above it were other rooms, used by William O'Reilly as his bedroom and study. The tower house had been added to by a three-storey Georgian wing and also an early nineteenth-century Gothic wing, to create a substantial house of some fifty rooms. O'Reilly further improved the property by constructing a third avenue to the Abbey, which he planted with lime trees and finished off with a lodge built at the new entrance gates. He took his place as a DL and JP for the county and in 1910 was on the role for high sheriff. His main recreations in middle life were hunting, shooting and golf, and for many years he was secretary to the Louth Horse Show. Like many other RMs, he was a member of the United Services Club in Dublin. In addition to being a resident magistrate from 1907 until 1922 he was at various times a member of Ardee Rural Council and of Louth County Council, and chairman of the Court of Referees instituted under the Insurance Act. His intellectual and political pursuits included writing occasional articles (published in the *New Ireland Review*) on such topics as religious persecution in France and Irish economic problems. Like his Father, William O'Reilly was particularly interested in Catholic education. He wrote and spoke publicly on the University question and gave evidence to the Royal Commission (1906) which resulted in the establishment of the National University. From 1906 to 1920, O'Reilly was one of the Commissioners of Intermediate Education. This interest was shared with Dr W.J. Walsh (1841-1921), the Catholic Archbishop of Dublin from 1885 until his death in 1921, who had been a close friend of O'Reilly's Father and who used Knock Abbey as his summer residence for some years after his appointment as archbishop. Dr Walsh was a member of the senate of the Royal University of Ireland (1883-84) and a keen advocate of a Catholic system of education. He became the first Chancellor of the National University in 1908. He was also an ardent nationalist who supported in turn the Land League, Parnell and the Irish Parliamentary Party, and Sinn Féin; he strongly opposed the Government of Ireland Act (1920) which partitioned the country.[15]

William O'Reilly did not marry and his two sisters, although frequent visitors to Knock Abbey, lived together independently at nearby Whitemills. Edmund O'Reilly joined the British army and was killed in action in South Africa during the closing stages of the Boer war, in March 1902. Francis O'Reilly was dimly recalled by Fris O'Reilly as something of a 'black sheep', living rather disreputably in Dublin, but her Uncle William took a special interest in his younger brother's eldest son, born in 1897, who became a Catholic priest. Charles Myles O'Reilly went to Sandhurst after his years in France and thereafter joined the Indian army. The Abbey was home to him when on leave and also to his wife and family when he was away on service. He married Sybil, fourth daughter of the Hon. B.J. Stapleton, in February 1899 and so formed another link between the O'Reillys and the English aristocracy.[16]

Charles and Sybil O'Reilly had four children: Brian (*b.*1900), Ida (*b.*1902), Frideswide ('Fris', *b.*1903), and Charles Hugh (*b.*1908). Frideswide was born in Oxford and named for the patron saint of that city. The children grew up thinking of Knock Abbey as their family home and they lived privileged lives

similar to those of English children born into a country estate, being rather
indulged by the servants and treated with deference by the few other social
inferiors with whom they came into contact. The gulf between them and the
bare-foot boys and girls they saw at Reaghstown chapel was instilled at an
early age by encounters such as that at Whitemills, where their Aunts Mary
and Edith entertained the schoolchildren of Dromin to an annual sportsday.
William O'Reilly usually acted as director of events, but in 1906 he was
unable to attend and his place was taken by Major C.M. O'Reilly and the six-
year old 'Master Brian'. Flat races, sack races, and egg and spoon races were
followed by country dancing and then the 'feasting' of tea and cakes. Before
the Major and his children left, Master Brian distributed the prizes and 'had
the pleasure of awarding himself and his two little sisters, Miss Biddy (Ida)
and Miss Baby (Fris), several prizes for the successes they had scored'. He
then made a short speech, telling all present 'I am glad you enjoyed the
games, so did I, and I hope we will all meet again next year.'[7] For the
O'Reilly children there were plenty of treats and amusements all year round
but their adored 'Mummy' was a rather remote figure and with their Father
away for long tours of duty it was Uncle William who largely filled the
paternal role in their lives, in which Nanny was an especially important
figure.

The O'Reilly estate had been reduced under the various land acts passed
since 1885. The acres in Galway were long gone and Knock Abbey was
diminished to a tenantless property of about 400 acres, run by a land steward
as a mixed farm. The farm labourers and their families lived in seven cottages
owned by O'Reilly, and an RIC pensioner and his elderly sister lived in the
lodge beside the gates to the main avenue. At the turn of the century the
Knock Abbey household included five living-in domestic staff (a cook, a
parlour maid, two housemaids, and a Dublin-born nurse for baby Brian)[18]
plus several daily maids and women who helped with the heavier chores. The
outdoor staff included a head gardener and under-gardener. There were some
forty outbuildings around Knock Abbey, set off to one side where a small
cottage between the big house and the stableyard was lived in by Nat Blackwell,
the head gardener, and his wife, Annie. There were coach houses, a harness
room, and a small forge as well as the stables around the yard. Beyond was
the farmyard, with barns and cow houses, calf sheds, the piggery, fowl house
and dairy, and stores for turf and potatoes. There was also an estate workshop
and a laundry. As well as the pleasure garden, with its borders and beds and
rockeries, there was a fern house, and shrubberies and 'walks' in chestnut
groves beyond which stretched wooded parkland bounded by the tree-lined
avenues. A walled kitchen garden and extensive greenhouses behind the farmyard kept the household supplied with most of its fresh vegetables and fruit.

As Fris remembers it, the laundry was unused in her childhood, when the washing was collected weekly by carrier and taken to the convent in Dundalk. There were other changes as the family grew, with the Dublin nurse being replaced by an English Protestant nanny (the only non-Irish, non-Catholic in the household or on the estate) and a succession of largely unmemorable governesses. None of the governesses stayed long ('we were too naughty, I suppose', Fris O'Reilly remarked) but one from Co. Wexford was remembered as departing even more quickly than was usual, within days of taking up her post. The neighbouring county families made up the immediate social circle of the O'Reillys at Knock Abbey, the Filgates at Lissrenny and the Bellews at Barmeath Castle, Dunleer, as well as Lord Louth at Louth Hall and the Vere Fosters at Glyde Court. The Vere Fosters' younger daughter ('little Dorothy in her red shoes', in the famous family portrait painted by William Orpen in 1907) was 'best friend' to Fris in her childhood and for many years after.[19]

The O'Reillys, like other families of their kind, were much less well-off by the early twentieth century than they had been in the middle nineteenth century and it was because 'he needed the money' that William O'Reilly sought appointment to the resident magistracy, or so his niece believed. She also understood that his connection with the Dease family helped him to obtain the post of RM in November 1907. He was stationed in the Killeshandra district of Co. Cavan and served there until 1917. There was at first little change in the routine at Knock Abbey, apart from the RM being away all week and at home for weekends, which suggests that he stayed in a hotel in Cavan during his first years as RM. There were several economies made, however, as the steward was dismissed about this time and some of the farmland was let. It seems that somewhat later, rather than run two households, the family and domestic staff moved between Co. Cavan and Co. Louth, leaving Knock Abbey partly closed up for much of the year.[20] At the time of the 1911 census the gardener Nat Blackwell and his wife were living in the big house, presumably as caretakers.[21] At the Abbey, Sybil O'Reilly fulfilled the role of lady of the house, taking the part of hostess when her brother-in-law entertained, holding the keys to the store cupboards, making decisions about household arrangements, and having considerable say over the design of the garden and such matters, and she seems to have done the same in Co. Cavan. The RM took a lease on a property called Rice Hill, in 1912,[22] and a note in Sybil O'Reilly's hand, found in her gardening book, listed 'curtains for Will . . . see about pictures for Will' among other domestic affairs needing attention.[23]

O'Reilly was a concientious but not over-zealous resident magistrate. The records show that in some years he contacted Dublin Castle only two or three times, other than submitting his monthly summary of duty, and he did so more often over a triviality (such as not having received his official diary) than to make any particular report on his district. He was not among those RMs recognised as qualifed to hear cases under the coercion acts and so never sat in a court of summary jurisdiction but he held an additional warrant for Belfast, and served there on special duty during the disturbed summer of 1912.[24] He reported in early 1914 that the Killeshandra district was 'satisfactory' but that 'a very acute divergence of feelings' was evident over the Home Rule Bill. Both the UVF and the Volunteers were 'strongly established' in Co. Cavan but he did not anticipate any danger to the peace until the Bill was 'definitely passed into law or definitely rejected.'[25] His petty sessions in the Killeshandra district provided entertainment for his nieces on occasion for sometimes, if there were only a few routine cases scheduled, he would take Fris and her sister to the courts to listen to the proceedings.

The family still spent much time at Knock Abbey. Sybil and her children were there during 1915 when Charles O'Reilly was home from India on a long leave. The boys went away to school but the last of the girls' governesses was one of the household that summer, a young French woman remembered by Fris as 'very pretty but very unhappy'. It did not occur to the twelve year old Miss O'Reilly to connect the governess's unhappiness with the Great War, or to ask where she went when she suddenly left, but there were other things worrying the young Fris at the time. There was some serious family disagreement going on, the cause of which was unknown in the schoolroom but that there was something wrong was apparent in 'Mummy's' withdrawn and occasionally tearful behaviour. The girls' later discovered that Sybil O'Reilly and the gardener, Nat Blackwell, had an acrimonious exchange at a garden party or public fete in the Abbey grounds, which ended with the autocratic Sybil dismissing him or threatening him with dismissal for what she considered to be insolence. Despite his devotion to Sybil, William would not hear of dismissing Nat, a trusted servant who had been with the family since he was a boy of ten, and this alone would surely have offended his sister-in-law. Mary and Edith O'Reilly were also at Knock Abbey then and it is possible that 'the old Aunts' made the situation worse, by accusing Sybil of having always presumed too much upon their brother's good will towards her. Mary and Edith O'Reilly may have resented the younger woman acting as mistress of Knock Abbey when she had less claim to do so than they themselves. Whatever the reason, Sybil O'Reilly decided that her position in the household was intolerable and that she would accompany her husband back to India, leaving the children variously at school or at Knock Abbey under the care of their Uncle William. Her husband was reluctant to agree to this because of the dangers at sea with the war on but he eventually booked their passage on the P&O steamship *Persia*. The vessel sailed from London for Bombay at the end of the year but on the 30 December it was torpedoed in the Mediterranean. The liner went down within minutes. Only four lifeboats were launched and some 400 passengers and crew were lost. Fifty-nine passengers, including Charles O'Reilly, were among the 153 survivors picked up and landed at Alexandria but Sybil O'Reilly was one of the dead.[26] This brought substantial changes to the O'Reilly children, whose Father turned to his sister-in-law, Veronica, for advice and guidance about his family. The governess was not replaced but for a while the local schoolmistress came up to the Abbey to give lessons, until the girls were sent to an English convent boarding school. In 1921, Charles O'Reilly married Veronica and the couple lived thereafter chiefly in Bath, England, although they continued to make long visits to the family home in Ireland.

William O'Reilly was transferred to the Navan district of Co. Meath in February 1917, and there rented a house called Beechmount at which his nieces sometimes stayed for school holidays. This was another comparatively quiet district although O'Reilly had responsibility for seventeen petty sessions or nineteen courts each month, four of them in Co. Cavan and one in Co. Westmeath. As the political situation deteriorated he became increasingly concerned to be at home, at Knock Abbey, and during 1918-1920 he made several requests to the authorities in Dublin for permission to run his Co. Meath district from his estate in Co. Louth.[27] This was not granted. There was some disruption to the courts in the Navan district, as elsewhere, and monthly summaries of duty show that from the beginning of 1920 O'Reilly's record of attendance fell off sharply. In January he went to only eight petty sessions and did 'no duty' on twelve days. He was 'at station' on eleven days but this vague term could cover time devoted to paper work or simply being available if any official matter required the attention of the RM. At the Oldcastle sessions on 19 January there was 'nothing of importance' and on 28 January he heard 'only two trifling cases' at the Dunboyne court. He was rather busier in May 1920, when in addition to his petty sessions he also attended a Quarter Sessions hearing and a sitting of the Court of Referees as well as being engaged for several days on 'office work'. On 26 May the RM was in Dublin for the RIC selection board and on 31 May he travelled to London for the same purpose, where the selection board conducted interviews for five days, until 5 June. In early October, O'Reilly was on sick leave for almost a fortnight and the rest of the month was enlivened only by the commital of a lunatic at Navan. He was again on sick leave in the last week of November and for virtually the whole of December. He worked only intermittently during the first months of 1921, when at the Virginia sessions in February he heard a police prosecution against Michael Fitzsimmons, who was 'living in a pig-sty at the end of the town'. The building was said to be 5' x 4', completely unfurnished and with no bedding of any sort for Fitzsimmons, his wife and four children. The RM imposed no penalty on the labourer but gave him one week to move out.[28]

In March 1921 O'Reilly was marginally involved in an incident that was perhaps of more significance than the press coverage suggests. During the night of 1-2 March a sentry at the Navan military barracks heard two shots fired in quick succession, and the guard was turned out to investigate but found nothing. Next morning the body of an unknown man, who had evidently been dead for several hours, was found dumped in the lane leading to the RMs house. The victim was a man in his thirties, who had been shot in the head and the chest, and his description matched that of a stranger seen the previous day in the town and on the Trim road. The man was reported to have 'got his tea from some people, and is alleged to have stated that he was a Black and Tan and had been dismissed'.[29] The murder was in itself not exceptional in the circumstances but the body was not found in the area from which the shots were heard. It was perhaps left on the avenue as a reminder to the RM of the possible fate of those who served the Crown, and it is not unreasonable to suppose that O'Reilly's part in recruiting Black and Tans in England was known to the IRA in Navan.

There is no documentary evidence of any direct threat ever being made by the IRA to the RM but a version of this incident passed into the O'Reilly family lore. Asked about her Uncle William's experiences during the troubles, his niece said that 'The only threat to William O'Reilly's life was while at Beechmount. While driving along the avenue, the Sinn Féin were going to shoot him. One man recognised him, and told them not to shoot. He said "he is one of us. A good man and a fair judge".'[30] This is of some interest because the event has been modified over many years of telling, to show the RM as a loyal man in danger yet as essentially at one with Catholic, nationalist Ireland despite his ascendancy status and his involvement with the administration of British rule in Ireland. As a Catholic from a family with a strong tradition of support for Home Rule, O'Reilly undoubtedly found his dual loyalty tested during this period. In the opinion of his niece, the RM became increasingly disillusioned with British policy in Ireland and was horrified by such atrocities as the sacking of Balbriggan. She believed, from later conversations with him, that by the time of the Truce he was sympathetic to Sinn Féin and had come to respect and admire Michael Collins, in particular. She had no recollection of his ill health from late 1921 and on into 1922 but suggested that it might have been of nervous origin, caused by the strain he was under. O'Reilly's recurring illness was commented on by Christopher Lynch-Robinson (resident magistrate for the Dundalk district), who covered for his sick colleague by attending many courts in the Navan district[31] over some six or seven months. O'Reilly was again on sick leave from shortly after the body was found on his avenue at Beechmount until 23 May 1921. During that time he made a lengthy visit to France, from where he wrote to Fris at school in England with descriptions of the battlefields in the north of that country but with no mention of his health or of the situation in Ireland.

Some news from Ireland reached Fris in letters from Nat Blackwell, who addressed her as Miss O'Reilly and signed off as 'old gardener'. In an undated letter apparently written in early 1921 he gave a detailed account of the plants in the conservatory and the snowdrops 'like snow' along the avenue and told Fris that her clematis from Navan was 'a grand plant now'. Mrs Campbell had bought her hen house, and Nat hoped she liked the price he had obtained for it; he had, as instructed, given the last of her hens to another of the cottagers, who was 'very glad of the bird'. Mr O'Reilly had bought a new hunter 'as black as night – I am shure if the Ladys was home you would have many a good spin', but there had not been much hunting for the gentlemen because of the troubles. Nat had 'a great time with Master Hugh' in the Christmas holidays but their sport had been affected by the removal of all weapons from Knock Abbey, 'so [we] had nothing better to catch our game and wildfowl but the rabbit trap as the gun was taken from us'. 'You know Erin is not as it should be', he wrote, 'when we go to town we do not know if we walk or be carried home' but 'every one that knew the Ladys, seems to me that is everyone round say four miles of the Abbey, be allways be asking for yous,' and Nat himself was looking forward to seeing Fris and her sister back in Ireland for the summer.[32]

It is not clear when the RM gave up Beechmount and left Navan but in Co. Louth after the resident magistrates were suspended in August 1922 he found himself in an area where there was considerable conflict between the forces of the Free State and the anti-Treaty Irregulars. Some 1,000 Irregulars descended on Dundalk in the early hours of 14 August and attacked the national army barracks and two police barracks. After heavy fighting for two hours they captured all three buildings but not without losses on both sides, and there were civilians among the dead and wounded. It was rumoured that Drogheda had also been taken by the anti-Treaty forces but this was not the case, although over the following days there were clashes in various places and railway bridges were blown up. Trim and Ardee were reported to be quiet but there was some fighting in Dunleer. The Irregulars evacuated Dundalk within three days and it was reported on 18 August that national troops were again in control, some of them pursuing the Irregulars 'to the mountain fastnesses' outside the town.[33] As the civil war progressed growing numbers of the big houses of Ireland were burned by the IRA. The houses of senators were particular targets but the Chief of Staff of the republican forces had ordered that the homes of "'Imperialists (ex-DL type)'" should also be destroyed.[34] Such arson attacks were often carried out as reprisals after the execution of IRA men, of which there were many, for the Irish Free State dealt ruthlessly with the men of violence. In Dundalk six Irregulars were executed within little more than a week during January 1923,[35] and a spate of attacks on the big houses of Co. Louth followed swiftly. One of those reduced to a gutted ruin was Milestown Castle near Castlebellingham, seven miles south of Dundalk. It was owned by an English army officer who was in residence, with his wife and four children and eight servants, when ten armed men (most of them said to be 'hardly seventeen years of age') raided the Castle.[36]

While the 'big burnings' were taking place in the Castlebellingham district it was rumoured several times that Knock Abbey had been similarly attacked but, as it was not raided at the height of the arson campaign, 'it was hoped that such a fine residence, owned by one of the principle Catholic families' would be spared.[37] This was not to be. The Abbey was at risk because of William O'Reilly's having been not only a DL but also a resident magistrate, and if it was known that he had helped in the recruitment of the Auxies and Black and Tans that, too, would have been held against him. Moreover, the family had a tradition of service in the British army and in the spring of 1923 Lt Colonel Charles Myles O'Reilly was back home in Ireland with his second wife. It may have been the presence of a senior British officer that provoked the attack on Knock Abbey, which came one Friday evening during the first week of March. Four men armed with revolvers and carrying tins of petrol came into the house at about ten o'clock, having 'gained entrance' through the kitchen. They were met by Charles O'Reilly and asked him if there were arms in the house. They were told there were not, and went on to the smoking room where they found William O'Reilly and informed him that they were there to burn the house. The family and servants were given time to gather some personal belongings, while the raiders sprinkled petrol on every floor and staircase. Then fires were started simultaneously in several places and flames were already shooting up as the O'Reillys' and their staff were told to clear out. The Abbey was well ablaze within minutes and the fire, fanned by a high wind, lit up the surrounding countryside for miles. William and Charles O'Reilly ran to the stables to quieten the frightened horses and were still trying to soothe them when they heard the rattle of machine guns. Young Pat Adams, the herd's son, had been quick to realise what was happening and he had the initiative to set off on his bicycle to alert the Free State force at Ardee. Troops were rushed to Tallinstown in a Crossley tender and dismounted at the lodge to make their way on foot up the avenue towards the burning Abbey. There were an unknown number of men posted in the shrubbery and around the house, who replied to machine gun fire from the troops with rifle and revolver shots. Two of the raiders, one of them slightly wounded in the thigh, surrendered but the others escaped. 'A peculiar story' was told by some of the eyewitnesses, who included the farm workers and villagers who had 'rushed to the conflagration'. It was said that when the fire was raging furiously like 'a furnace' one of the young raiders was seen disappearing through the main door, walking directly into the heart of the blaze, and he 'was not observed leaving again'. William O'Reilly paid high tribute to the prompt and plucky action of his neighbours, whose efforts helped to save some parts of the building and a considerable amount of the furniture, but the original tower was 'almost a heap of ruins' and the total damage was estimated to be between £20,000 and £30,000. The barrel-vaulted ceiling over the stone hall of the tower survived intact but all that was saved from the chapel above was a chalice. In the rest of the house the beautiful carved oak of the back hall and staircase was destroyed, as was the valuable library.[38] It was reported that the Pope's table, a treasured family heirloom, had also been lost to the flames but it had actually been carried out into the garden for safety and survives to this day.

The story of the IRA raider walking into the flames was well remembered by O'Reilly's niece, who recalled that it was generally believed in the family that the attackers were all strangers to the district. It was assumed that they knew nothing of the private chapel in the old tower house until too late to change their plans, and that it was the realisation that they were committing a sacrilege that explained the action of the raider who walked into the blazing abbey. The notion that such raids, and other kinds of attack on the owners of the estates of Ireland, were carried out by strangers seems to have been common among victims who took some comfort from convincing themselves that the people of their own locality were personally loyal or held the family in too high esteem to act against them with violence. Yet the two who surrendered to the troops were from the immediate area (Christopher Mullins lived in the village of Louth and Denis Murphy was from Rossmakea) and, many years later, a local inhabitant told one of the O'Reilly descendants that the four men who fired the Abbey were well known to him.

For William O'Reilly, as for his kinsman Edmund Dease, there had never been any thought of leaving the country and this attack on his home did not shake his faith in the new Ireland. The burning of Knock Abbey 'resulted in rendering a well-known and highly respected family homeless' and it added 'many thousands of pounds to the heavy burden which the Irish ratepayers already have to bear'.[39] The problem of where to live was quickly solved when Lord Louth, domiciled in London, offered his old friend the use of

Louth Hall and although O'Reilly was understandably very distressed by the event he did rebuild the damaged parts of Knock Abbey when the compensation was paid. The refurbished house was somewhat smaller and the repairs did not incorporate any replicas of the fine woodcarvings or other notable features of the earlier building. During the later 1920s the Knock Abbey estate dwindled to some 200 acres around the gardens, parklands and woods, after 'the Land Commission gave the land to the workmen . . . also the houses they lived in', as Fris O'Reilly remembered it, but the Catholic democracy that emerged from the struggle for freedom seems to have suited William O'Reilly rather well. He was a devout Catholic and held papal office as 'Privy Chamberlain of the Cape and Sword' to Pope Pius XI, a post which involved entertaining cardinals visiting Dublin and entailed spending some time at the Vatican each year.

Following the Censorship of Publications Act (1929) he was appointed to the Board of literary censors. The appointments were announced in February 1930, six months after the Act was passed, and even in sections of the press in favour of censorship there was some criticism of the calibre of the five men who were to sit on the Censorship Board. They were Canon Patrick Boylan, the chairman, who was a distinguished scriptural scholar and professor of Eastern languages at UCD; Professor W.E. Thrift, a member of the Evil Literature Committee, a Dáil deputy for Dublin University and later Provost of Trinity College; William O'Reilly, and W.B. Joyce and P.J. Keawell. The *Irish Statesman* supported the Act but it did not wholly approve the composition of the Board. 'After prolonged delay incidental to finding people so exalted in mind that they could be trusted to supervise the reading of the Irish people', it reported, 'the composition of our Board of Censors has been announced. Two of these are entities, the other three are nonentities. . . . We shall await with interest the first list of books which we are to be prohibited reading. The nonentities can outvote the entities'. This provoked a letter from a Jesuit priest, who set out the credentials of two of the 'nonentities'. Joyce was Principal of the Marlborough Street Training College and Central Model Schools, and an active member of library committees in Dublin and Limerick. He was also honorary treasurer of the Central Catholic Library, a Dublin institution recently founded by the Jesuit priest, Fr S. Browne. Keawell had the postgraduate qualification of MA and was chief clerk of the Department of Posts and Telegraphs, modest enough qualifications for a literary censor but apparently better than those of O'Reilly about whom the priest had nothing to say.[40] At the end of March 1932, 179 books and five periodical publications were on the banned list.[41] The *News of the World*, a Sunday paper famed for its reporting of sex scandals, was prohibited reading as was the magazine *Health and Strength*, which featured photographs of nudists and scantily clad physical fitness enthusiasts. Marie Stopes' *Wise Parenthood*, a manual on family limitation by the use of contraceptive measures, was among the books banned from Ireland but so too were works such as Stella Gibbons' *Cold Comfort Farm* (banned in November 1932) and novels by D.H. Lawrence, Colette, Maxim Gorky, Ethel Mannin, Erich Maria Remarque, and Somerset Maugham.[42] It became something of an accolade for a writer, especially an Irish writer, to feature in the censors' list but the deadening effect of such a narrow cultural outlook was deeply dispiriting to many intelligent readers of literature, and to native-born creative writers. Sean O'Faolain recalled in his autobiography that his satisfaction about the publication of his collection of short stories, *Midsummer Night Madness* (1932), was soured by reading in the press (while in France) that it had been banned by the Irish censors as obscene: 'Outwardly I laughed at the news. In my heart I felt infuriated and humiliated. Above all I felt frightened that I was soon to return to live with these stupid, boorish, dispirited people who publicly disowned and insulted me.'[43]

One beneficiary of O'Reilly's appointment was his niece, who from 1926 until her marriage in 1937 lived permanently at Knock Abbey with her Uncle. There she acted as housekeeper and hostess, in much the same role that her mother had taken on, albeit in somewhat reduced circumstances. Life was pleasant enough, with the customary social round and tennis parties in the summer followed by plenty of hunting in the winter, and there was the added diversion of sneaking Uncle William's reading matter from his study, although he was always very cross if this was discovered. His role in the life of the new Ireland was not confined to his duties as a papal representative and a literary censor. He also contributed to the growth and development of the tourist industry by inspecting hotels for Bord Fáilte or its forerunner. William O'Reilly was now truly at home in his own country and finding satisfaction in an undivided loyalty to the Irish Free State and its people but by the beginning of 1937, in his early seventies, his health was failing. He went to England to stay in Bath with his brother and his wife, hoping to recuperate in the spa town, but his condition worsened and he did not live to return to Knock Abbey. He died on 25 May 1937 and was buried in Bath.

Notes and references

1 Origins and Early Years

1 Information on the magistrates is taken from Galen Broeker, *Rural Disorder and Police Reform in Ireland, 1812-36*, Routledge & Kegan Paul, London, 1970, Chapter III, 'The failure of the magistracy, 1812-13', pp. 39-47, passim, and Virginia Crossman, 'Emergency legislation and agrarian disorder in Ireland, 1821-41', *Irish Historical Studies*, xxvii, 108 (Nov. 1991), pp. 309-23, p. 312. On the administrative system in general see R.B. McDowell, *The Irish Administration, 1801-1914*, Routledge & Kegan Paul, London, 1964, reprinted by Greenwood Press, Westport, Connecticut, USA, 1976; Laurence McBride, *The Greening of Dublin Castle: the transformation of bureaucratic and judicial personnel in Ireland, 1892-1922*, Catholic University of America Press, Washington DC, USA, 1991.

2 McDowell, *Irish Administration*, p 114. More information on police magistrates can be found in Broeker, *Rural Disorder*, Chapter IV, 'The Peace Preservation Force, 1813-14', and Crossman, 'Emergency legislation', passim.

3 *The Irish Resident Magistrates. Statement of the Irish Bar, with respect to the qualifications and appointments of Irish Resident Magistrates*, King, Law Printer, Dublin, 1908.

4 Returns (Resident Magistrates, Ireland) to the House of Commons (HC), 1837 (254), xlvi. 335; 1844 (131), xliii. 539.

5 Ibid., HC 1837 (254), xlvi. 335; 1852-3 (107), iv.615; 1860 (288), lvii.879.

6 Cited in McDowell, *Irish Administration*, pp. 114-15. The influence of the RMs reports in shaping policy has been considered by Margaret O'Callaghan, *British High Politics and a Nationalist Ireland: Criminality, Land and the Law under Forster and Balfour*, Cork University Press, Cork, 1994.

7 The title 'Resident Magistrate' was first used in the Bill (16 Vict.) to Amend the Acts regulating the salaries of resident magistrates, Parliamentary Papers (PP), HC 1852-3 (623), vi.

8 Return (Resident Magistrates, Ireland), HC 1872 (284), i. 269.

9 Report of Inquiry into the Civil Service in Ireland (Resident Magistrates), PP, HC 1874 (923), xvi. 723.

10 Bill to Amend . . . salaries of RMs, PP, HC 1874 (117), iii. 249.

11 No institutional history of the RIC has been published since that of R.Curtis, *The History of the Royal Irish Constabulary*, Moffat, London, 1869. For personal accounts of the RIC in the late nineteenth and early twentieth centuries see G. Garrow Green, *In the Royal Irish Constabulary*, Hodges, Figgis & Co., Dublin, 1905 and John D. Brewer, *The Royal Irish Constabulary. An Oral History*, Institute of Irish Studies, Belfast, 1990. See also W.J. Lowe and E.L. Malcolm, 'The domestication of the RIC, 1836-1922', *Irish Economic and Social History*, 19 (1992), pp. 27-48.

12 This was a popular name for the Society for the Education of the Poor in Ireland, a Protestant organisation founded in 1811. From 1817 the Society received state support and although its declared aim was to provide non-denominational education it was widely regarded as an organisation seeking to convert Catholics to the Church of Ireland.

13 Sir Robert Peel (1822-95) was Liberal Chief Secretary 1861-5; he later moved to the Conservative party but lost his parliamentary seat at the election of 1885, when he supported Home Rule.

14 Larcom MSS, National Library of Ireland (NLI), MS 7618, letters and papers on constabulary duties etc., 1852-62; 7618/99, copy of letter from Peel to Carlisle, 20 May 1862.

15 Peel to Carlisle, 24 May 1862, NLI MS 7618.

16 Return (Stipendiary Magistrates . . . over 60), HC 1862 (459), xlvi. 493. It was Mr Gonne Bell, stationed at Castle Connell, Co. Limerick, who sent a supporting letter. He was aged sixty-eight and had been a resident magistrate since 1841.

17 Larcom's memo on Peel's letters to Carlisle, NLI MS 7618/99.

18 Ibid.

19 See Charles Townshend, *Political Violence in Ireland. Government and Resistance since 1848*, Clarendon Press, Oxford, 1984, Chapter I, 'Resisters and Rebels', iii, 'Fenianism', pp. 24-38.

20 Letters from Larcom to OC Cork Division, 5 December and 11 December 1866, Kilmainham MSS 1059, cited in Townshed, *Political Violence*, p. 91.

21 Report of the 31st Regiment, 5 March 1867, Kilmainham MSS 1059, cited in Townshend, op. cit., p. 93. Townshend draws attention to the fact that the question of who took command when the military was called to the aid of the civil power was never definitively answered.

22 Return (Stipendiary Magistrates . . . over 60), HC 1862 (459), xlvi. 493; Return (Resident Magistrates, Ireland), HC 1872 (284) l.269.

23 Mayo MSS, NLI MS 11248-58, letters applying for posts, 1866-8.

24 Mr Cole to Lord Mayo, 2 November 1867, NLI MS 11248-58

25 Ibid., 19 September 1868.

26 Royal Irish Constabulary records, RUC Museum, RUC HQ, Knock Road, Belfast. RIC records are also held in Home Office papers (HO) at Public Record Office (PRO), London.

27 Hamilton MSS, D901, Public Record Office of Northern Ireland (PRONI), miscellaneous papers.

28 Larcom's memo on Peel's letters to Carlisle, NLI MS 7618/99.

29 *Burke's Guide to Country Houses*, vol.1, Ireland, Burke's Peerage Ltd., London, 1978, p. 67; the Ffrench family bought back the Castle in 1919.

30 *Burke's Irish Family Records*, Burke's Peerage Ltd., London, 1976. Biographical information on the RMs and their families is drawn from relevant entries in the works of reference listed in the bibliography, unless otherwise acknowledged in the notes.

31 Report of the Inquiry into the Civil Service in Ireland (Resident Magistrates), PP, HC 1874 (923), xvi. 723.

32 U.H. Hussey de Burgh, *The Landowners of Ireland*, Hodges, Foster & Figgis, Dublin, *c.*1878.

33 Sir Henry Robinson, *Further Memories of Irish Life*, Herbert Jenkins, London, 1924, p. 195.

34 Ibid., pp. 195-6.

2 A Decade of Drama

1 See Peter Collins (ed.), *Nationalism and Unionism. Conflict in Ireland, 1885-1921*, Institute of Irish Studies, Belfast, 1994, especially Brian Walker, 'The 1885 and 1886 General Elections: a milestone in Irish history', pp. 1-15.

2 For an account of the historical period see D. George Boyce, *Ireland, 1828-1923, From Ascendancy to Democracy*, Historical Association Studies, Blackwell, Oxford, 1992; on the land agitation see Townshend, *Political Violence*, 'Land War', pp. 104-80 and Margaret O'Callaghan, *British High Politics and a Nationalist Ireland. Criminality, Land and the Law under Forster and Balfour*, Cork UP, Cork, 1994, especially chapter three, 'A Liberal Dilemma', pp. 61-94.

3 Memorandum on increase in numbers of RMs, 17 December 1879, Treasury Papers, Ireland [TI], PRO TI 17101.

4 Return (Resident Magistrates, Ireland), HC 1889 (83) LXI. 475

5 Information and biographical details from Donald E. Jordan Jr., *Land and Popular Politics in Ireland. County Mayo from the Plantation to the Land War*, Cambridge UP, Cambridge, 1994, 'The Boycott Affair', pp. 285-93, passim, and Joyce Marlow, *Captain Boycott and the Irish*, Andre Deutsch, London, 1973.

6 *Connaught Telegraph*, 25 September 1880, cited in Jordan, *Land and Popular Politics*, p. 288.

7 Jordan, *Land and Popular Politics*, p. 289

8 David Harrel was a former police officer who was later appointed Chief Commissioner of the Dublin Metropolitan Police, 1883-93, and subsequently served as Under-Secretary 1893-1902.

9 Jordan, *Land and Popular Politics*, p. 290.

10 *Freeman's Journal*, 24 August 1922. Traill was first appointed in March 1880 and this incident probably took place in 1883 or 1884; his name reappears in returns from the later 1880s and in RIC lists, which show that he went on to serve in counties Meath and Monaghan before retiring in 1894.

11 Return (Resident Magistrates, Ireland), PP, HC 1880 (417) LX. 547.

12 Return showing numbers of persons receiving special police protection on 31 December 1880, PP, HC 1881 (76) LXXVI. 641.

13 Townshend, *Political Violence*, p. 138.

14 Circular to resident magistrates, 22 June 1882, PRO TI 14022.

15 C.D.C. Lloyd, *Ireland under the Land League. A narrative of personal experiences*, Blackwood, Edinburgh, 1892. Cf. Wilfred Scawen Blunt, *The Land War in Ireland. Being a Personal Narrative of Events*, Stephen Swift & Co., London, 1912.

16 O'Callaghan, *British High Politics and a Nationalist Ireland*, p. 87, pp. 88-9.

17 Townshend, *Political Violence*, p. 174, n. 4.

18 Lloyd, *Ireland under the Land League*; the narrative was written while Lloyd was unemployed prior to taking up his post in Egypt, and published posthumously. He died in Armenia of pneumonia, aged forty-seven, on 7 January 1891.

19 See, for example, Parliamentary debates (PD), HC, [330] 1819/1821, 22 November 1881.

20 Memo to Dublin Castle from Treasury office, n.d., c.November 1885, PRO TI 15392.

21 Townshend, *Political Violence*, p. 164 and p. 226, n. 1; information on the careers of the RMs is taken from appointments and transfers listed in the *Dublin Gazette*, from details of RMs stations etc. given in the RIC annual lists (HO 184 at PRO, London), and from the various returns made to the House of Commons.

22 Cited in Townshend, op. cit, pp. 170-3 and p. 195, n. 1.

23 Lloyd, *Ireland under the Land League*, pp. 212-13.

24 U.H. Hussey de Burgh, *The Landowners of Ireland*, Hodges, Foster & Figgis, Dublin, c.1878.

25 Letter to Treasury from the Under-Secretary's office, 16 March 1883, PRO TI 15392.

26 Ibid., an exceptional payment of £45 (in addition to the standard disturbance allowance of £33) was made to McTernan becuse of extra expenses incurred as a result of the boycott.

27 Townshend, *Political Violence*, pp. 183-4.

28 Return (Commissions of the Peace, Ireland), PP, HC 1884 (13) LXIII. 331

29 See Paul Buckland, *Irish Unionism: the Anglo-Irish and the New Ireland, 1885-1922*, Gill and Macmillan, Dublin, 1972; the initial manifesto of the ILPU, as published in the *Irish Times*, is given in Appendix A, pp. 302-8. The ILPU became the Irish Unionist Alliance in 1891.

30 Dr Anthony Traill (1838-1914) was the first medical man to hold the office of Provost of Trinity College, Dublin, in 1904-14.

31 PD, HC [333] 841, 4 March 1889.

32 PD, HC [338] 1431, 26 July 1889, Mr Flynn drew attention to a resolution of protest passed in his North Cork constituency.

33 Brian Walker, 'The 1885 and 1886 General Elections', p. 3, in Collins (ed.), *Nationalism and Unionism*.

34 Report of the Belfast Riots' Commission, PP, HC 1887 (4925) XVIII, 1.

35 Ibid.

36 See Laurence M. Geary, *The Plan of Campaign, 1886-91*, Cork University Press, Cork, 1986.

37 A.J. Balfour succeeded his uncle, Lord Salisbury, as Prime Minister; he was leader of the Conservative party until replaced by Andrew Bonar Law in 1911. His political career is recounted in several readily available biographies; for an interesting analysis of his role in shaping modern Ireland see Catherine B. Shannon, 'The Legacy of Arthur Balfour to Twentieth-century Ireland', in Collins (ed.), *Nationalism and Unionism*, pp. 17-33.

38 See Geary, *Plan of Campaign*, for a full account of the incident.
39 Blanche Dugdale, *Arthur James Balfour*, Hutchinson, London, 1936, pp. 141-3.
40 According to Colonel A. Turner, *Sixty Years of a Soldier's Life*, Methuen & Co., London, 1912; Turner was commissioner for counties Kerry and Clare, and served on the court of inquiry into the Mitchelstown affair.
41 PD, HC [332] 830/32, 19 December 1888.
42 PD, HC [332] 812/19, 19 December 1888.
43 PD, HC [332] 820/26, 19 December 1888.
44 PD, HC [334] 409/10, 21 March 1889.
45 PD, HC [336] 513, 20 May 1889
46 PD, HC [336] 514/6, 20 May 1889.
47 *The Times*, 18 March 1889.
48 Return (Resident Magistrates, Ireland), HC 1889 (83) LXI. 475.
49 The commissioners were Major General Sir Redvers Buller and Colonel Turner, who was not wholly unsympathetic to Home Rule. See Turner, *Soldiers Life*, passim, and Townshend, *Political Violence*, p. 209, n. 1; p. 215; pp. 217-19
50 Kieran Flanagan, 'The Chief Secretary's Office, 1853-1914: a bureaucratic enigma', *Irish Historical Studies*, xxiv, 94 (Nov.1984), pp.197-225, p.221.
51 Hamilton held the clerkship from July 1881 until September 1882, when he was appointed RM for Belfast. He claimed that he had taken the post in the CSO on the understanding that when his services were no longer required there he would still be entitled to a salary of £800, rather than the £675 paid to senior RMs. Correspondence relating to Thomas Hamilton of CSO, appointed RM for Belfast, PRO TI 14022.
52 R.C. Hamilton McMurray, undated typescript entitled 'Reminiscences in the Life of a Brave Man', PRONI D901.
53 Agreement was reached in early November 1882, when the Treasury granted Hamilton an extra £25 per annum to bring his salary up to £700. With the commuted forage and postage allowances (£108) and the Belfast lodging allowance (£100) his annual income was therefore £908, PRO TI 14022. Documents relating to Hamilton's pension position are held in the National Archive, Dublin, Chief Secretary's Office, Registered Papers 1889/5676.
54 Letter from RIC, Donegal, to CSO, Dublin Castle, 18 February 1889, PRONI D901.
55 *The Times*, 8 April 1919. The Major's name is variously spelled but he is listed as Neild in Return (Resident Magistrates, Ireland), HC 1887 (129) LXVII. 465
56 S.M. Hussey, *The Reminiscences of an Irish Land Agent, Being Those of S.M. Hussey*, compiled by Home Gordon, Duckworth & Co., London, 1904, p. 253.
57 *Freeman's Journal*, 24 August 1922.
58 Sir Henry Robinson, *Further Memories of Irish Life*, Herbert Jenkins Ltd., London, 1924, p. 196.

3 Major Yeates and the Irish RMs

1 For works by Somerville and Ross see their entry in Robert Hogan (ed.), *Dictionary of Irish Literature*, Gill & Macmillan, Dublin, 1979; for a survey of critical studies see Richard J. Finneran, *Anglo-Irish Literature. A Review of Research*, MLA, New York, 1976, and later editions. See also Declan Kiberd, *Inventing Ireland*, Johnathon Cape, London,1995, 'Somerville and Ross – Tragedies of Manners', pp. 69-82; Thomas Flanagan, 'The Big House of Ross-Drishane', *Kenyon Review*, 28, 1 (Jan. 1966), pp. 54-78; Conor Cruise O'Brien, *Writers and Politics*, Parthenon Books, New York, USA, 1965, Part IV, 'Ireland. Somerville and Ross', pp. 106-15.
2 John Cronin, *Somerville and Ross*, Bucknall UP, New Jersey, USA, 1972, 'Family Backgrounds and the Beginning of Collaboration', pp. 11-24; Gifford Lewis, *Somerville and Ross. The World of the Irish RM*, Penguin Books, Middlesex, 1987.
3 Hilary Robinson, *Somerville and Ross. A Critical Appreciation*, Gill & Macmillan, Dublin, 1980, pp. 134-5.
4 A.C. Partridge, *Language and Society in Anglo-Irish Literature*, Gill and Macmillan, Dublin,1984, p.271.
5 Guy Fehlman, 'The Composition of Somerville and Ross's Irish RM', pp. 103-11, in Patrick Rafroidi and Terence Brown (eds), *The Irish Short Story*, Universite de Lille, France, 1979.
6 Partridge, *Language and Society*, pp. 271-2.

7 Letter from Edith Somerville to her brother, Col. John Somerville, 1 February 1899, Somerville and Ross Papers, QUB Library (Special Collections), MS17 (877); Cronin, *Somerville and Ross*, pp. 51-2.

8 Somerville and Ross Papers, QUB. Letter from Edith Somerville to Col. John Somerville, 4 October 1899.

9 Quotation from E.OE. Somerville and Martin Ross, *Irish Memories*, Longman Green, London, 1917, cited in Cronin, *Somerville and Ross*, pp. 51-2.

10 From Frank O'Connor, *The Lonely Voice*, cited in Fehlman, 'Composition of Somerville and Ross', pp. 105-6.

11 Julian Moynahan, *Anglo-Irish. The Literary Imagination in a Hyphenated Culture*, Princeton UP, New Jersey, USA, 1995, p.196.

12 The text used for this study is the Penguin Books, Middlesex, 1984 edition of the *Irish RM*.

13 Moynahan, *Anglo-Irish*, pp. 196-7.

14 Stephen Gwynn, *Today and Tomorrow in Ireland. Essays on Irish Subjects*, Hodges Figgis, Dublin, 1903, pp. 110-15.

15 Cronin, *Somerville and Ross*, pp. 59-60.

16 Ibid., p. 57.

17 Moynahan, *Anglo-Irish*. Moynahan challenges post-colonial assumptions, arguing that the Anglo-Irish since 1800 were indelibly Irish, not mere colonial servants of Imperial Britain. Cf. Richard Cairns and Shaun Richards, *Writing Ireland. Colonialism, Nationalism and Culture*, Manchester UP, Manchester, 1988. See also Liam Kennedy, 'Modern Ireland: post-colonial society or post-colonial pretensions?', *The Irish Review*, No. 13 (1992-3), pp. 107-21 and Colin Graham, '"Liminal Spaces": post-colonial theories and Irish culture', *The Irish Review*, No. 16 (1994), pp. 29-43.

18 Moynahan, *Anglo-Irish*, Chapter IX, '"The Strain of the Double Loyalty". Edith Somerville and Martin Ross', pp. 162-97, p.192.

19 Sir Christopher Lynch-Robinson, *The Last of the Irish RMs*, Cassell & Co., London, 1951, preface. The author was plain Mr Robinson during his service as RM but later added 'Lynch' to his name; he inherited his father's title.

20 From the opening paragraphs of the first

of the stories, 'Great-Uncle McCarthy'.

21 Lawrence W. McBride, *The Greening of Dublin Castle. The Transformation of Bureaucratic and Judicial Personnel in Ireland, 1892-1922*, Catholic University Of America Press, Washington DC, USA, 1991, p.ix.

22 PD, HC [7] 327, 11 August 1892.

23 Unless otherwise acknowledged in the end notes all biographical information in the text is taken from relevant entries in works of reference (eg *Burke's Irish Landed Gentry*) listed in the bibliography.

24 U.H. Hussey de Burgh, *The Landowners of Ireland*, Hodges, Foster & Figgis, Dublin, *c.*1878.

25 PD, HC [148] 1312, 6 July 1905.

26 PD, HC [185] 552, 3 March 1908.

27 PD, HC [62] 32, 4 May 1914.

28 McBride, *Greening of Dublin Castle*, p.48.

29 See Eamon Pheonix (ed.), *A Century of Northern Life. The Irish News and 100 Years of Ulster History, 1890s-1990s*, Ulster Historical Foundation, Belfast, 1995.

30 PD, HC [90] 198, 1 March 1901.

31 PD, HC [107] 1363, 12 May 1902.

32 Figures given by Chief Secretary, PD, HC [173] 1169, 3 May 1907.

33 *Irish Catholic*, 6 November 1909, cited in McBride, *Greening of Dublin Castle*, p.36.

34 PD, HC [18] 469-70, 23 June 1910.

35 PD, HC [101] 144-5, 16 January 1902; 177-8, 17 January 1902.

36 Maurice Headlam, *Irish Reminiscences*, Robert Hale Ltd., London, 1947.

37 Lynch-Robinson, *Last of the Irish RMs*, p.93.

38 Boyce, *Ireland 1828-1923*, p.69; Part 5, 'Makers of a new Ireland, 1891-1910', pp. 62-78, gives a brief but informative survey of cultural nationalism.

39 Joseph Lee, *The Modernisation of Irish Society*, 1848-1918, Gill and Macmillan, Dublin, 1989, pp. 137-41; first published 1973.

40 Boyce, *Ireland 1828-1923*, p.70.

41 Geroid O'Tuataigh, 'The Celts II', pp. 40-54, in P. Loughrey (ed.), *The People of Ireland* (Appletree Press / BBC Northern Ireland: 1989), p. 45.

42 Lee, *Modernisation of Irish Society*, pp. 137-41.

43 The continuing relevance of 'identity' in the new Ireland is discussed by Margaret O'Callaghan, 'Language, nationality and

cultural identity in the Irish Free State, 1922-7: the *Irish Statesman* and the *Catholic Bulletin* reappraised', in *Irish Historical Studies*, xxiv, 94 (Nov. 1984), pp. 226-45.

44 Bence-Jones, *Twighlight of the Ascendancy*, passim; Moynahan, *Anglo-Irish*, p.163.

45 John Eglinton, *Anglo-Irish Essays*, Talbot Press, Dublin & London, 1917, p. 4.

46 Lynch-Robinson, *Last of the Irish RMs*, p. 9.

47 All three were former RIC officers, two Protestants born in England and a Presbyterian Scot from Aberdeenshire.

48 C.P.Crane, *Memories of an Resident Magistrate, 1880-1920*, T. & A. Constable, Edinburgh, 1938.

49 Lynch-Robinson, *Last of the Irish RMs*, pp. 27-8; p. 94.

4 Public Duties

1 Katherine Tynan, *The Times*, 28 August 1922.

2 Resident Magistrates (Belfast) Bill, PP, HC 1904 (17), IV. 199. The Act came into operation on 1 January 1905.

3 *The Times*, 28 August 1922.

4 Royal Commission on the Civil Service, Fourth Report, Second Appendix (Evidence), PP, HC 1914 (7340), XVI. 363.

5 Crane, *Memories of a Resident Magistrate*, chapters XIII and XIV cover the South African or Boer war, pp.154-80.

6 Return (Resident Magistrates, Ireland), HC 1911 (277) LXV. 461.

7 Committee of Inquiry into the RIC & DMP, Evidence and Appendices, PP, HC 1914 (7637), XXXII. 359.

8 Lynch-Robinson, *Last of the Irish RMs*, pp. 93-4; p.142.

9 PD, HC [28] 457-8, 9 August 1894

10 PD, HC [24] 1160, 24 May 1894.

11 Somerville and Ross, 'Great Uncle McCarthy'.

12 Lynch-Robinson, *Last of the Irish RMs*, p.101.

13 NAI CSO, RMs Monthly Summaries, Jan-June 1916, H. Hinkson, February 1916.

14 NAI CSO, RMs Monthly Summaries, 1915, Box 21, 3/406, H. Hinkson, October 1915.

15 Lynch-Robinson, *Last of the Irish RMs*, p.145.

16 Major Herries Crosbie's summary of duty for April 1914 and the ensuing correspondence can be found in CSO, RMs Monthly Summaries, Jan-June 1915, Box 21, 3/406. This box also contains other papers from 1914.

17 When the RM for Lisbellaw, Co. Fermanagh, heard and determined a case of assault, out of petty sessions, the Attorney General ruled that his order was illegal (such cases requiring the presence of two magistrates) and it was not enforced. PD, HC [136] 145, 15 June 1904.

18 Lynch-Robinson, *Last of the Irish RMs*, p.95.

19 NAI CSORP 1890/17253, Reports on the Condition of the Poor (Counties Donegal, Mayo and Waterford; part of Co. Cork).

20 above, pp.

21 Captain Welch's original handwritten report survives for the Bantry-Skibbereen district of west Cork.

22 *The Times*, 22 July, 23 July 1890.

23 *The Times*, 11 November 1890.

24 See Townshend, *Political Violence*, pp. 226-34.

25 Crane, *Memories of a Resident Magistrate*, p.182.

26 PD, HC [98] 234, 26 July 1901; the RMs name was given as 'Crean', presumably a mis-spelling for Crane.

27 PD, HC [111] 523, 17 July 1902.

28 PD, HC [110] 694-5, 3 July 1902

29 PD, HC [110] 1200, 9 July 1902.

30 PD, HC [111] 1027-8, 23 July 1902.

31 PD, HC [111] 1071-2, 23 July 1902.

32 Gifford Lewis (ed.), *Selected Letters of Somerville and Ross*, Introduction, p. xxix.

33 Cited in Lewis, op. cit., p. xxix.

34 E.OE. Somerville and Martin Ross, *The Irish RM and his Experiences*, Faber & Faber, London, 1928.

35 Crane, *Memories of a Resident Magistrate*, pp. 194-5.

36 Lynch-Robinson, *Last of the Irish RMs*, pp. 103-4.

37 Crane, *Memories of a Resident Magistrate*, p.195.

38 Somerville & Ross, 'Great Uncle McCarthy'.

39 Crane, *Memories of a Resident Magistrate*, p. 193.

40 Townshend, *Political Violence*, p. 48.
41 Stephen Gwynn, *Today and Tomorrow in Ireland*, pp. 110-15.
42 Note to H. Hinkson from clerk to Killala petty sessions, 29 November 1914, NAI CSO, RMs Monthly Summaries, Jan-June 1915, Box 21, 3/406.
43 Lynch-Robinson, *Last of the Irish RMs*, pp. 105-12.
44 Ibid., p.189.
45 CSO, RMs Monthly Summaries, Jan-June 1919, 29/9.
46 *The Times*, 28 August 1922.
47 Letters between A. Newton Brady and O'Farrell, February 1912, Colonial Office Papers [CO], PRO CO 904/28.
48 Lynch-Robinson, *Last of the Irish RMs*, p. 116.
49 Sir Henry Robinson, *Further Memories of Irish Life*, p. 199.
50 NAI CSO, RMs Monthly Summaries, Jan-June 1915, Box 21, 3/406.
51 NAI CSORP 1915/20096.
52 Lynch-Robinson, *Last of the Irish RMs*, pp. 116-17.
53 NAI CSORP 1915/20096.
54 Lynch-Robinson, *Last of the Irish RMs*, pp. 142-4.
55 MacBride, *Greening of Dublin Castle*, pp. 48-9.
56 Crane, *Memories of a Resident Magistrate*, p.192.
57 Somerville and Ross, 'Occasional Licenses'.
58 Mr Sparrow's note is dated June 1916 (NAI CSORP 1916/17042) but is filed in Box 5759 (3/691) of RMs Monthly Summaries for 1918.
59 NAI CSORP 1918/21774, papers relating to conduct of Mr Rice, JP.
60 NAI CSO, RMs Monthly Summaries, Jan-June 1919, 29/9, C.P. Crane, February 1919.
61 NAI CSO, RMs Monthly Summaries, 1916, W. Maxwell Scott Moore, February 1916.
62 Marilyn Silverman and P.H. Gulliver, *In the Valley of the Nore. A Social History of Thomastown, County Kilkenny, 1840-1983*, Geography Publications, Dublin, 1986, 'The Lads in the Band: An Episode in 1890', pp.159-62.
63 *The Times*, 28 August 1922.
64 Ibid.

5 Private Lives

1 PD, HC [350] 478-9, 12 February 1891.
2 U.H. Hussey de Burgh, *Landowners of Ireland*.
3 *Kildare Observer*, 22 March 1890.
4 *Kildare Observer*, 5 April 1890.
5 PD, HC [350] 479, 12 February 1891.
6 Crane, *Memories of a Resident Magistrate*, pp. 148-9.
7 Ibid., p. 187
8 Ibid., p. 203.
9 Ramsay Colles, *In Castle and Court House: Being Reminiscences of Thirty Years in Ireland*, Werner Laurie, London, 1911, pp. 21-2.
10 *Who Was Who*, 1916-28; *Thom's Irish Who's Who*, 1923.
11 Maurice Headlam, *Irish Reminiscences*, Robert Hale, London, 1947, p. 109.
12 Katherine Tynan, *Years of the Shadow*, Chapter XVIII, 'The county of Mayo', pp. 161-9, passim; *Wandering Years*, Chapter IV, 'Mayo and Resident Magistrates', pp. 28-37, passim.
13 Eunan O'Halpin, *The Decline of the Union. British Government in Ireland 1892-1920*, Gill and Macmillan, Dublin, 1987, pp.95-6.
14 *The Times*, 28 August 1922.
15 Lionel Fleming, *Head or Harp*, Barrie & Rockliffe, London, 1965: in the world of the Anglo-Irish at the turn of the century 'nobody ever thought of himself as "middle class"', p. 17.
16 Nora Robertson, *Crowned Harp*, Allen Figgis & Co., Dublin, 1960, pp. 74-5.
17 Bence-Jones, *Twilight of the Ascendancy*, pp. 53-5. Information on club membership from *Thom's Irish Who's Who* 1923 and other works of reference in the bibliography.
18 Stephen Gwynn, *Today and Tomorrow in Ireland*, pp. 106-7.
19 Bence-Jones, *Twilight of the Ascendancy*, p. 56.
20 Tynan, *Years of the Shadow*, p. 163.
21 *King's County Chronicle*, 18 September 1890.
22 Crane, *Memories of a Resident Magistrate*, p. 154.
23 *King's County Chronicle*, 7 August 1890.
24 Crane, *Memories of a Resident Magistrate*, p. 183.

25 *Mayo News*, 28 March 1896.
26 Tynan, *Years of the Shadow*, pp. 243-5.
27 Somerville & Ross, 'Philippa's Fox-Hunt'.
28 Somerville and Ross, 'The Maroan Pony'.
29 Tynan, *Years of the Shadow*, p. 163.
30 Ibid, p. 300.
31 Bence-Jones, *Twilight of the Ascendancy*, pp. 58-9.
32 Crane, *Memories of a Resident Magistrate*, p. 155.
33 Ibid, p. 181.
34 Lynch-Robinson, *Last of the Irish RMs*, p. 151.
35 Gwynn, *Today and Tomorrow*, pp. 110-12.
36 Headlam, *Reminiscences*, pp. 109-12.
37 Lynch-Robinson, *Last of the Irish RMs*, p. 151.
38 Crane, *Memories of a Resident Magistrate*, p. 190.
39 Ibid., pp. 151-2.
40 Lynch-Robinson, *Last of the Irish RMs*, p. 99.
41 Crane, *Memories of a Resident Magistrate*, pp. 187-8 and passim.
42 Tynan, *Years of the Shadow*, Chapter XXXV, 'The coming of the Soldiers', pp. 310-19. For the experience of officers and troops in Ireland before the Great War see Elizabeth A. Muenger, *The British Military Dilemma in Ireland. Occupation Politics 1886-1914*, University of Kansas Press and Gill and Macmilllan, Dublin, 1991.
43 Tynan, *Wandering Years*, pp. 30-1; *Years of the Shadow*, p. 163.
44 Tynan, *Years of the Shadow*, pp.161-9, passim, p.269, pp. 302-4.
45 Fleming, *Head or Harp*, p. 17.

6 Troubled Times

1 Synopses of Reports from Resident Magistrates on the State of Ireland, PRO CO 904/227.
2 Intelligence Notes 1915-19, Report of RIC County Inspector, Monaghan, 1915, PRO CO 903/19.
3 Lynch-Robinson, *Last of the Irish RMs*, p. 129.
4 Ibid., pp. 132-3.
5 Ibid., pp. 134-5.
6 Tynan, *Years of the Shadow*, p. 30
7 NAI CSO, RMs Monthly Summaries,

1915, W.M. Scott Moore, April and May, 1915.
8 Tynan, *Years of the Shadow*, pp. 204-5
9 Lynch-Robinson, *Last of the Irish RMs*, pp.137-8.
10 Tynan, *Years of the Shadow*, pp. 204-5.
11 Lynch-Robinson, *Last of the Irish RMs*, p. 141.
12 Summary of Reports on the State of the Country, 1916-18, PRO CO 904/157/1.
13 Ibid.
14 Official Memorandum, condition of County Tipperary and the working of Sinn Féin in Ireland, 4 July 1919, PRO CO 904/225.
15 Ibid., Arrest of J.A. Burke, Sinn Féin MP, for using violent language.
16 E. Holt, *Protest in Arms. The Irish Troubles, 1916-23*, Putnam, London, 1960, p. 192.
17 The other members of the secret committee were the chief commissioner of the DMP, the acting inspector general of the RIC, and assistant under-secretary, Sir John Taylor. C. Andrew and D. Dilks (eds), *The Missing Dimension. Governments and Intelligence Communities in the Twentieth Century*, Macmillan, London, 1984, E.O. Halpin, 'British Intelligence in Ireland, 1914-21', pp.71-2.
18 Alan Bell's report of inquiry into attempted assassination of Lord French, PRO CO 904/188.
19 W.J. O'Reilly (below, chapter 11) was one RM who served on the RIC selection board. The Auxiliary Division was first commanded by a former UVF officer, Brigadier Crozier, who was a grandson of Major Percy RM. Crozier later resigned over ADRIC indiscipline, although Townshend suggests that he almost certainly helped to establish the pattern of 'economic' reprisals, Townshend, *Political Violence*, p. 350, n. 2. Brigadier General F.P. Crozier, *Impressions and Recollections*, Werner Laurie, London, 1903, p. 9.
20 Mark Bence-Jones, *Twilight of the Ascendancy*, p. 187.
21 J.G. Farrell, *Troubles*, Johnathan Cape, London, 1970, pb. edition, Phoenix, London, 1993; Elizabeth Bowen, *The Last September*, Constable, London, 1929; pb. edition, Penguin, Middlesex, 1942, current reprint. For some critical analysis see

Margaret Scanlan, 'Rumours of War: Elizabeth Bowen's *Last September* and J.G. Farrell's *Troubles'*, *Eire-Ireland*, xx, 2 (Summer 1985), pp. 70-89.

22 *Kilkenny Journal*, 14 January 1920.

23 Alan Bell's investigation into Dail funding, transcripts of evidence given by managers of various Dublin banks, PRO CO 904/227.

24 *Freeman's Journal*, 27 March, 29 March 1920; *The Times*, 27 March 1920.

25 PD, HC [127] 1090-1, 28 March 1920. Papers relating to Bell's murder can be found in NAI CSORP 1920/8051, 8052.

26 *Cork Examiner*, 12 May 1920.

27 *Cork Examiner*, 21 June 1920.

28 Lynch-Robinson, *Last of the Irish RMs*, p. 152.

29 NAI CSO, RMs Monthly Summaries, July-December 1920, 32/12, C. Robinson, July 1920.

30 Lynch-Robinson, *Last of the Irish RMs*, p. 167.

31 PD, HC [115] 302-3, 1 May 1919.

32 Resident Magistrates (Ireland) Bill, Report and Proceedings of Standing Committee B, PP, HC 1920 (171), VIII. 507, 1920; Resident Magistrates (Ireland), Estimate of Probable Expenditure, PP, HC 1920 (750), XL. 811.

33 Correspondence relating to Kilbride's application to Treasury, PRO TI 92/7.

34 Crane, *Memories of a Resident Magistrate*, pp. 252-5, 260-1.

35 *Freeman's Journal*, 23 September 1920.

36 *Freeman's Journal*, 27 & 28 September 1920.

37 *The Times*, 2 October 1920.

38 *Freeman's Journal*, 30 September 1920.

39 *Freeman's Journal*, 2 October 1920.

40 Lynch-Robinson, *Last of the Irish RMs*, p. 157.

41 Anon., *Tales of the RIC*, Blackwoods, Edinburgh, 1921; Farrell, *Troubles*.

42 One in twelve members of the RIC was injured and one in twenty killed in just over two years; John D. Brewer, *The Royal Irish Constabulary*, p. 9.

43 *Freeman's Journal*, 5 October 1920.

44 Lynch-Robinson, *Last of the Irish RMs*, pp. 156-7.

45 NAI CSO, RMs Monthly Summaries, July-Dec 1920, 32/12, W.M. Scott Moore, October 1920.

46 *Freeman's Journal*, 22 December 1920.

47 PD, HC [136] 2102, 23 December 1920.

48 *Freeman's Journal*, 16 & 17 December 1920.

49 Charles Townshend, *The British Campaign in Ireland 1919-21. The Development of Political and Military Policies*, Oxford UP, Oxford, 1975, p. 139.

50 War Office (WO) Papers relating to Court of Inquiry into the deaths of Canon Magner and Timothy Crowley, PRO WO 35/155B.

51 Cited in Townshend, *British Campaign in Ireland*, p. 139.

52 *Freeman's Journal*, 6 January 1921.

53 PD, HC [139] 2784, 24 March 1921.

54 Lynch Robinson, *Last of the Irish RMs*, pp. 152-66, passim.

55 Position of Certain RMs in Cork, enquiries as to duties, PRO WO 35/66.

56 NAI CSORP 1921/332, P.S. Brady, sick leave from 17 January for six months.

57 *The Times*, 23 June 1921.

58 *Freeman's Journal*, 8 & 21 July 1921.

7 The RMs and the New Ireland

1 Lynch-Robinson, *Last of the Irish RMs*, p. 170.

2 PD, HC [151] 1518, 9 March 1922

3 Lynch-Robinson was one of the party when Long toured Ireland with Sir Henry Robinson in 1905. Sir Henry's unofficial notes on their travels are published as an appendix to Lord Long's memoirs, Rt Hon Viscount Long, *Memories*, Hutchinson, London, 1923. For an account of Long's life and career see Charles Petrie, *Walter Long and his Times*, Hutchinson, London, 1936.

4 Letter to Lord Long from Christopher (Lynch) Robinson, 27 May 1922, Long MSS, Irish Papers 1914-24, Wiltshire County Record Office [WRO], 947/42/174.

5 Copy of memorandum prepared for the Resident Magistrates' Association, WRO 947/42/174.

6 *Freeman's Journal*, 5 August 1922.

7 *Freeman's Journal*, 22 & 24 August 1922.

8 Letter to Lord Long from Murray Hornibrook, 30 August 1922, WRO 947/43/86.

9 *The Times*, 30 September 1922.
10 For the Dáil debate see *Freeman's Journal*, 30 September 1922.
11 *Freeman's Journal*, 27 October, 28 October 1922.
12 Letter to J. Crotty from Ministry of Home Affairs, Dublin, 20 October 1922, Cork University Library, Special Collections, U256, and *Freeman's Journal*, 27 October 1922.
13 Lynch-Robinson, *Last of the Irish RMs*, pp. 95-6.
14 Ibid., p. 174.
15 Ibid., pp. 171-3, passim.
16 Ibid., pp. 174-5, passim.
17 *The Times*, 22 March 1922.
20 *Who Was Who, 1929-40*; Crane, *Memories of a Resident Magistrate*, p. 262.
21 *Thom's Irish Who's Who* (Alexander Thom & Co, Dublin:1923). The listings seem to have been updated after mid 1922. That there would have been little future for Catholic resident magistrates in the North is suggested by the fact that in 1931 only one of the eleven in office was a Catholic, while of 600 lay magistrates appointed since 1921 only twenty were Catholic, Eamon Pheonix, *Northern Nationalism. Nationalist Politics, Partition and the Catholic Minority in Northern Ireland, 1890-1940*, Ulster Historical Foundation, Belfast, 1994, p. 451, n. 28.
22 Return of RMs transferred to provisional government on 1 April 1922, Long MSS, WRO 947/86/433; *Belfast Gazette*, 1922, 1923.
23 NAI CSORP 1919/792, Toppin's request for demobilization; NAI CSORP 1919/10516, Mr Toppin not to be released from army service.
24 Letter from J.B. Wroughton, GHQ Ireland, to Under-Secretary, 13 October 1920, PRO WO 35/65.
25 Letter from Macready to Under-Secretary, 12 October 1920, PRO WO 35/65.
26 Lynch-Robinson, *Last of the Irish RMs*, p. 174.
27 Sir Henry Robinson, *Further Memories of Irish Life*, Herbert Jenkins, London, 1923.
28 Lynch-Robinson, *Last of the Irish RMs*, pp. 188-9.
29 See Annabel Davis-Goff, *Walled Gardens. Scenes from an Anglo-Irish Childhood*, Picador pb. ed., Pan Books, London, 1991.
30 Bence-Jones, *Twilight of the Ascendancy*, p. 236.
31 Peter Somerville-Large, *The Irish Country House. A Social History*, Sinclair-Stevenson, London, 1995, p. 358.
32 *The Times*, 28 August 1922.
33 *Cork Examiner*, 8 September 1936.

8 John Charles Milling, 1873-1919

1 R. Curtis, The *History of the Royal Irish Constabulary*, Moffat, London, 1869, pp. 162-65.
2 Somerville-Large, *Irish Country House*, p. 235.
3 See V.S. Pritchett, *The Living Novel*, Chatto & Windus, London, 1949, 'A Plymouth Brother', pp. 109-15.
4 Census data, 1900, in the possession of Dr & Mrs Shearer, Belfast.
5 Michael Quane, 'Ranelagh Endowed School', *Journal of the Old Athlone Society*, vol. 1, No 1 (1969), pp. 24-34.
6 Regulations under which 'Gentlemen are to be admitted as Cadets of the RIC' and details of the examination are published in the RIC lists, vol. 13 (74-9), July 1878-January 1881, PRO HO 184/93.
7 For an account of the training and life of an officer in the RIC see G. Garrow Green, *In the Royal Irish Constabulary*, Hodges, Figgis & Co., Dublin, 1905.
8 Illuminated address in the possession of Dr & Mrs Shearer, Belfast; Crane, *Memories of a Resident Magistrate*, p. 248.
9 Walsh was later Assistant Inspector General of the RIC and served with Alan Bell RM on the committee set up to improve British intelligence gathering; he was knighted in the New Year honours' list of 1922.
10 The accident and compensation case are reported in the *Mayo News*, 18 April, 25 April, 19 December 1903.
11 An obituary to Oliver Milling can be found in *The Times*, 18 September 1906.
12 J.C. Milling, *The RIC ABC or Police Duties in Relation to Acts of Parliament in Ireland*, John Adams, Belfast, 1908, copy in the possession of Dr & Mrs Shearer, Belfast.
13 *Belfast Telegraph*, 14 July 1909.
14 Military Aid to the Civil Power in Belfast,

July to September 1912, PRO WO 35/60.
15 *Irish News*, 16 July 1912.
16 *Irish News*, 5 October 1912.
17 *Daily News and Leader*, extract reprinted in *Irish News*, 5 November 1912.
18 *Irish News*, 1 November 1912.
19 *Irish News*, 2 November 1912.
20 *Irish News*, 5 November 1912.
21 Ibid., extract reprinted from *Daily News and Leader*.
22 *Irish News*, 22 November 1912.
23 *Mayo News*, 9 January 1915.
24 Katherine Tynan, *Wandering Years*, p. 52.
25 *Mayo News*, 16 January 1915.
26 *Mayo News*, 13 February 1915.
27 *Mayo News*, 2 October 1915.
28 *Mayo News*, 26 June 1915.
29 *Mayo News*, 13 March 1915.
30 *Mayo News*, 11 December 1915.
31 Katherine Tynan, *Wandering Years*, p. 36.
32 Ibid., pp. 51-2.
33 Ibid., p. 53.
34 NAI CSORP 1915/9403, emigration from Westport district, 12 June 1915.
35 NAI CSORP 1915/20096, Sinn Féin disruption of recruiting meeting, 28 November 1915.
36 Intelligence Notes, 1915-19, PRO, CO 903/19.
37 *Mayo News*, 25 March 1916.
38 *Mayo News*, centenary supplement, 2 March 1994.
39 *Connaught Telegraph*, 14 August 1915.
40 *Mayo News*, 6 May 1916.
41 Katherine Tynan, *Wandering Years*, p. 52.
42 *Mayo News*, 13 May 1916.
43 *Mayo News*, 3 June 1916.
44 Katherine Tynan, *Wandering Years*, p. 51, p. 54.
45 *Mayo News*, 17 February 1917.
46 *Mayo News*, 3 May 1917.
47 *Mayo News*, 10 March 1917.
48 *Mayo News*, 14 April 1917.
49 *Mayo News*, 19 May 1917.
50 *Mayo News*, 1 December 1917.
51 *Connaught Telegraph*, 19 January 1919.
52 *Mayo News*, 16 March 1918. Milling's correspondence with the Castle about the disturbances of March 1918 and his request that sections of DORA be enforced in Westport can be found in NAI CSORP 1918/7982.
53 *Mayo News*, 23 March 1918.
54 Ibid.

55 Press Censor to Chief Secretary, Dublin Castle, and for the attention of Attorney General and others, PRO CO 904/160/5.
56 *Mayo News*, 3 August 1918.
57 Katherine Tynan, *Years of Shadow*, p. 52. Henry Hinkson died on 11 January and an obituary appeared in *The Times*, 13 January 1919. Documents relating to his illness and death are recorded in the annual index to CSORP but they are among the many that cannot actually be found in the archives.
58 NAI CSORP 1919/3918, Milling's report of disturbances at Lowpark petty sessions and minutes thereon.
59 Ibid.
60 Information on the shooting is taken from *Mayo News* reports of the incident and the inquest, 5 April 1919, 12 April 1919, and reports of the compensation claim hearing, 28 June 1919. Documents relating to the sentencing of Joe Ring in 1918 and related matters, to Milling's death and funeral in 1919, and to Lilla Milling's compensation claim are among the many listed in the annual index to CSORP but not surviving in the archives. It seems probable that, in this case, all papers of relevance to the Milling affair were assembled for investigation into his killing and it may be that they are mislaid in the archives, having been filed under an unrecorded number.
61 *Irish Times*, 2 April 1919.
62 John Milling's grave was not marked and neither was that of his brother, buried at Westport in 1903. The Protestant cleric in Westport has no records showing burial places in the cemetary but it is assumed that the RM was buried with his sister. His name has recently been added to the headstone, by Dr and Mrs Shearer.
63 *Belfast Telegraph*, 31 March 1919.
64 *The Times*, 3 April 1919.
65 PD, HC [114] 1513, 3 April 1919.
66 *Irish Times*, 2 April 1919.
67 *Connaught Telegraph*, 5 April 1919.
68 *Mayo News*, 5 April 1919.
69 Criminal Injuries (Ireland) Bill, to amend the enactments relative to compensation for Criminal Injuries in Ireland, PP, HC 1919 (55) I. 381.
70 *Mayo News*, 28 June 1919.
71 Lilla Milling lodged a fresh claim for

£8,000 but this was not, it seems, proceeded with; it was scheduled for hearing
at Castlebar in October but no reports can
be found in local papers. *Mayo News*, 28
June, 12 July, 19 July, 2 August 1919.
72 Jarlath Duffy (ed.), *My Stand For Freedom. Autobiography of an Irish Republican
Soldier*, by Joe Baker, Westport Historical
Society, Westport, Co. Mayo, 1988. See
also J. Duffy, 'Joe Ring', *Cathair na Mart*,
Westport Historical Society, vol. 7, No. 1
(1987), pp.5-20 and Anthony J. Jordan,
'Major John MacBride, 1865-1916, "Mac-
Donagh, and MacBride and Connolly and
Pearse"', Westport Historical Society,
Westport, Co. Mayo, 1991.
73 *Connaught Telegraph*, 17 May 1919, 24 May
1919.
74 PD, HC [116] 2185-6, 5 June 1919; [117]
1182, 3 July 1919.
75 *Mayo News*, 25 October 1919.
76 Lynch-Robinson, *Last of the Irish RMs*, p.
167.
77 *Connaught Telegraph*, 5 April 1919.

9 *James Woulfe Flanagan, 1864-1922*

1 U.H. Hussey de Burgh, *The Landowners
of Ireland*.
2 The season is described in Bence-Jones,
Twilight of the Ascendancy, pp. 43-5.
3 Letter from Jenny to John Woulfe Flanagan, 4 February, 1882, Woulfe Flanagan
Papers, 1189/16/8.
4 Bence-Jones, *Twighlight of the Ascendancy*,
p.46; see also E.M. Fingall, *Seventy Years
Young. Memories of Elizabeth, Countess of
Fingall*, told to Pamela Hinkson, The
Lilliput Press, Dublin, 1991, first published
by Collins, London, 1937. (Pamela
Hinkson was the daughter of Katherine
Tynan and Henry Hinkson RM.) The
fate of girls in the marriage market is a
theme of George Moore in, *A Drama in
Muslin. A Realistic Novel*, Colin Smythe,
Gerrads Cross, 1981; the novel was first
published in 1886.
5 Bence-Jones, *Twilight of the Ascendancy*,
pp. 56-7.
6 Letter from James to John Woulfe
Flanagan, 9 February 1892, private correspondence of John Woulfe Flanagan,
Tedworth Square, Chelsea, London, NAI

1189/6/1.
7 Letters dated 17 January, 18 January, 28
February 1892, NAI 1189/6, letters 1891-
3.
8 Ibid., letter dated 5 March 1892.
9 Letter dated 14 Jan 1894, NAI 1189/7/1.
10 Letter, from Italy, 6 October 1898, NAI
1189/11.
11 Letter from Dublin, 22 Oct 1898, NAI
1189/11.
12 Letter from Dublin, 1 November 1898,
NAI 1189/11.
13 Letter fron Listowel, Co. Kerry, 24 December 1898, NAI 1189/11.
14 Letters from Listowel, 7 February and 17
February 1899, NAI 1189/12.
15 Letter from Listowel, 17 February 1899,
NAI 1189/12.
16 Letters from Listowel, January-February
1899, NAI 1189/12.
17 Letter from Kenmare, 15 July 1900, NAI
1189/14.
18 Letter from Hayes Hotel, Tullamore, 26
July 1900, NAI 1189/14.
19 Letter from Tullamore, 20 August 1900,
NAI 1189/14.
20 Letter from Tullamore, 10 September
1900, NAI 1189/14.
21 Ibid.
22 For an account of the Lynchehaun affair
see James Carey, *The Playboy and the Yellow Lady*, Poolbeg Press, Dublin, 1986.
23 Letter from Jack Woulfe Flanagan, Canada,
to James Woulfe Flanagan, 3 April 1908,
NAI 1189/18.
24 *Belfast Telegraph*, 5 June 1922.
25 *Cork Examiner*, 28 August 1920.
26 *Newry Reporter*, 16 June 1921.
27 *Newry Reporter*, 7 July 1921.
28 *The Times*, 7 June 1922.
29 NAI CSORP 1921/24194, Major Woulfe
Flanagan for appointment as RM.
30 One surviving page from a letter to John
Woulfe Flanagan from Stephen, NAI
1189/16/8.
31 *Newry Reporter*, 7 July 1921.
32 *Freeman's Journal*, 8 March 1922.
33 *Freeman's Journal*, 12 February 1922.
34 *Freeman's Journal*, 8 March 1922.
35 *The Times*, 3 April 1922.
36 Lynch-Robinson, *Last of the Irish RMs*, p.
152-66, passim.
37 *Freeman's Journal*, 4 February 1922.
38 *Belfast Telegraph*, 5 June 1922.

39 *The Times*, 5 June 1922.
40 Ibid.
41 *The Times*, *Belfast Telegraph*, and *Newry Reporter* all mentioned the car travelling towards the border.
42 Letter to John Woulfe Flanagan, written from Athaneum Club, signature illegible, 8 June 1922, NAI 1189/16/8.
43 Letter to Sister Scholastica from secretary of AOH, 13 June 1922, NAI 1189/16/8.
44 *Newry Reporter*, 15 June, 22 June 1922.
45 *Belfast Telegraph*, 5 June 1922.
46 *The Times*, 6 June 1922.
47 *The Times*, 5 June 1922.
48 *Newry Reporter*, 22 June 1922.
49 Letters from Sr Scholastica to John Woulfe Flanagan, 28 June, 16 July 1922, NAI 1189/16/10. On the civil war see Michael Hopkinson, *Green against Green. The Irish Civil War*, Gill and Macmillan, Dublin, 1988.
50 *Belfast Telegraph*, 5 June 1922.
51 Draft of letter from John Woulfe Flanagan to Mr Gartlan, solicitor, 16 September 1922, NAI 1189/16/11.
52 Letter from Newry RIC District Inspector to John Woulfe Flanagan, 15 November 1922, NAI 1189/16/8.
53 Letter from Mr Gartlan, solicitor, to John Woulfe Flanagan, 1 May 1923, NAI 1189/17.
54 Letter from parish priest, Newry, to John Woulfe Flanagan, 1 June 1923, NAI 1189/17/3.
55 Letter to John Woulfe Flanagan from unidentified Dublin correspondent, NAI 1189/17/3.

10 Edmund James Charles Dease, 1861-1945

1 Charlotte Jerningham's younger sister, Ida, married Myles O'Reilly, father of William O'Reilly RM, below, chapter 11. For the Jerningham connection with the English aristocracy see *Burke's Peerage*, STAFFORD, B.
2 See *Burke's Peerage*, HAREWOOD, E.
3 S.M. Hussey, *Reminiscences of an Irish Land Agent*, p. 95.
4 Countess Fingall, *Seventy Years Young*, p. 85.
5 Ibid., pp. 63-4.
6 Ibid., p.68.
7 A. Norman Jeffares gives an account of this in his introduction to the 1981 edition of *Drama in Muslin*, Colin Smythe, Gerrards Cross, pp. ix-xi, referring to and citing from Joseph Hone, *The Life of George Moore*, Victor Gollancz Ltd., London, 1936.
8 Fingall, *Seventy Years Young*, p.226.
9 John Biggs-Davison and George Chowdharay-Best, *The Cross of Saint Patrick. The Catholic Unionist Tradition in Ireland*, Kensal Press, Bourne End, Bucks., 1984, p. 249, pp.257-8.
10 Ambrose Richard More O'Ferrall was a DL and JP for Co. Kildare; see that family in *Irish Family Records*.
11 Townshend, *Political Violence*, p. 232.
12 Synopsis of Reports from the Resident Magistrates on the State of Ireland (Tipperary North Riding, Nenagh District, Major Dease), PRO CO 904/227.
13 NAI CSORP 1915/9463, minutes relating to Rathdowney petty sessions.
14 Official printed list of RMs in Ireland, 15 November 1919 (with information on petty sessions in each district, and distances from headquarters to petty sessions), Brennan MSS, NLI MS 26153/3454.
15 Letter from Edmund Dease to Walter Long, 11 June 1918, WRO 947/429.
16 Copies of letters from Walter Long to Edmund Dease, to Lord Lieutenant and to Chief Secretary, 14 June 1918, WRO 947/433.
17 Letter from Edmund Dease to Walter Long, 6 November 1918, WRO 947/433.
18 Copy of letter from Walter Long to Edmund Dease, 11 November 1918, WRO 947/433.
19 Townshend, *Political Violence*, pp. 331-2.
20 Official Memorandum, condition of County Tipperary and the working of Sinn Féin in Ireland, 4 July 1919, PRO CO 904/225; see Townshend, *Political Violence*, 'Guerilla Struggle', pp.322-64, passim.
21 NAI CSO, RMs Monthly Summaries, Jan-June 1920, Edmund Dease; C. Townshend, 'The Irish railway strike of 1920: industrial action and civil resistance in the struggle for independence', *Irish Historical Studies*, xxi, 83 (March 1979).
22 Letter from Edmund Dease to Walter Long, 4 May 1922, WRO 947/429

23 NAI CSO, RMs Monthly Summaries, May 1920, W.J. O'Reilly, Navan District.
24 Letter from Edmund Dease to Walter Long, 4 May 1922, WRO 947/429.
25 Edmund Dease's daughter, Marion (1900-63), inherited the property which after her death passed to the son born of her marriage to William Bland of Blandsfort, Co. Laois.

11 William Joseph O'Reilly, 1864–1937

1 J.C. Knoulty, *A Biographical Dictionary of Ireland from 1500* (bound typescript), QUB Library, Special Collections; Anthony Mathews, *Origin of the O'Reillys*, Athony Mathews, Rathmines, Dublin, n.d., *c.*1980, pp.10-2. See also Robert Lynd, *Irish and English. Portraits and Impressions*, Francis Griffiths, London, 1908, p. 119.
2 John O'Reilly (d.1801) was Lt Col of the Hibernia regiment in the service of King Charles IV of Spain and his nephew, James O'Reilly, was a captain in the 15th British Regiment who later served as colonel in a Spanish regiment; he was killed in action in Spain. On Irishmen serving in foreign armies see Maurice Hennessy, *The Wild Geese. The Irish Soldier in Exile*, Sidgewick and Jackson, London, 1973.
3 Derek Beales, *From Castlereagh to Gladstone 1815-1885*, Sphere Books pb. edition, London, 1971, pp. 120-2.
4 U.H. Hussey de Burgh, *The Landowners of Ireland*.
5 See *Burke's Peerage*, STAFFORD, B.
6 Hennessy, *The Wild Geese*, pp.137-43, passim; G.F-H. Berkeley, *The Irish Battalion in the Papal Army of 1860*, Talbot Press, Dublin, 1929, Chapter VII, 'Major O'Reilly's Work at Spoleto', pp. 76-83.
7 *The Times*, 20 February 1862.
8 *The Times*, 24 February 1862.
9 *The Times*, 28 February 1862.
10 *The Times*, 3 March 1862.
11 *The Times* (reports of the election and its immediate aftermath), 6 March, 7 March, 10 March 1862; (on the petitition) 24 March, 27 March 1862.
12 PD, HC [166], 2116-36, 23 May 1862.
13 Information from the late Mrs F. McQuillan, Co. Louth.
14 David Sweetman, *Irish Castles and Forti-fied Houses*, Town House and Country House, Dublin, 1995, p.36.
15 D.J. Hickey and J.E. Doherty, *A Dictionary of Irish History 1800-1980*, Gill and Macmillan, Dublin, 1980 (1987 reprint), pp. 595-6.
16 See *Burke's Peerage*, BEAUMONT, B.
17 Press cutting in the family memorabilia of the late Mrs F. McQuillan, Co. Louth.
18 Census Schedules, 1901, (NAI), 4/DED. 5, Thomastown 1-11.
19 Orpen spent most of the summer of 1907 at Glyde Court working on the painting; for a brief account of his experiences see Bence-Jones, *Twilight of the Ascendancy*, pp. 114-6.
20 Mrs McQuillan was recalling events from her very early childhood, aged four and five, and could not be sure what periods of time were spent in Co. Cavan or at Knock Abbey. The Abbey was never left, she thought, for very long and it was usually the case that Sybil was there with the children but made frequent visits to Co. Cavan.
21 Census Schedules, 1911, (NAI), 4/DED. 5, Thomastown 1-8.
22 O'Reilly notified Dublin Castle that he had taken up residence at Rice Hill in early 1912, NAI CSORP 1912/278.
23 Note in the family memorabilia of the late Mrs F. McQuillan, Co. Louth.
24 O'Reilly appointed to Commission of Peace for Belfast, to act with the military if required, NAI CSORP 1912/13289; appointed additional RM for Co. Down, CSORP 1912/13593; directed to special duty in Belfast, CSORP 1912/16283. One of his rare communications with the Castle was a complaint about the inconvenience caused by having to make prior application for 'occasional days' of leave, CSORP 1915/4524.
25 Synopsis of Reports from Resident Magistrates on the State of the Country, PRO CO 904/227.
26 *Freeman's Journal*, 3 January 1916.
27 For permission to work his district from Knock Abbey, CSORP 1918/22594; for permission to reside in Co. Louth, CSORP 1920/7016, CSORP 1920/7965.
28 *Dundalk Democrat*, 14 February 1921.
29 *Freeman's Journal*, 3 March 1921.
30 The late Mrs F. McQuillan, Co. Louth, in conversation May 1994.

31 Lynch-Robinson, *Last of the Irish RMs*, p.151.
32 Letter to 'Miss O'Reilly' from 'old gardener, Nat Blackwell', in the family memorabilia of the late Mrs F. McQuillan, Co. Louth.
33 *Freeman's Journal*, 15 August, 17 August, 18 August 1922.
34 Bence-Jones, *Twilight of the Ascendancy*, p. 232.
35 *Dundalk Democrat*, 20 January, 27 January 1923.
36 *Freeman's Journal*, 31 January 1923.
37 *The Times*, 5 March 1923.
38 *Dundalk Democrat*, 10 March 1923.
39 Ibid.
40 Michael Adams, *Censorship: the Irish experience*, Scepter Books, Dublin, 1968, pp.64-5 and n.2, p.209. *Irish Statesman*, 1 March 1930, cited by Adams, p. 64.
41 Éire. Department of Justice. Register of Prohibited Publications (Books) as on the 31 March 1932 (Censorship of Publications Act 1929), QUB Library, Special Collections, hp Z109 EIRE.
42 See Adams, *Censorship*, Appendix 2, pp. 240-3 for a selection of books prohibited 1930-46.
43 Sean O'Faolain, *Vive Moi! An Autobiography*, Rupert Hart-Davis, London, 1965, p.263.

Bibliography

UNPUBLISHED PAPERS

Brennan MSS National Library of Ireland (NLI)
Chief Secretary's Office, Registered Papers. National Archive (NAI)
CSO, RMs Monthly Summaries of Duty. (NAI)
Colonial Office Papers Public Record Office (PRO]
Hamilton MSS Public Record Office, Northern Ireland (PRONI)
Home Office Papers, PRO
Larcom MSS, NLI
Mayo MSS, NLI
Long Papers County Record Office, Trowbridge, Wiltshire (WRO)
Treasury Papers, PRO
War Office Papers, PRO
Woulfe Flanagan Papers, NAI

OFFICIAL PAPERS AND PUBLICATIONS

Return of Stipendiary Magistrates in Ireland, HC 1831-2 (360), XXXIII.561.
Returns of Resident Magistrates, Ireland, HC 1837 (254), XLVI. 335; HC 1844 (131),
    XLIII. 539; HC 1852-3 (107), XCIV. 615; HC 1860 (288), LVII. 879; HC 1862
    (459), XLVI. 493; HC 1872 (284), I.269; HC 1880 (417), LX. 547; HC 1887 (129),
    LXVII. 465; HC 1889 (83), LXI. 475; HC 1892 (107), LXV. 397; HC 1895 (262),
    LXXXII. 73; HC 1911 (277), LXV. 461.
Bill (16 Vict.) to Amend the Acts regulating the salaries of Resident Magistrates, 1874
    (923), XVI. 723.
Report of Inquiry into the Civil Service in Ireland (Resident Magistrates), 1874 (923),
    XVI. 723.
Return Showing Numbers of Persons Receiving Special Police Protection on 31 De-
    cember 1880, 1881 (76), LXXXVI. 641.
Return of Commissions of the Peace in Ireland, by county, 1884 (13), LXIII. 331.
Report of the Belfast Riots Commission, with Evidence and Appendices, 1887 (4925),
    XVIII.
Royal Commission on the Civil Service, Fourth Report, Second Appendix (Evidence),
    1914 (7340), XVI. 363.

Report of the Committee of Inquiry into the RIC and DMP, Evidence and Appendices, 1914 (7637), XXXII. 359.
Resident Magistrates (Ireland) Bill, report and proceedings of Standing Committee B, 1920 (171), VIII. 507.
Resident Magistrates (Ireland), estimate of probable expenditure, 1920 (750), XL. 811.
Belfast and Ulster Directory, vol. XLIII, compiled at the Belfast News Letter office, 1923.
Belfast Gazette.
Dublin Gazette.
Parliamentary Debates, House of Commons, Series 3, 4 and 5.
RIC Annual Lists, bound volumes (PRO, HO 184).

WORKS OF REFERENCE

Bateman, John, *The Great Landowners of Great Britain and Ireland*, Leicester UP, Leicester, 1971 (first published 1876).
Burke's Guide to Country Houses, vol. I, Ireland, London, 1978.
Burke's Irish Family Records, London, 1976.
Burke's Landed Gentry of Ireland, London, 1958.
Burke's Peerage, London, 1975.
Doherty, J.E., and Hickey, D.J., *A Chronology of Irish History since 1500*, Gill & Macmillan, Dublin, 1989.
Gibbs, Vicary (ed.), *The Compleat Peerage by G.E.C.*, vol. II, London, 1912.
Hickey, D.J., and Doherty, J.E., *A Dictionary of Irish History 1800-1980*, Gill and Macmillan, Dublin, 1980.
Knoulty, J.C., *A Biographical Dictionary of Ireland from 1500* (bound typescript presented to the Queen's University of Belfast in memory of J.C. Knoulty, 1991), QUB Library, Special Collections.
Thom's Irish Who's Who 1923, Alexander Thom & Co., Dublin.
Walford's County Families of the United Kingdom, Spottiswoode, London, 1912.
Who Was Who, Adam and Charles Black, London, vol. II, 1916-28 (1929, 4th. ed. 1967); vol. III, 1929-40 (1941, 4th. ed. 1967); vol. V, 1951-60 (1961, 3rd. ed. 1967).

BOOKS, ARTICLES AND PAMPHLETS

Adams, Michael, *Censorship: the Irish experience*, Scepter Books, Dublin, 1968.
Andrew, C., and Dilks, D. (eds), *The Missing Dimension. Governments and Intelligence Communities in the Twentieth Century*, Macmillan, London, 1984.
Anonymous, *Tales of the RIC*, Blackwoods, Edinburgh, 1921.
Beales, Derek, *From Castlereagh to Gladstone 1815-85*, Sphere Books pb. edition, London, 1971.
Bence-Jones, Mark, *Twilight of the Ascendancy*, Constable, London, 1987.
Berkeley, G.F-H., *The Irish Battalion in the Papal Army of 1860*, Talbot Press, Dublin, 1929.

Biggs-Davison, John, and Chowdharay-Best, George, *The Cross of St Patrick. The Catholic Unionist Tradition in Ireland*, Kensal Press, Bourne End, Bucks., 1984.

Blunt, Wilfred Scawen, *The Land War in Ireland, Being a Personal Narrative of Events*, Stephen Swift, London, 1912.

Bowen, Elizabeth, *The Last September*, Constable, London, 1929; Penguin Books, London, 1942.

Boyce, D. George, *Ireland, 1828-1923, From Ascendancy to Democracy*, Blackwells, Oxford, 1992.

Brewer, John D., *The Royal Irish Constabulary. An Oral History*, Institute of Irish Studies, Belfast, 1990.

Broeker, Galen, *Rural Disorder and Police Reform in Ireland 1812-36*, Routledge and Kegan Paul, London, 1970.

Buckland, Paul, *Irish Unionism: the Anglo-Irish and the New Ireland 1885-1922*, Gill and Macmillan, Dublin, 1972.

Cairns, Richard, and Richards, Shaun, *Writing Ireland. Colonialism, Nationalism and Culture*, Manchester UP, Manchester, 1988.

Carey, James, *The Playboy and the Yellow Lady*, Poolbeg Press, Dublin, 1986,

Colles, Ramsay, *In Castle and Court House: Being Reminiscences of Thirty Years in Ireland*, Werner-Laurie, London, 1911.

Collins, Peter (ed.), *Nationalism and Unionism. Conflict in Ireland 1885-1921*, Institute of Irish Studies, Belfast, 1994.

Cook, Scott B., 'The Irish Raj: social origins and careers of Irishmen in the Indian Civil Service, 1855-1914', *Journal of Social History*, vol. 20,3 (1987).

Crane, C.P., *Memories of a Resident Magistrate, 1880-1920*, T. & A. Constable, Edinburgh, 1938.

Cronin, John, *Somerville and Ross*, Bucknell UP, New Jersey, 1972.

Crossman, Virginia, 'Emergency legislation and agrarian disorder in Ireland, 1821-41', *Irish Historical Studies*, xxvii, 108 (Nov. 1991).

Crozier, Brigadier General F.P., *Impressions and Recollections*, Weirner Laurie, London, 1930.

Curtis, R., *The History of the Royal Irish Constabulary*, Moffat, London, 1869.

Duffy, Jarlath, 'Joe Ring', *Cathair na Mart*, vol. 7, No. 1 (1987); Duffy (ed.), *My Stand for Freedom. Autobiography of an Irish Republican Soldier*, by Joe Baker, Westport Historical Society, Westport, Co. Mayo, 1988.

Dugdale, Blanche, *Arthur James Balfour*, Hutchinson, London, 1936.

Eglinton, John, *Anglo-Irish Essays*, Talbot Press, Dublin and London, 1917.

Farrell, J.G., *Troubles*, Jonathan Cape, London, 1970, pb. edition, Phoenix, London, 1993.

Fingall, E.M., *Seventy Years Young. Memories of Elizabeth, Countess of Fingall*, told to Pamela Hinkson, Lilliput Press, Dublin, 1991, first published by Collins, London, 1937.

Finneran, Richard J., *Anglo-Irish Literature. A Review of Research*, MLA, New York, 1976.

Flanagan, Kieran, 'The Chief Secretary's Office, 1853-1914: a bureaucratic enigma', *Irish Historical Studies*, xxiv, 94 (Nov. 1984).

Flanagan, Thomas, 'The Big House of Ross-Drishane', *Kenyon Review*, 28, No. I (Jan. 1966).

Fleming, Lionel, *Head or Harp*, Barrie and Rockliffe, London, 1965.

Geary, Laurence M., *The Plan of Campaign 1886-91*, Cork UP, Cork, 1986.

Goff-Davis, Annabel, *Walled Gardens. Scenes from an Anglo-Irish Childhood*, Picador pb. edition, Pan Books, London, 1991.

Graham, Colin, ' "Liminal Spaces": post-colonial theories and Irish culture', *Irish Review*, No. 16 (1994).

Green, G. Garrow, *In the Royal Irish Constabulary*, Hodges & Figgis, Dublin, 1905.

Gwynn, Stephen, *Today and Tomorrow in Ireland. Essays on Irish Subjects*, Hodges & Figgis, Dublin, 1903.

Headlam, Maurice, *Irish Reminiscences*, Robert Hale, London, 1947.

Hennessey, Maurice, *The Wild Geese. The Irish Soldier in Exile*, Sidgwick and Jackson, London, 1973.

Hogan, Robert (ed.), *Dictionary of Irish Literature*, Gill and Macmillan, Dublin, 1979.

Holt, E., *Protest in Arms. The Irish Troubles 1916-23*, Putnam, London, 1960.

Hopkinson, Michael, *Green against Green. The Irish Civil War*, Gill & Macmillan, Dublin, 1988.

Hussey de Burgh, U.H., *The Landowners of Ireland*, Hodges, Foster and Figgis, Dublin, *c.*1878.

Hussey, S.M., *The Reminiscences of an Irish Land Agent, Being Those of S.M. Hussey*, compiled by Home Gordon, Duckworth, London, 1904.

Jeffery, Keith (ed.), *'An Irish Empire'? Aspects of Ireland and the British Empire*, Manchester UP, Manchester, 1996.

Jordan, Anthony J., *Major John MacBride, 1865-1916, 'MacDonagh and MacBride and Connolly and Pearse'*, Westport Historical Society, Westport, Co. Mayo, 1991.

Jordan Jr., Donald E., *Land and Popular Politics in Ireland. County Mayo from the Plantation to the Land War*, Cambridge UP, Cambridge, 1994.

Kennedy, Liam, 'Modern Ireland: post-colonial society or post-colonial pretensions?', *Irish Review*, No. 13 (Winter 1992-3).

Kiberd, Declan, *Inventing Ireland*, Johnathon Cape, London, 1995.

Lee, Joseph, *The Modernisation of Irish Society 1848-1918*, Gill and Macmillan, Dublin, 1989 edition.

Lewis, Gifford, *Somerville and Ross. The World of the Irish RM*, Penguin Books, Middlesex, 1987.

Lloyd, Clifford D.C., *Ireland Under the Land League. A Narrative of Personal Experiences*, Blackwood, Edinburgh, 1892.

Long, Viscount Walter, *Memories*, Hutchinson, London, 1923.

Loughrey, P. (ed.), *The People of Ireland*, Apple Tree Press / BBC Northern Ireland, Belfast, 1989.

Lowe, W.J., and Malcom, E.L., 'The domestication of the RIC 1836-1922', *Irish Economic and Social History*, 19 (1992).

Lynch-Robinson, Sir Christopher, *The Last of the Irish RMs*, Cassell, London, 1951.

Lynd, Robert, *Irish and English. Portraits and Impressions*, Francis Griffiths, London, 1908.

Marlow, Joyce, *Captain Boycott and the Irish*, Andre Deutsch, London, 1973.

McBride, Lawrence, *The Greening of Dublin Castle: the Transformation of Bureaucratic and Judicial Personnel in Ireland 1892-1922*, Catholic University of America Press, Washington DC, 1991.

McDowell, R.B., *The Irish Administration 1801-1914*, Routledge and Kegan Paul, London, 1964, reprinted by Greenwood Press, Westport, Connecticut, 1976.

McFadden, J.J., and Keeler, D., '"Abstracted in his dreams." Katherine Tynan's W.B. Yeats', *Modern Psychology*, vol. 88 (1991).

Moore, George, *A Drama in Muslin. A Realistic Novel*, Colin Smythe, Gerrards Cross, 1981 edition, first published 1886.

Muenger, Elizabeth A., *The British Military Dilemma in Ireland. Occupation Politics 1886-1914*, University of Kansas Press, Lawrence / Gill and Macmillan, Dublin, 1991.

O'Brien, Conor Cruise, *Writers and Politics*, Parthenon Books, New York, 1965.

O'Callaghan, Margaret, 'Language, nationality and cultural identity in the Irish Free State, 1922-7: the *Irish Statesman* and the *Catholic Bulletin* reappraised', *Irish Historical Studies*, xxiv, No. 94 (Nov. 1984); *British High Politics and a Nationalist Ireland: Criminality, Land and the Law under Forster and Balfour*, Cork UP, Cork, 1994.

O'Faolain, Sean, *Vive Moi! An Autobiography*, Rupert Hart-Davis, London, 1965.

O'Halpin, Eunan, *The Decline of the Union. British Government in Ireland 1892-1920*, Gill and Macmillan, Dublin, 1987.

Partridge, A., *Language and Society in Anglo-Irish Literature*, Gill and Macmillan, Dublin, 1984.

Petrie, Charles, *Walter Long and his Times*, Hutchinson, London, 1936.

Phoenix, Eamon, *Northern Nationalism. Nationalist Politics, Partition and the Catholic Minority in Northern Ireland 1890-1940*: Ulster Historical Foundation, Belfast, 1994; Phoenix (ed.), *A Century of Northern Life. The Irish News and 100 Years of Ulster History 1890s-1990s*, Ulster Historical Foundation, Belfast, 1995.

Pritchett, V.S., *The Living Novel*, Chatto and Windus, London, 1949.

Quane, Michael, 'Ranelagh Endowed School', *Journal of the Old Athlone Society*, vol. I, No. 1 (1969).

Rafroidi, Patrick, and Brown, Terence (eds), *The Irish Short Story*, Université de Lille, 1979.

Robertson, Nora, *Crowned Harp*, Allen Figgis & Co., Dublin, 1960.

Robinson, Sir Henry, *Memories Wise and Otherwise*, Cassell, London, 1923; *Further Memories of Irish Life*, Herbert Jenkins, London, 1924.

Robinson, Hilary, *Somerville and Ross. A Critical Appreciation*, Gill and Macmillan, Dublin, 1980.

Scanlan, Margaret, 'Rumours of War: Elizabeth Bowen's *Last September* and J.G. Farrell's *Troubles*', *Eire-Ireland*, xx, 2 (Summer 1985).

Silverman, Marilyn, and Gulliver, P.H., *In the Valley of the Nore. A Social History of Thomastown, County Kilkenny, 1840-1983*, Geography Publications, Dublin, 1986.

Somerville, E.OE., and Ross, Martin, *The Irish RM*, Penguin Books, London, 1984 edition; *The Irish RM and his Experiences*, Faber and Faber, London, 1928.

Somerville-Large, Peter, *The Irish Country House. A Social History*, Sinclair-Stevenson, London, 1995.

Sweetman, David, *Irish Castles and Fortified Houses*, Town House and Country House, Dublin, 1995.

Townshend, Charles, *The British Campaign in Ireland 1919-21*, Oxford UP, Oxford, 1975; 'The Irish railway strike of 1920: industrial action and civil resistance in the struggle for independence', *Irish Historical Studies*, xxi, No. 83 (March 1979); *Political Violence in Ireland. Government and Resistance since 1849*, Clarendon Press, Oxford, 1984.

Turner, Sir Alfred, *Sixty Years of a Soldier's Life*, Methuen, London, 1912.

Tynan, Katherine, *The Years of the Shadow*, Constable, London, 1919; *The Wandering Years*, Constable, London, 1922.

Index

Mitchell, Arthur, 23
Moane, Ned, 144, 152
Monaghan James, 167
Moore, George, 176
Moore, William M. Scott, 81, 105, 115
Moran, D.P., 49, 57
Morley, John, 79
Moynahan, Julian, 47-8
Murney, Michael, 167

Naas, Lord (later 6th Earl Mayo) 19
Nagle, Garrett, 76, 137
national identity, 57
National League, 32
Neild, Major, 41
News of the World, 196

O'Brien, William, 35-6, 70, 141, 159
O'Connell, Daniel, 21
O'Connor, Frank, 44
O'Connor, Henry, 92
O'Faolain, Sean, 197
O'Farrell, Edward, 76-7, 78
O'Growney, Fr Eugene, 57
O'Malley, William, 145
O'Reilly, Brian (nephew of William),
   187
O'Reilly, Charles Hugh (nephew of
   William), 187
O'Reilly, Edith (sister of William), 184
O'Reilly, Edmund (brother of William),
   185
O'Reilly, Francis (brother of William),
   185
O'Reilly, Frideswide (niece of William),
   185
O'Reilly, Ida (niece of William), 185
O'Reilly, Ida *née* Jernigham (mother of
   William), 184
O'Reilly, Mary (sister of william), 184
O'Reilly, Myles William (father of
   William), 183
O'Reilly, Sybil (sister-in-law of
   William), 187

O'Reilly, William Joseph, 80, 180, 182-
   97
O'Sullivan, Morty, 21
Olivier, Sir Sydney, 60
Olphert, Robert, 51
Orange Order, 33
Orr, William, 112

Parliament Act, 1911, 100
Parliamentary Irish Party, 40
Parnell, Charles S., 26
Peel, Robert, Chief Secretary, 17-18;
petty sessions, 67
Plunkett, Sir Horace 29, 98, 127, 177
Plunkett, T.O., 29
Protection of Persons and Property
   (Ireland) Act, 1881, 25

Real Charlotte, The, 43, 44, 47, 48
Redmond, John, 54, 70, 72, 103, 141
Remarque, Erich Maria, 197
Representation of the People Act, 1918,
   108
resident magistrates (RMs): origins, 11-
   24; suitability of candidates, 11, 20,
   53; origins of term 'RM', 12; full
   numerical strength, 13, 50; duties,
   13-14, 62-81; leave and salary, 14-
   15, 22, 62-3; horses, 15; retirement,
   16, 124-5; qualifications of, 16, 40,
   52; nepotism, 16, 19-20, 56;
   relations with RIC, 16-17, 18, 53,
   75-6, 78; and JPs, 17, 79-80; Peel's
   reforms, 17; and land war, 26-7;
   'Special Resident Magistrates', 29-
   30; support of ILPU, 33; Belfast
   Riots of 1886, 34-5; Somerville and
   Ross stories, 43-61; religion of, 39,
   50, 54-5; patronage, 56; nationality
   of, 59; social class, 19, 59, 82-3, 88-
   91, 91-2; transfers, 64-5; famine
   report of 1890, 68; nature of cases,
   74-5; relations with Dublin
   administration, 76-8; and
   sectarianism, 95-6; and World War

White, Jasper, 87
Willis, Colonel, 118
Woulfe Flanagan, Edward (brother of
James), 154
Woulfe Flanagan, Elizabeth (sister of
James), 154, 169
Woulfe Flanagan, Frances (sister of
James), 154
Woulfe Flanagan, James, 59, 99, 123,
154-81
Woulfe Flanagan, Jane (sister of
James), 154, 155
Woulfe Flanagan, Johanna (sister of
James), 154, 155
Woulfe Flanagan, Mary (sister of
James), 154

Woulfe Flanagan, Richard (brother of
James), 154
Woulfe Flanagan, Stephen (brother of
James), 154, 156-7
Woulfe Flanagan, Stephen (father of
James), 154
Woulfe Flanagan, Terence (brother of
James), 154
Wood, Albert, 118
Woods, Captain, W.A., 130
Wyndham, George, Chief Secretary, 56,
72
Wyndham Land Act, 1903, 70
Wynne, Edward, 111

Yeats, W.B., 85